Doing Research

*The Complete
Research Paper Guide*

Second Edition

Doing Research

The Complete Research Paper Guide

Dorothy U. Seyler

Northern Virginia Community College

McGraw-Hill College

Boston   Burr Ridge, IL   Dubuque, IA   Madison, WI   New York
San Francisco   St. Louis   Bangkok   Bogotá   Caracas   Lisbon
London   Madrid   Mexico City   Milan   New Delhi   Seoul
Singapore   Sydney   Taipei   Toronto

McGraw-Hill College

A Division of The **McGraw·Hill** *Companies*

DOING RESEARCH: THE COMPLETE RESEARCH PAPER GUIDE

This book is printed on acid-free paper.

9 0 DOC/DOC 0 9 8 7 6 5 4

ISBN 0-07-057979-2

Editorial director: *Phillip A. Butcher*
Sponsoring editor: *Tim Julet*
Developmental editor: *Alexis Walker*
Marketing manager: *Lesley Denton*
Project manager: *Jim Labeots*
Production supervisor: *Lori Koetters*
Senior designer: *Crispin Prebys*
Supplement coordinator: *Nancy Martin*
Compositor: *Shepherd Incorporated*
Typeface: *10/12 Century Book*
Printer: *R. R. Donnelley & Sons Company*

Library of Congress Cataloging-in-Publication Data

Seyler, Dorothy U.
  Doing research : the complete research paper guide / Dorothy U.
Seyler. — 2nd ed.
    p.   cm.
  Includes bibliographical references (p.) and index.
  ISBN 0-07-057979-2 (alk. paper)
  1. Report writing. 2. Research. I. Title.
  LB2369.S46 1999
  808'.02—dc21   97-53292

http://www.mhhe.com

Contents

Chapter 2   Locating Sources 27

Chapter 3 Preparing a Bibliography 73

Chapter 4 Understanding Sources and Taking Notes 111

Chapter 5   Presenting and Documenting Research 153

Chapter 6 Writing the Paper 193

Chapter 7 Observing Other Styles of Documentation 247

Preface

As its subtitle suggests, *Doing Research* offers a complete guide to preparing documented papers in the humanities, social sciences, and science fields. The MLA, APA, and footnote/endnote documentation styles (used in the humanities, social sciences, and some science fields) are thoroughly explained and illustrated. Explanations are supported by sample students' papers in MLA and APA formats. Instructors will find a sample paper with footnotes in the *Instructor's Manual*, a paper they can use for overhead instruction in the classroom or copy to make it available to students. In addition, documentation in several science fields is explained and illustrated so that science students can comfortably read documented sources and prepare documented papers in their specialized field. Illustrations of the various documentation styles are supported by detailed guidelines for formatting papers in the various disciplines and for handling numbers and preparing visuals. *Doing Research* really can serve students as a reference text for research throughout their college careers.

Equally important, perhaps more important, *Doing Research*, as its title establishes, explains and illustrates the *doing* of research, the steps in the research process. Although faculty are necessarily—and appropriately—concerned that students prepare completed papers that conform to an expected scholarly format, many students fall by the wayside long before struggling to prepare a paper's page of references. Many students cannot finish because they do not know how to get started, because they are overwhelmed by an academic library, or because they do not understand how to use sources. A process that seems obvious to instructors is decidedly not obvious to many college freshmen who are, for the first time, asked to engage in academic writing. *Doing Research* is based on the belief that a thoughtfully organized, clearly written, and amply illustrated text can guide the less prepared students through the research and writing process while not condescending to the more prepared student who needs help primarily with technical details of documentation and manuscript conventions. This text strikes the proper balance between explaining the process and providing guidelines and checklists for completing a paper. This text shows students how to do their own research, how to blend sources with their own thinking into papers, so that they begin to taste the pleasures of investigation and problem solving—what doing research is really all about.

THE TEXT'S ORGANIZATION

Doing Research is organized into chapters that correspond to what can roughly be called stages in the research process: selecting a topic, searching for sources and preparing a bibliography, reading and taking notes, writing and documenting. This organization does not imply, however, that the research process can be completed by merely checking off a series of unrelated steps. Rather, the recursive nature of research—*re-search*—is stressed and illustrated throughout the text.

The documentation style illustrated in preparing a working bibliography (Chapter 3) and documenting research (Chapter 5) is the in-text author/page number style of the Modern Language Association (MLA). Thus, those instructors who want to teach the research process in detail and want students to use—or at least be aware of—MLA style can assign Chapters 1 through 6 in order. Other documentation patterns are explained in Chapter 7. So, those instructors planning to use a style other than MLA can use the appropriate section of Chapter 7 instead of the sections of Chapters 3 and 5 that illustrate MLA style. Guidelines for preparing a working bibliography have been placed at the beginning of a separate chapter (Chapter 3)—not mixed in with locating sources (Chapter 2)—so that students using a style other than MLA can read about finding sources without the constant intrusion of sample cards and source-citing guidelines in a documentation style not used in their papers.

Several other features of the text's organization and content should be noted. Chapter 4 devotes ample space to the note-taking process and types of notes, but this information comes after a discussion of the researcher's relationship to sources and preparing a preliminary outline to guide the use of sources. Many students have some difficulty framing a thesis and developing a preliminary plan that will direct them to a paper meeting the expectations of their research assignment. This chapter explains how sources are to be used to meet different types of research assignments so that students can go beyond the fruitless exercise of merely copying passages from several sources and pasting them together into a paper. Chapter 4 also presents an annotated bibliography and a review-of-the-literature essay, projects frequently assigned instead of, or along with, a documented argumentative paper.

The technicalities of referring to authors and titles, presenting quotations and visuals, handling numbers and punctuation, and documenting sources are presented when they need to be: in Chapter 5, *before* guidelines for writing the paper. If the biggest problem is getting started with a good topic choice and tentative thesis, the second biggest problem is presenting the results of research clearly and without awkwardness. Although not all elements of presentation covered in Chapter 5 will be relevant to every writer or every paper, and the specifics of format cannot be learned all at once, students need to review this material and have a general understanding of what their papers should look like before they start to draft the paper.

Chapter 6 organizes writing the research essay into a clear process of drafting, revising, editing, and proofreading. It provides detailed guidance on writing opening, body, and concluding paragraphs, on revising, and on editing. The chapter concludes with two annotated student essays, one a literary analysis, the other an argument on a current public policy issue. Examples of possible topics used throughout the text come from a range of disciplines, and many are used again and again so that students can see how a researcher actually progresses from topic to sources to outline and so on. The text concludes with additional information in two appendices, one listing many common abbreviations, the other providing a list of reference sources, including online databases, by discipline.

CHANGES IN THE SECOND EDITION

Some important changes from the first edition will be found throughout this second edition. First, Chapter 2, Locating Sources, has been heavily revised to become current with today's technological library. The assumption is made that most researchers will now be using an online book catalog, CD-ROM, and online databases as indexes to sources, and the Internet for some sources. Included in the revised chapter is a discussion of the advantages of print, CD-ROM, and online sources for research. And Chapter 3 now shows bibliographic citations for full-text articles from CD-ROM or online databases and for Internet sources—along with a clear warning that citation patterns for some of these sources are still in flux. Additionally, the widespread use of personal computers requires that discussions of the retrieval of sources, bibliography preparation, and note taking be updated to include the possible use of a PC throughout the research process, not just as a form of "typewriter" to prepare the completed paper. *Doing Research* integrates guidelines for using a PC into the traditional stages of the research process. This new edition also places emphasis on evaluating sources and selecting the best sources for every topic and purpose in writing; this emphasis includes a recognition of what the Internet can provide—and ways in which it adds to the task of evaluating sources. Finally, examples throughout the text have been updated, all the student essays are new, and the book has the convenient design features of a spiral binding and tabs to locate key information in the research process. These changes to the second edition of *Doing Research* mirror the technological changes in today's library: both are current and even more user-friendly.

A WORD ABOUT THE TABS

Eight tabs have been provided to locate sections of the text that are important either because students are likely to turn to that section frequently or because the section contains especially significant information. For example, students will use the many examples of citations frequently as they prepare their bibliographies and then the Works Cited page. And, while students may not return many times to guidelines for preparing a research proposal, they do need to study this section and be able to find it readily when they are ready to write their research proposal. In addition to providing easy access to key passages in the book, the tabs reinforce the information they mark with brief reminders or guidelines. Thus, the student turning to the section on plagiarizing will find, on the tab, a "quick warning" of seven writing strategies that lead to plagiarism. The brief list distills the more detailed discussion—and illustration—of plagiarism found in the text.

ACKNOWLEDGMENTS

No book of value is written alone. Friends and colleagues have helped me with *Doing Research*, and I am happy to thank them publicly. The editor who first signed the book for McGraw-Hill, Steve Pensinger, deserves recognition for his faith in my ability to handle this project. I also want to thank McGraw's current English Editor, Tim Julet, for his enthusiasm and guidance through the second edition, as well as Developmental Editor Alexis Walker for her many good suggestions. I am also grateful to colleagues Pamela Monaco and Karla Eaton for sharing student papers and favorite exercises, and to Professor Michael Hughes of Virginia Polytechnic Institute and State University for sending me so many excellent papers—to illustrate APA style—from his sociology students. My gratitude is once again due to the reference staff at the Annandale campus of Northern Virginia Community College, especially to Marian Delmore, Ruth Stanton, Carol Simwell, and Ellen Wertman. These generous women read the original Chapter 2 and made suggestions for updating, read my revision of Chapter 2, and read a revision of Appendix B to keep me straight on all the new databases. (Of course I alone am responsible for any flaws in the final version of these sections.) I do not want to overlook the help closest to home: my daughter Ruth has been a good—and patient—sounding board and has offered helpful suggestions after reading the entire manuscript. I appreciate as well the advice and specific suggestions of the following reviewers:

Karen Wilkes Gainey
Limestone College

Connie G. Rothwell
UNC—Charlotte

Kathy Howlett
Northeastern University

James Stokes
University of Wisconsin—Stevens Point

Kathleen Kelly
Northeastern University

Kim Brian Lovejoy
*Indiana University at
Indianapolis*

Robert Esch
University of Texas at El Paso

Finally, I want to acknowledge the students who have allowed me to use their papers. They worked hard on their essays and deserve to be proud to have achieved an audience beyond the classroom.

Dorothy U. Seyler

About the Author

Dorothy U. Seyler is Professor of English at Northern Virginia Community College. A Phi Beta Kappa graduate of the College of William and Mary, Dr. Seyler holds advanced degrees from Columbia University and the State University of New York at Albany. She taught at Ohio State University, the University of Kentucky, and Nassau Community College before moving with her family to Northern Virginia.

She has co-authored *Introduction to Literature* and *Language Power*, both in second editions. She is the author of *The Writer's Stance, The Reading Context, Steps to College Reading, Understanding Argument, Read, Reason, Write*, in its fifth edition, and *Patterns of Reflection*, in its third edition. In addition, Professor Seyler has published articles in professional journals and popular magazines. She enjoys tennis and golf, traveling, and writing about both sports and travel.

1

UNDERSTANDING RESEARCH

W riters, and teachers of writing, are fond of assuring students that getting started is the hardest part of any writing task. If they are right, then you have your research assignment under control because, by opening this guide, you have begun. Before you complain that you are not that naïve, let us agree that doing research is a complex, challenging, and sometimes frustrating activity. It can also be an exciting, rewarding activity. If you will also agree that complex tasks are handled best when organized into steps or stages and when you seek help for the difficult stages, then you must already be feeling less anxious. For the help is here: This handbook will lead you through the research process and explain how to handle each part of the task.

Remember, too, that some anxiety is good. It is what gets you to the library or your computer and keeps you reading or writing to stay on schedule. To keep anxiety in check, take comfort that you will be guided through the process of research. As you see results from your efforts, your confidence will grow and the excitement of discovery will carry you forward.

WHAT DOING RESEARCH MEANS

Doing research means obtaining information about a subject so that you can know something that you did not know before. Doing research *well* means finding the *best* information as a result of thinking critically about what you need to know and what sources can best provide that information. Doing research *well* means that what you know when you are finished gives you the best possible understanding of the subject.

Clearly we do research all the time. You probably did not decide just to appear on your college campus one August afternoon. You probably did some research before selecting your college. You spoke to high school friends who were attending the college, read the college's catalogue, perhaps visited the campus and talked with admissions personnel or someone in the field of your interest. When you are ready to buy a car, you will (if you are smart) do some research. You may have been looking over friends' cars for some time, so you already have some ideas. Now you need to supplement your knowledge with information from a variety of sources: brochures from car dealers, comparative evaluations in consumer magazines, remarks on the Web, conversations with owners of the cars you are considering. Your study will be limited by how quickly you need a new car and, most importantly, by how much money you have to spend. Your goal is to collect and study the best information about the models you are considering so that you can make a wise choice in the car you purchase.

What can we learn about research from these examples? We engage in research to explore an interest, answer a question, solve a problem, make a decision. Research is goal-oriented. The success of your market research into colleges and cars will be measured by how happy you are with your choices.

will be measured by the new knowledge you have and the excitement of discovery. (Just how did the dinosaurs die? Or, do they live on in today's birds?)

When we do research—in part—for others, for an academic, business, or professional community, then instead of acting on the research by making a purchase, we act by sharing the results of that research in some way: at a meeting, in a memo or report, or in a more formal paper. Most of you have had at least one experience of presenting the results of research in a library, term, or research paper, one that involved the use of sources and some form of documentation acceptable to the academic community. You may also have shared your knowledge through a class presentation. Frequently in college courses, as well as in business and professional settings, both oral and written reports of research are expected. Unfortunately, under the pressure of finding good information, coping with the technicalities of format, and meeting a deadline, student researchers sometimes lose sight of the purpose of doing research. As you begin your project, keep in mind the goals of research:

1. New knowledge
   - The biochemical triggers of alcoholism
   - Data on the contents of network news programs collected and analyzed
   - A comparison of shopping habits in urban, suburban, and rural communities
   - The discovery and publication of an artist's drawing notebooks
2. New understanding
   - Better methods for preventing and treating alcoholism
   - A recommendation for in-depth coverage of lead stories, based on the analysis of current news programs
   - A shopping-center plan based on the study of shopping habits
   - A reevaluation of the artist's work based on the study of the published notebook

The research *paper* is the written presentation of the researcher's new knowledge or understanding. Some college research projects in the sciences and social sciences involve experiments, case studies, field research, or questionnaires. These result in new knowledge for both the researcher and readers. Other research projects, such as those listed under 2 above, offer new understanding or new approaches for readers (and new knowledge for the researcher). Whether you are presenting new knowledge or new understanding, you are expected to find the best information, to understand that information, and to present it in an organized, fresh, and thoughtful way. You are also expected to prepare your completed paper to conform to an appropriate format for academic writing. The success of your project will come from your care in selecting and studying sources, your insight into the topic, and your clarity and thoroughness in presenting the results of your research.

THE REWARDS OF RESEARCH

We usually write our best when we keep in mind the nature of the writing project. Writers also profit from considering the benefits of their writing, especially as they "gear up" for the task of doing research. A few minutes' reflection on the benefits of your project may help you get started with the positive attitude that can lead to a first-class paper you will be proud to share with others.

New Knowledge/New Understanding

Remember that the purpose of research is to learn something you did not know before, not just to complete an assignment and get a grade. When you finish, you will have new information and perhaps a whole new perspective on the subject you studied. See yourself as in the process of becoming an expert on your topic. Discuss what you are learning with anyone who will listen—classmates, friends, family, your instructor—so that you develop a sense of pride in your new expertise.

Research Skills

Each time you take on a research assignment, you refine your research skills—skills that you will use in your personal life and probably, in some form, in your work as well. More specifically, each time you complete an assignment, you refine your skills in this particular type of academic writing. Skills are sharpened only with practice. Even research papers become easier each time through.

Critical Thinking Skills

Much of research is asking the right questions about a subject and then finding ways to get the answers. These are basic problem-solving skills that we need throughout our lives. To choose a career path, to find the right job, to decide where to live—and how we want to live our lives: These decisions require our best efforts at critical thinking. When you no longer remember the title of every college paper you wrote, you will still be drawing on the skills you developed in thinking through a problem and finding the best strategies for completing a task.

Participation in the Academic Community

Every time you do research and present your results in a paper or discuss your project with classmates, you take an active part in the community of scholars. Do not underestimate your contribution, your special perspective, on the topic you have studied. Many instructors learn as much from the fresh insights of their students as they do from their own research. In addition, you are learning the correct forms of documenting sources and presenting papers for the scholars in your discipline. Prepare your results with care so that you feel a part of the academic community.

TYPES OF RESEARCH PROJECTS

We have defined research on the basis of the results—new knowledge or new understanding. We can also make distinctions on the basis of the researcher's purpose in writing. Different purposes lead to papers that are primarily *expository, analytic,* or *argumentative.*

Expository

The expository or informative paper is sometimes called a report. Its purpose is to impart information, to explain to readers what the researcher has learned from the study. Scholarly reports in many disciplines include annotated bibliographies and reviews of the literature (what has already been written) on a given topic. (See pages 140–43 and 144–52 for an annotated bibliography and a review of literature.) In the sciences, reports include the results of experiments. Market research and technical reports are important kinds of informative writing in business. Reports usually serve as starting points for further research or as decision-making guides.

College students are sometimes assigned expository research papers, usually when instructors want them to

- read widely on a topic
- gain greater understanding of complex topics
- improve research skills (typically in a composition class).

If you are assigned a report, remember that a good report in any field reveals the writer's critical thinking in selecting and arranging the information so that both researcher and reader gain some new understanding.

Analytic

The analytic paper goes beyond an organized reporting of information with the purpose of explaining a topic to an examination of the implications of that information. For example, a report on problems in American education will assemble the results of recent tests that reveal some weaknesses in math and science. An analytic paper will present and discuss the causes for these weaknesses. Many literary studies are analyses. An analysis of light and dark imagery in Shakespeare's *Romeo and Juliet*, for example, will show how this imagery helps develop the play's theme. Analytic papers explore causes (what led to the dinosaurs' extinction), classify data (techniques used in print advertising), and explain processes (how journalists decide what's news).

Argumentative/Persuasive

The argumentative research essay uses information and analysis to support a thesis, to argue for a claim. An argumentative paper on problems in American education may use recent test results and an analysis of their causes to support an agenda for change. The researcher may seek to support the position, for example, that American schools should adopt elements of the Japanese school system. Another researcher studies violence on television and then seeks to persuade readers to support restrictions on programming. Compare these topics to see how they differ according to writing purpose:

Expository: Report on debate over relationship of modern birds to dinosaurs.

Report of recent literature on infant speech development.

Analytic: Account of the processes used to identify and classify animals based on the fossil record.

Explanation of process of infant speech development.

Argumentative: Support of claim that modern birds descended from dinosaurs.

Argument for specific actions by parents to aid infant speech development.

THE PROCESS OF RESEARCH WRITING

As you read through the following outline of stages in the research process, keep in mind that complex intellectual activities rarely fit neatly into a rigid sequence. No one can map your particular thinking processes, the development of ideas that will cause you to refocus your study and return to the library. Research writing means *re-searching*, *re-thinking*, and perhaps *re-writing* as well. Still, there is a basic process that can be described. Having an overview of this process will give you a sense of where you are headed and serve as a reminder of the technical elements of research writing. The following six stages provide that overview. Note, as you read, how the outline emphasizes the recursive nature of thinking, reading, and writing about a topic.

Stage 1. Select and Limit. Select and limit a topic consistent with assignment guidelines. Clear up any confusion about the assignment by asking questions of the instructor. Review some sources as necessary to aid in limiting a topic. Also consider purpose or type of research, audience, and required length or number of sources or amount of data when selecting.

Stage 2. Focus and Plan. Choose an approach or focus for your research. Decide on a tentative thesis, hypothesis, or question to answer. Think, talk, and read to complete this stage. Think about the kinds of sources needed and where to find them. Write a statement of purpose or research proposal that highlights your purpose and approach.

Stage 3. Gather Sources. In a systematic manner, locate potential sources in the library or from other appropriate places. (In addition to the library, consider the Internet, government publications, interviews, and doing your own data gathering by questionnaire.)

Stage 4. Read and Think. Read and evaluate sources and/or study original data. Take notes on relevant information and ideas. Learn about the topic. Re-think about what needs to be covered and what you need to learn to complete your study. Re-search as necessary. Develop a preliminary outline. Obtain additional information as necessary. Think some more.

Stage 5. Organize and Draft. Plan in detail the structure of your paper. With notes arranged according to a possible order, write a first draft. Include documentation as you draft to be certain that acknowledgment appears in all the right places.

Stage 6. Revise, Edit, and Format Correctly. First revise the draft and then edit to remove errors. Prepare the completed paper in an appropriate format with correct documentation of sources according to the style expected by your instructor.

FINDING A WORKABLE TOPIC

As Stage 1 indicates, to begin you need to select and limit your research topic. One key to success is finding a *workable* topic. No matter how interesting or clever your topic, it is not workable if it does not meet the guidelines of your assignment. So, start with a thorough understanding of the writing context created by the assignment.

Understand Purpose, Audience, and Constraints

As soon as you are given a research assignment, recognize the type of project assigned. Is the purpose expository, analytic, or argumentative? How would you classify each of the following possible topics?

1. Explain the chief solutions proposed for increasing the Southwest's water supply.
2. Compare the Freudian and behavioral models of mental illness.

3. Respond: Is *Death of a Salesman* a tragedy?

4. Consider: What twentieth-century invention has most dramatically changed our personal lives?

Did you recognize that the first topic calls for a report, that is, expository writing? The second topic requires an analysis of the views of two schools of psychology on the issue of mental illness. This means that you cannot report on only one model. Neither can you argue that one is superior to the other. Both topics 3 and 4 call for argument. Just reporting on what others have written on either topic will not fulfill assignment guidelines.

A sense of audience is also important. Even though, in most cases, your actual audience is the instructor who has assigned the research project, you should still give some thought to the implications of that audience for you as a writer. If you are doing research in a specific discipline, then imagine your instructor as a representative of that field, a reader who has knowledge of the subject area but is open to fresh ideas. If you are learning about the research process in a composition course, then your instructor may advise you to write to a general reader, someone who reads newspapers and magazines and knows today's issues and problems but may not have the exact information and perspective you have. Specialized terms and concepts need definition and illustration for a general reader but not for a "colleague." In some courses students discuss at least parts of their projects with classmates, or present their papers to the class. In this situation you actually have the multiple "readers" you have prepared for in your reflections on audience.

> Regardless of your purpose in writing or the number of readers you will have, you need to consider the expectations of readers of research papers. A research essay is not like a personal essay. A research essay is not about you; it is about a subject. The reading, thinking, and writing are yours, but your personality is less on display in research writing. Your reader comes to your paper to learn about a subject, not about you. So, keep yourself more in the background than you might in a more informal piece of writing.

The required length of the paper, the time given for the project, and the availability of sources are three constraints you must also consider when selecting a research topic. Most instructors establish guidelines regarding paper length. Undergraduate research papers generally range from six to twelve typed pages of text. (Instructors in upper-division courses in which the only grades will be for one paper and a final exam will expect longer papers.) Knowing length requirements is crucial to selecting an appropriate topic, so if your instructor does not specify, be sure to ask. Suppose, for example, that you must argue for solutions to either an educational or environmental problem. Your paper needs to be about six pages and is due in three weeks. Do you have the space or the time to explore solutions to all the problems caused by overpopulation? Definitely not. Limit your study to one issue, such as coping with trash. You could further limit this topic by exploring waste management solutions for your particular city or county.

Along similar lines, be careful about selecting topics that are dependent on source materials obtained only through interlibrary loan or the mails. If you have only a few weeks for a project, you may not receive government reports, for example, in time to use them in your study. (Fax machines, databases that provide full texts of articles, and the Internet have eliminated many but not all time constraints.)

Finally, several kinds of research topics are best avoided because they usually produce disasters, no matter how well the student handles the rest of the research process. Here is a list of types of topics to avoid.

1. *Topics that are irrelevant* to your interests and to the course. If you are not interested, your writing is likely to be uninspired. If you insist on selecting a topic far removed from the course content or from the specified subject areas listed on the assignment sheet, you may create some hostility in your instructor, who will wonder why you are unwilling to become engaged in the course.

2. *Topics that are broad subject areas.* These result in general surveys that lack appropriate detail and support.

3. *Topics that can be fully researched with only one source.* You will produce a summary, not a research paper that involves synthesizing information from several sources.

4. *Biographical studies.* Short undergraduate papers on a person's life usually turn out to be summaries of one or two major biographies.

5. *Topics that evoke strong emotions from you.* If there is only one "right" answer to the abortion issue and you cannot imagine counterarguments, do not choose to write on abortion. Probably most religious topics are best avoided.

6. *Topics that are too technical for you* at this point in your college study. If you do not understand the complexities of the federal tax code, then arguing for a reduction in the capital gains tax may be an unwise topic choice.

Use Invention Strategies to Generate and Limit Topics

Instructors vary in their control of topic selection. Assignments usually fit into one of three categories:

1. Course-related topics. For example: for a U.S. history course, you must explore the impact of any law passed in the twentieth century.

2. Topics selected from a specific list or from several broad groupings. For example, you must argue for solutions to an environmental or educational problem.

3. No restrictions on topic choice (but often a restriction on the *type* of topic). For example, you must write a review of the literature on your chosen subject.

If your instructor restricts topics or focuses the assignment in particular ways, consider this a benefit, for the instructor has simplified a difficult step in the research process. Regardless of the degree of focus of a given assignment, you will still need to select a subject and limit it to a specific topic. So, you may need to use one or more invention strategies to direct your selection. Here are some suggestions.

Think about What Interests You

While working within assignment guidelines, try to write about what interests you. See how the following assignments have been turned into topics that are influenced by the student's interests.

Assignment	*Interest*	*Topic*
1. Trace the influence of any twentieth century event, development, invention.	Music	The influence of the Jazz Age on modern music.
2. Support an argument on some issue of pornography and censorship.	Computers	Censorship of pornography on the Internet.
3. Demonstrate the popularity of a current myth and then discredit it.	Science fiction	The lack of evidence for the existence of UFOs.

Think about the Course

As soon as a research project is assigned, start thinking about topic possibilities. If the assignment is course-related, begin by thinking about what you already know or are learning in the course. Look over your class notes and think about subjects covered that have interested you. Or, take a different approach and reflect on topics that you could benefit from studying in detail. For example, for your art history course you must show how one artist is representative of a period or school of painting. Rather than choosing to write on your favorite impressionist, why not select a surrealist so that you can learn more about surrealism? What you discover may help you on the final exam, and your choice might set you apart from other students in the class.

To help you apply your interests and your knowledge of the course to topic guidelines, whether fairly general or quite specific, consider thinking on paper or on your personal computer. Some people can think through topic possibilities in their heads, but many are aided by getting ideas down and then reflecting on what they have written. Three writing strategies to generate topics include freewriting, brainstorming, and asking questions.

Freewrite

Freewriting forces you to get some ideas on paper, for the "rule" is that you cannot stop writing until you have filled a page or written for, say, 10 minutes. The student considering a paper for her art history course might begin her freewriting as illustrated in Figure 1. Notice that her freewriting reveals both an understanding of the course and her particular interest in the artist Chagall.

```
    I need to select an artist for my research
paper. My favorite is Van Gogh, but he's so
special—maybe he doesn't make a good
representative of a school. I could write about
Monet, but everybody likes the impressionists
and besides I think I can handle this term.
    What should I be studying? What about the
expressionists? The surrealists? Dadaism? These
terms run together in my thinking right now.
Maybe picking someone from one of these schools
would help me understand the differences,
because I'll have to be able to define these
categories. Let's see—who are some artists?
Dali? Miró? Escher? What about Chagall? I like
his cow jumping over the moon. Is this
surrealism or magic realism? Maybe I can
approach this topic by explaining
characteristics of some of the school's
subcategories and then show elements of the
subcategories in different Chagall paintings.
```

Figure 1 Sample of Freewriting on a Computer.

Brainstorm

Many people find brainstorming, another strategy that encourages thinking and imagination, preferable to freewriting, perhaps because it resembles a shopping list. Indeed, the strategy is similar to making a shopping list—of possibilities in this case—and it works much the same way. When starting to make a list, you may think you need only a few items at the store, but as you jot them down, others come to mind. And that is the idea: to range through possibilities, letting one idea generate another. Suppose your assignment is to study any current problem and then present and defend the best solutions to that problem. What problems concern you? You can get started by generating a list similar to the one in Figure 2.

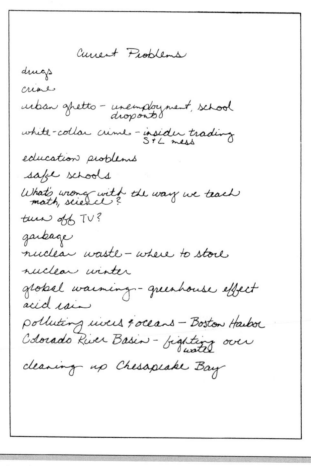

Figure 2 Sample of Brainstorming List.

Many problems worth studying are listed in Figure 2. Now you need to analyze the list, perhaps grouping similar kinds of problems and crossing out those you reject—and thinking about why you are rejecting them. In other words, have a conversation with yourself about the list. Your conversation will probably look something like the one illustrated in Figure 3. Figure 3 shows a process that combines listing, analyzing, and debating about ideas and interests to help the student reach a decision to study a local environmental problem. When thinking about current problems, try to get beyond just those in the national news. You may want to consider both college-based and community or statewide issues as alternatives.

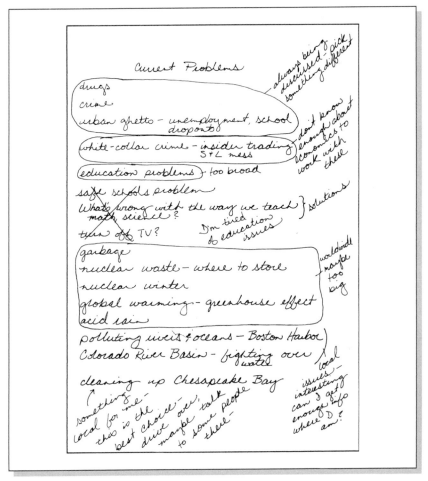

Figure 3 Interaction with Brainstorming List.

Ask Questions

One way to focus a narrowed topic from a broad subject is to ask questions. Contemplating the topic Prohibition for your U.S. history course, you may generate these questions:

Who wanted Prohibition?

Who opposed it?

Who benefited from it?

What forces created the climate for its passage?

What were the consequences?

Where did the temperance movement originate? Where was it most influential?

When was the law passed? When rescinded?

Why did people defy the law?

Notice that these questions use all the questions we associate with the journalist's list: *Who? What? Where? When?* and *Why?* A sixth question to consider for some topics is *How?*

Examine Printed Sources

If reflecting on the assignment and your interests and exploring ideas on paper do not lead to a workable topic, you can turn to various printed sources for help.

Scan a Book's Table of Contents or Index

Your textbook's table of contents or index can help you find a course-related topic. Similarly, a library book may suggest a workable topic, or help you narrow a broad topic. The table of contents entries in Figure 4 and the index entries in Figure 5 suggest several topics on environmental problems. Reading the appropriate pages in the text can give you an approach to such topics as coping with radioactive wastes and the need for earthquake prediction capabilities.

Explore Encyclopedia Indexes and Articles

Your library's multivolume general encyclopedias and specialized encyclopedias, handbooks, and dictionaries can serve as aids in topic selection and in narrowing a topic. They can also serve as places to begin learning about your topic.

One good choice is *The New Encyclopaedia Britannica*, considered one of the best of the general encyclopedias. This is a 32-volume work with four distinct parts. The *Micropaedia*, in volumes 1–12, contains brief articles on topics. The *Macropaedia*, in Volumes 13–29, contains long essays on topics, each

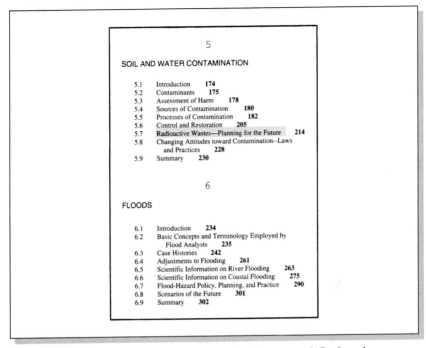

Figure 4 Table of Contents Entries from *Environmental Geology* by Lawrence Lundgren. Prentice, 1986.

Figure 5 Index Entries from *Environmental Geology* by Lawrence Lundgren. Prentice, 1986.

followed by a bibliography. Volume 30, called the *Propaedia*, is an outline of knowledge with suggestions for appropriate reading in the first 29 volumes. Volumes 31 and 32 contain the *Index*. If you are considering several broad subjects but need help in seeing how one might be narrowed, the volume to explore first is the *Propaedia*. If the student who needs to write on the impact of a federal law in the twentieth century had not decided on Prohibition by thinking about the course and his interests, he could have examined the outline of history. As the excerpt in Figure 6 reveals, Prohibition—as well as other possible topics—is suggested in the outline.

The student already thinking about a study of Prohibition can begin with the Index (see Figure 7) both to locate the volume and page number for the main article on his subject and to get ideas for narrowing and focusing his topic. The main article, a part of which appears in Figure 8, provides some answers to questions the student generated about his topic and suggests a possible strategy for exploring the effects of Prohibition: examining its differing effects on rural and urban areas and on various classes in society.

You may also use encyclopedias online if you have computer access. The *Britannica* is online as is *World Book Encyclopedia*. Online versions, updated frequently, are more current than the book versions. Sometimes books in your library's reference section are the most efficient tools. For others, the online encyclopedia has been a comfortable companion for years. For those, online is the place to be.

Section 973.

The United States and Canada Since 1920

A. The United States since 1920

   1. The post-World War I Republican administrations

      a. Politics and economics under Harding and Coolidge (1921-29): favouritism toward big business, restriction of immigration, "Coolidge prosperity"

      b. Social conditions in the 1920s: prohibition, growth of organized crime, and the jazz age

      c. Hoover's administration (1929-33) and the Great Depression: the stock market crash, domestic and international repercussions, Hoover's attempts to effect economic recovery

   2. The effects of the New Deal and World War II: the presidency of Franklin D. Roosevelt (1933-45)

      a. Comprehensive New Deal measures for economic recovery, relief, and reform

      b. Reform measures of the second New Deal and the election of 1936

Figure 6 From the *Propaedia* of *The New Encyclopaedia Britannica*, 1992 Edition.

---

prohibition (alcohol suppression)
  9:722:3b
  non-uniformity of regulations
    13:222:1a
  for a list of related subjects see
      PROPAEDIA: Section 522
Prohibition (U.S. hist.)
  major ref. in prohibition **9:**723:1a
  effect on
      bootlegging **2:**376:1b
      organized crime **8:**994:3b;
        29:255:1b
      police **25:**943:2a
      Saint Valentine's Day Massacre
        10:336:1a
  popularization of
      jazz **24:**642:2b
      stock-car racing **11:**277:1a
  role of
      Capone **2:**833:2b
      Ness **8:**611:1b
  support by Anti-Saloon League
        1:448:1b
Prohibition Amendment (U.S.
        Constitution): *see* Twenty-
        first Amendment

Figure 7 From the Index of *The New Encyclopaedia Britannica*, 1992 Edition.

☑ Encyclopedias are useful to researchers seeking to limit and focus topics and needing background information. You should understand, though, that college-level research essays cannot be developed from encyclopedias and other reference books. Encyclopedias are for preliminary research only.

Explore Computerized Sources

If your search for a topic has brought you to the library to examine encyclopedias, you may also be helped by using some of your library's CD-ROM and online materials. What you are looking for is a tool that will provide a list of subjects with subtopics suitable for a research paper. Two possibilities include *InfoTrac*, the CD-ROM version of *Magazine Index Plus*, and the library's online book catalog.

The drive for national prohibition emerged out of a renewed attack on the sale of liquor in many states after 1906. The underlying forces at work to support national prohibition included antipathy to the growth of cities (the presumed scene of most drinking), evangelical Protestant middle-class anti-alien and anti-Roman Catholic sentiment, and rural domination of the state legislatures, without which ratification of the Eighteenth Amendment would have been impossible. Other forces included the corruption existing in the saloons and the industrial employers' increased concern for preventing accidents and increasing the efficiency of workers.

The Anti-Saloon League, founded in 1893, led the state prohibition drives of 1906–13. During World War I a temporary Wartime Prohibition Act was passed to save grain for use as food. By January 1920 prohibition was already in effect in 33 states covering 63 percent of the total population. In 1917 the resolution for submission of the Prohibition Amendment to the states received the necessary two-thirds vote in Congress; the amendment was ratified on Jan. 29, 1919, and went into effect on Jan. 29, 1920. On Oct. 28, 1919, the National Prohibition Act, popularly known as the Volstead Act (after its promoter, Congressman Andrew J. Volstead), was enacted, providing enforcement guidelines.

Federal government support of enforcement of Prohibition varied considerably during the 1920s. Illegal manufacture and sales of liquor went on in the United States on a large scale. In general, Prohibition was enforced wherever the population was sympathetic to it. In the large cities, where sentiment was strongly opposed to Prohibition, enforcement was much weaker than in rural areas and small towns. Increased price of liquor and beer, however, meant that the working classes probably bore the restrictions of urban Prohibition to a far greater degree than the middle-class or upper class segments of the population.

Figure 8 Excerpt from "Prohibition," *The New Encyclopaedia Britannica*, 1992 Edition.

Examine *InfoTrac*

Magazine Index Plus, usually called by its trade name *InfoTrac* when the CD-ROM format is referred to (*Magazine Index Plus* is also online), is a combined author/subject index to periodicals, similar to *The Reader's Guide to Periodical Literature*, except that it is limited to more recent years. Find the library's appropriate terminal and type in various possible subjects to see what this index can suggest. For example, if your assignment requires a current controversial subject, and you remember an early fascination with dinosaurs, type in *dinosaur* to see what subheadings might suggest a topic. A partial list, in Figure 9, highlights two possible controversies: dinosaur behavior (were they warm-blooded, active animals?) and dinosaur extinction (what caused their demise?).

Writing a Thesis or Research Proposal

Make your thesis:

- A complete sentence
- A statement of an attitude or position
- Narrowed and concrete
- Consistent with assignment guidelines

Make your proposal:

- Extend at least 3–5 sentences
- Include your thesis
- Suggest an approach to the topic
- Suggest types of sources to be explored

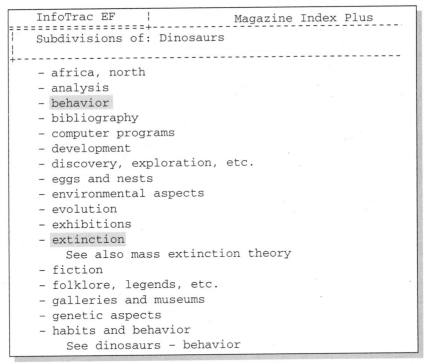

Figure 9 Excerpt from *Magazine Index Plus (InfoTrac.)*

Examine the Online Public Access [Book] Catalog

A library's online book catalog (usually referred to as OPAC because it usually catalogs more than just the book collection), can be used for a topic search by typing in a subject in which you are interested—perhaps dinosaurs or Hemingway or television violence. The catalog will provide headings and subheadings, as Figure 10 demonstrates, guiding you to limited topics within larger subject categories. (OPAC also gives you some insight into the relative size of a topic. If you see that your library has many books on a particular subheading, you may have to narrow your topic further to make it workable in a paper. If only one source is listed, your topic may be too narrow. Scan the headings and subheadings to look for ways to expand your potential topic. Observe in Figure 10 that there are 275 entries under the large subject *pollution*. Suggestions for narrowing include focusing on prevention or limiting the topic to one region.)

Talk with Others

Some people find that they do their best thinking when testing their ideas in conversation with others. If dialogue stimulates your thinking, then find a

```
Search Request: S=POLLUTION                          NVCC Library Catalog
Search Results: 264 Entries Found                         Subject Guide
-------------------------------------------------------------------------
      POLLUTION
 184  --LAW AND LEGISLATION--UNITED STATES--STATISTICS
 185  --MATHEMATICAL MODELS
 186  --MEASUREMENT
 190  --MEASUREMENT--LABORATORY MANUALS
 191  --MEASUREMENT--STANDARDS
 192  --MEDITERRANEAN REGION
 193  --MORAL AND ETHICAL ASPECTS
 194  --NEW YORK STATE
 195  --NEW YORK STATE--NIAGARA FALLS
 196  --PERIODICALS
 199  --PHYSIOLOGICAL EFFECT
 205  --POPULAR WORKS
 206  --PREVENTION
 208  --PSYCHOLOGICAL ASPECTS
-------------------------------------------- CONTINUED on next page  ----
STArt over      Type number to begin display within index range
HELp            INDex                          <F8>  FORward page
OTHer options   CHOose                         <F7>  BACk page

NEXT COMMAND:
4-©              1 Sess-1    164.106.130.4                       24/16
```

Figure 10 One Screen of a Subject Search of the Topic *pollution.*

classmate or friend who will listen to your ideas for topics and ask good questions that may help you select and focus one topic. Because of their knowledge, instructors also make good sounding boards. Most are happy to discuss possible topics with students and may provide good suggestions for narrowing and focusing a topic and locating useful sources. Instructors (and probably friends, too) will be most receptive if you have some topics to propose and are seeking help in choosing one or in deciding on an approach to a chosen topic. If you confess to having no ideas for a course-related topic, be prepared for your instructor to suggest that you try some of the search strategies discussed here first and then return to the office for conversation about several concrete possibilities.

WRITING A THESIS OR RESEARCH PROPOSAL

Once you have selected and narrowed a topic, you need to write a tentative thesis, research question, or research proposal to guide your planning and search for sources. Some instructors will ask to see a statement—from a sentence to a paragraph long—to be approved before you proceed. Others may require as much as a one-page proposal that includes a tentative thesis, a basic organizational plan, and a description of the types of sources to be used. Even if your instructor does not require anything in writing, you need to write something for *your* benefit—to direct your reading and thinking. Let's use the

Marc Chagall topic as an example to distinguish among subject, narrowed topic, thesis, and research proposal:

Subject: the painter Marc Chagall

Topic: Marc Chagall as a surrealist

Thesis: Marc Chagall is a representative of the surrealist school of modern art.

Research Proposal: I propose to show that Marc Chagall is a representative of the surrealist school of modern art. I will define "surrealism" and related terms such as "expressionism," "dadaism," and "magic realism" and show that characteristics of these elements of modern art can be found in Chagall's paintings. I plan to explore some of the sources included in the textbook's list of references as well as indexes to art journals.

This example illustrates several key ideas. First, the initial subject is both too broad (whole books have been written on Chagall) and unfocused (what about Chagall?). Second, the thesis is more focused than the topic statement because it asserts a position, a claim the student must demonstrate in her paper. Third, the research proposal is more helpful than the thesis statement because it includes a strategy for developing and supporting the student's thesis.

Not all researchers start with as much understanding of their subject as the art student. At times students select topics that intrigue them but about which they know very little. When this is the case, you will need a research question rather than a tentative thesis, or a more open-ended research proposal. Take, for example, the history student studying the effects of Prohibition. Although an encyclopedia article suggested an approach, he cannot, at this stage, write a tentative thesis. He can write a research question or, better yet, a research proposal that suggests some possible approaches to the topic.

Topic: The effects of Prohibition

Research Question: What were the effects of Prohibition on the United States?

Statement of Purpose: I will examine the effects of Prohibition on the United States in the 1920s (and possibly consider some long-term effects, depending on the amount of material on the topic). Specifically, I will look at the varying effects on urban and rural areas and on different classes in society.

Some Strategies for Focusing a Topic and Writing a Research Proposal

Ask Questions

Researchers generating their own data from questionnaires, case studies, or other strategies, will not be able to write a tentative thesis, but they, too, will need to begin with a research question and a strategy or methodology for obtaining and analyzing data. For example, for a course in marketing or communications or composition, you decide to answer this research question: Do the various techniques or appeals used in advertisements for liquor change when the audience for the ads changes? How do you proceed? Ask yourself some key questions to limit and focus your project:

All forms of liquor advertising?
Mixing forms really complicates any study, so you decide to examine print ads only, at least to start.

All kinds of liquor?
For the moment you decide yes, but this decision can be reexamined after you start collecting ads.

All kinds of audiences?
You remember that your initial interest in this study stemmed from an awareness that ads for station wagons seem to appear in women's magazines, but not men's magazines. You decide to limit your study to these same two audiences.

How will I collect my data?
To see if advertising changes with a change in audience, you need to collect liquor ads from representative men's and women's magazines, choose a time period (the last year?), and then collect all the liquor ads in each of the selected magazines for each of the selected months.

What else do I need to do?
You also need to study relevant sources on advertising strategies to expand your understanding of selling techniques used in print ads.

If you put together the answers to the questions you have asked, you can write a sound research proposal. Asking yourself questions is a good strategy for focusing a research topic and writing a research proposal.

Use the Language and Approaches of the Course to Focus and Write Your Proposal

The student who wants to do a paper "on Hemingway" for her literature class limits her study, because of time constraints, to *The Sun Also Rises* and one other Hemingway novel, *A Farewell to Arms*. Now what? We can analyze elements of a literary work such as *setting, character, style* and *symbol*. We can also apply concepts about a writer's approach in one work to other works by that writer, or test someone else's ideas about a writer based on our own reading and analysis. Our student is interested in Hemingway's female *characters* Brett Ashley and Catherine Barkley. She has also learned in class about the traits of the "Hemingway hero." She can now move from the broad and unfocused topic—something on Hemingway—to the following:

Topic: Brett and Catherine and the idea of the Hemingway hero

Research Proposal: I will analyze Brett Ashley and Catherine Barkley, the female lead characters in *The Sun Also Rises* and *A Farewell to Arms,* to see if they qualify as Hemingway heroes. I will read the chief Hemingway scholars who define the Hemingway hero and see if (and why or why not) Brett and Catherine meet the definition.

Use Various Fields of Study to Focus and Write Your Proposal

Your assignment is to defend a position on a current social issue. You think you want to do something "on television." Using some of the strategies for generating a topic, you decide on the following:

Topic: Television and violence

Research Proposal: I will explore the problem of violence on TV. I will read articles in current magazines and newspapers and see what's on the Internet.

Do you have a focused topic and a proposal that will guide your thinking and research? Not yet. Observe how working with fields of study (think of your college catalog of departments) can sharpen your thinking about the topic.

Literary/Humanities: What kinds of violence are found on TV? Children's cartoons? Cop and mystery shows? The news? How are they alike? How different? Do any have merit?

Sociology: What are the consequences to our society of a continual and heavy dose of violence on television?

Psychology: What are the effects of television violence on children? Do they become more aggressive? Less sensitive? Why are we drawn to violent shows?

Politics/Government: Should violence on television be controlled in any way? If so, how?

Education: What is the impact on the classroom when children grow up watching a lot of violence on TV? Does it impede social skills? Learning?

Structuring your thinking about the topic in these ways can help you focus your attention on a specific approach. After reflecting, you decide on the following more focused topic:

Topic: The negative effects of television violence on children and some solutions

Research Proposal: I will demonstrate that children suffer from their exposure to so much violence on TV and propose some solutions. Until I read more, I am not certain of the solutions I will propose; I want to read arguments for and against the V-Chip and ratings and other possibilities.

Do not settle for an unfocused topic and vague research proposal. To do so is only to put off the task of thinking about what you want to study and how you will proceed. Although your writing at this point is tentative—research may result in your changing your position on an issue—you still need a clear topic to research and some guidelines for getting started.

KEEPING A RESEARCH JOURNAL

The place to start work on your research proposal is in your *research notebook* or *journal*. Some instructors will require a journal or log as part of the project; others will recommend that you keep a journal for your own benefit. Keeping a journal means having a place to record new ideas, vent frustrations, prepare a work list for each week, and rejoice in stages completed. As you review what you have written, you can be encouraged by seeing progress made—or alerted to the fact that you need to pick up speed. Your completed journal provides a detailed account of the evolution of your paper. As such, it can be a guide to future projects, telling you much about how you think and work, perhaps even what steps should be handled differently another time. For example, if your journal reveals many problems in gathering sources, the dates of your recorded frustrations may also reveal that you did not start your search for sources promptly enough.

Keep your journal in a separate notebook, in a separate file in your word processor, or on the blank pages provided for this purpose at the end of the text. Prepare pages in a log format: Have two narrow columns on the left for recording each date and the amount of time spent and then use the rest of each page for recording your entries. Follow these guidelines for writing entries:

- **Record all work sessions**, including time spent locating sources, reading, thinking, taking notes, writing, and typing. Remember to include the time you spend reading this handbook. Make entries specific, dividing a block of time spent in the library, for example, into time searching for sources and that spent reading.

- **Record ideas on your topic**. Use your journal as a place for freewriting or brainstorming, for drafting a proposal, for noting ideas as they develop throughout your study.

- **Record the completion of any required steps in the process**. For example, note when you met the due dates for a research proposal, a working bibliography, and/or a first draft. Reward yourself for work accomplished.

- **Record problems, frustrations, distractions**. Take out your frustrations on your journal, not on the librarian or your roommate, neither one of whom is responsible for the book you need not being on the shelf. After recording problems, take time to think about solutions, and record those, too, when they are found.

- **Record plans for work**. Draw up weekly work sheets, listing specific research tasks in the library or online, or the time you will set aside for writing.

- **Record entries on a regular, frequent basis**, preferably after each work session. Let your journal writing be a way to keep you involved in and progressing through your project.

ESTABLISHING A SCHEDULE

To avoid being overwhelmed by a complex task such as a research project, you need to establish a plan. Your instructor may help you in this by setting dates for completing some stages of the process. Instructors often require a conference with each student, at which time the student must have a tentative thesis or research proposal and, possibly, a partial list of sources as well. If a conference date is set as well as a due date for the project, then you need to set two more dates for yourself: a date for completing your research and a date for completing your first draft. Make sure to set a draft completion date that is several days—at least—before the project's due date so that you have time to revise your paper and prepare a completed version to submit on time.

If your instructor does not expect to see a research proposal or a working bibliography, then you need to add completion dates for these steps to your schedule. Although "poking around" in the library can be fun as you search for ideas for topics, you must be practical, too, and set a deadline for deciding on a topic. Similarly, you can spend considerable time reading about your topic, but at some point you must get on with the writing of the paper. Deadlines will keep you moving forward toward your goal: a completed research paper.

2

LOCATING
SOURCES

O ccasionally student researchers have trouble locating enough sources for their research topic. (If this happens, you need to broaden your topic.) More typically, the available resources seem overwhelming. For this reason, you need a good research proposal, one that points you in the direction of what you will need to find and study. Indeed, you really need three types of information to work effectively in this next stage in the research process. You need to know:

- your search strategy—how and what to find, as determined by the needs of your topic

- your choice of method and format for recording information about potential sources

- your library—what is available and how information is organized and accessed

DETERMINING A SEARCH STRATEGY

Reflect on the sample research proposals presented in Chapter 1. Each one includes some thoughts about what the student needs to cover or how the student will go about developing the topic. You need similar guidelines before starting a search for sources. Let's revisit the study of liquor ads. The student made key decisions about what ads to study in what types of magazines. To gain additional understanding of advertising strategies, the student also needs to do some reading. Where to begin? A good choice would be a textbook on advertising. Several chapters may have relevant information. Which ones? The student is not interested in advertising costs or the process of designing the ads. The student *is* interested in the effects of ads on viewers, so only relevant sections about how ads "work" need study. In addition, the text is likely to contain references to works on advertising the author studied in preparing the text. One good source with a bibliography leads to other sources.

If you are writing on a course-related topic, your starting place may well be your textbook both for relevant sections and for possible sources. (Your text may be where you began the process of selecting and narrowing a topic.) Also, do not overlook the reference guides in the lists by discipline in Appendix B of this book. Those basic books and indexes will give you a place to start your library search. If you are doing research for a composition course, you probably have some information and possible sources from the process of selecting and focusing your topic. To aid both types of researchers, here is a general guide to library reference sources that may be useful for different kinds of searches.

Using Library Reference Sources: A General Guide

To Narrow and Focus a Topic, Use:
general encyclopedias, in paper or electronic format (CD or online)

book indexes
book tables of content
periodicals indexes, especially CD-ROM indexes such as *InfoTrac* or online
    indexes such as those found through *Information Access, UMI, Silver-*
    platter, etc.

To Obtain Background Information on a Topic, Use:
specialized encyclopedias, handbooks, etc.
biographical dictionaries
other specialized dictionaries
atlases, almanacs
histories

*To Obtain Sources on Current Topics—for Assignments in Composition
Courses—Use:*
the book catalog (OPAC)
The Reader's Guide to Periodical Literature
Magazine Index/Plus (*InfoTrac* on CD), *Information Access* (*SearchBank*
    online), and other current online indexes
Newspaper Index or *New York Times Index* or other news sources
Full-text databases such as *ProQuest*
Statistical sources such as *Matter of Fact* or *Fact Search*
the Internet
government documents (often available through the Internet)
interviews; correspondence; television programs—as appropriate

*To Obtain Sources for Topics in a Subject Area—for Assignments in Spe-
cific Disciplines—Use:*
the book catalog
general periodicals indexes and full-text databases listed above, as
    appropriate
specialized indexes for discipline, e.g., *Art Index, PAIS, Social Sciences
    Index, MLA International Bibliography*
citation indexes for discipline
Dissertation Abstracts International
the Internet
sources outside the library as appropriate

SELECTING A METHOD AND FORMAT
FOR DOCUMENTING SOURCES

Before starting a systematic search for sources, you need to know both how
you are going to keep a record of possible sources and what documentation
format you will use in your paper. As Chapter 3 discusses, you have two good
choices of recording method: the always reliable 3 × 5-inch index cards or a
bibliography file in your personal computer. Read pages 74–76 of Chapter 3
before continuing with this chapter if you need to weigh the two methods to

select the best one for you. (**Note:** If your instructor requires bibliography cards, then the decision has been made for you.).

You should know what documentation format you will be using before beginning your research. If you are in a composition class, you may be assigned the MLA (Modern Language Association) format, or perhaps be given a choice between MLA and APA (American Psychological Association). In an upper-level course, you may be expected to use the format common to that discipline, for example, CBE (Council of Biology Editors) for biology, APA for psychology. If you are uncertain, ask your instructor. Then skim the appropriate pages in Chapter 3 or Chapter 7 to get an overview of both style and content for the format you will use. When listing bibliographic information for possible sources, refer to the inside front and back covers of this text for models of basic formats for MLA and APA styles. If you record all needed information in the correct format the first time, you will save time and make fewer mistakes.

☑ A collection of printouts, slips of paper, and backs of envelopes is not a method! You will end up having to return to the library for needed information. And you risk making serious errors in documentation. Choose your method and know the basics of your format: then stick to both faithfully as you gather potential sources.

KNOWING YOUR LIBRARY

If knowledge of your campus library is limited, you need to take a little time to learn about the library's arrangement, hours of operation, and procedures for obtaining materials. You will save time in the long run if you take time at the beginning to learn your way around and understand how to find the sources you need. What you may discover is that your campus library has embraced new computer technology. Most computer applications actually make research easier and provide access to materials not previously available in many libraries. For example, you may find that your library is part of a group of libraries sharing resources and that you can check, while in your library, if another school has a book you need. The rest of this chapter will instruct you in both the standard tools of research and the new technology, but first you need a quick tour of the library.

Circulation Desk

Located in the center of the library or near the main entrance is the circulation desk. Here you can receive information about the library's procedures and also check out and return materials, a process probably now handled on a computer terminal.

Book Catalog (OPAC)

The chief guide to your library's book collection is the book catalog, tradition-ally called the card catalog because at one time book catalogs were on 3×5 cards in drawers. Now most book catalogs are online. Online catalogs are usually referred to as Online Public Access Catalogs or OPAC, in part because they are online and in part because the catalogs include audiovisual and other materials in addition to the book collection. OPAC terminals will probably be near the circulation desk or near the reference desk.

Stacks

A library's book collection is generally divided into three categories. First is the general collection, those books housed on long rows of shelves, usually called *stacks*. These books, making up most of the book collection, circulate for a several-week period and can sometimes be renewed for an additional period. Most but not all college library stacks are open to students; that is, you are expected to find the books you need by using their classification or "call" number and then bring them to the circulation desk for processing.

If the stacks are not open, then you must complete a request slip for each book and wait for runners to bring the requested books to the circulation desk.

Reference Collection

Placed in a separate area or room is the reference collection, those books of a general nature essential to research that therefore cannot be checked out. Included in the reference collection are general encyclopedias and dictionar-ies, atlases, bibliographies, and many handbooks, manuals, and specialized encyclopedias arranged in the reference area by classification number. Refer-ence books are listed in the book catalog but designated by the abbreviation *Ref* as part of the classification number. Located in the reference area are the reference desk and, behind it, the single most valuable resource in the room: the reference librarian. Although reference librarians cannot find research topics for you, they can help you find information or the right research tools for your project.

Reserve Collection

In large libraries the collection of books, articles, and audiovisual materials on reserve will be located in a separate reading room; in smaller libraries reserve materials will usually be found behind the circulation desk. Some reserve materials can be checked out for overnight or up to several days; others, on "closed" reserve, must be used in the library—or retrieved on your PC from electronically stored and accessed sources. The reserve collection consists of works that instructors consider essential aids to their courses. The checkout times have been limited so that more students have access to these works.

Periodicals Collection

A library's periodicals collection consists of popular magazines (*Newsweek; Consumer Reports*), scholarly journals (*New England Journal of Medicine; Modern Fiction Studies*), and newspapers (*New York Times; Wall Street Journal*)—works that are issued periodically. The collection can generally be found in a separate area or room in the library. Periodicals are stored in their original paper format, on microfilm or microfiche, and on CD. Check to see if volumes of indexes to periodicals are located in the reference area or in the periodicals area. (Other periodical indexes will be online, accessed on the OPAC terminals or their own terminals.)

Interlibrary Loans

As impressive as your library's collection seems, it still may not have a particular work that you need. Before despairing, explore interlibrary loan procedures. In many areas where several colleges are found, the schools have formed consortia, allowing students at one school to check out books at another's library. Other cooperative arrangements include statewide catalog listings in each library (indicating if there is a library in the state with the book or periodical you need that can be requested on loan). For books at a nearby school, your best choice is to go yourself to obtain the work rather than wait for delivery. If you start your search for sources early, you can take advantage of a statewide loan service. Needed articles found at other schools can be faxed or e-mailed to you.

Nonprint Collection

Your library's book and periodicals collection is enhanced by a variety of audio and multimedia materials. Learn the location and general content of the records, tapes, and discs, for these are designed to supplement courses, especially in languages, art, and music. Nonprint works can also be valuable for some research projects.

Photocopiers, Printers, E-mail

Most libraries provide coin- or card-operated photocopying machines and even change machines as well. These give you one strategy for studying noncirculating materials in your room. Additionally, many articles, available electronically, can be printed in the library, and other materials can be downloaded from the Internet.

Once acquainted with your library's layout and services, you want to understand in detail how to use its major tools for locating sources. Because you are likely to need books, regardless of your research topic, the discussion of locating sources will begin with the book catalog.

> ✓ Remember: All works, regardless of their source or the format in which you obtain them, must be fully documented in your paper, and there are restrictions on copyrighted materials beyond your personal use.

LOCATING BOOKS

Regardless of the catalog's format—card, microform, online—the information provided is much the same, and the ways of accessing are similar. All catalogs use author, title, and subject access points. Online catalogs can also be accessed by using keywords—and other possibilities, depending on who has prepared the catalog.

Card or Microform Catalogs

You can locate books in a card or microform catalog by looking up author, title, or subject. So, in a card or microform catalog, you will find at least three entries for each book: the author entry, the title entry, and one or more subject entries. In some catalogs, all entries are filed together in one alphabetical listing. Others create three catalogs or combine author and title entries in one listing and subject entries in another. Knowing which catalog to use will speed your search.

Author Catalog

Authors are filed alphabetically with the last name first. This catalog also includes editors, translators, illustrators, and organizations that "author" publications. If you know the author's name, use this catalog.

Title Catalog

Title entries contain the same information about each book as author entries but include the title repeated across the top. Title entries are filed alphabetically (usually) word by word, excluding *A*, *An*, and *The* at the beginning of titles. Thus *The Great Gatsby* is filed under *G*, not *T*. If you know the title of a book (for example, *The Story of Art*) but not its author, use the title catalog (or an undivided catalog) and look under *S*.

Subject Catalog

This catalog contains entries filed alphabetically according to the subject heading, printed at the top of the entry in capital letters. Subject headings include people (WILLIAMS, TENNESSEE; ROOSEVELT, ELEANOR), topics (GOVERNMENT AND THE PRESS; POP ART), and place names (CANADA; SAN FRANCISCO). Since most academic libraries use the Library of Congress subject heading system for books, you can most efficiently use the subject catalog by first looking in the *Library of Congress Subject Headings (LCSH)*. This three-volume work lists subject headings used in the subject catalog, so you do not have to try to guess what headings have been used that would be relevant to your topic. Using the *LCSH* eliminates the frustration similar to looking in the Yellow Pages of the phone book under *Gas Stations* when you need instead to look in the *S*'s under *Service Stations*. Figure 11 illustrates part of a page from the *LCSH* and explains the abbreviations used. If you wanted to find books on the subject of the care and treatment of animals in zoos, the passage in Figure 11 would direct you to the correct subject headings to use. (**Note:** For many library catalogs, the *LCSH* is still a useful tool. However, online catalogs are becoming increasingly "user-friendly" to keyword rather than LC subject heading searches).

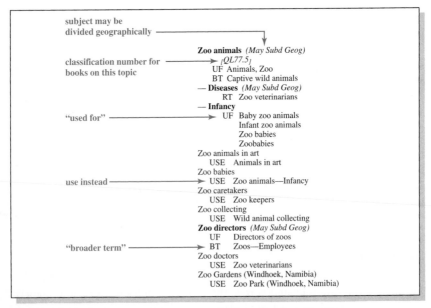

Figure 11 Excerpt from *Library of Congress Subject Headings*.

Catalog Entries

Each catalog entry contains a wealth of helpful information in addition to a book's author, title, and classification or call number (the number by which the book is shelved in the library).

Card or Microform Catalogs

Figure 12 shows a sample entry for card or microform catalogs with an explanation of its details. When preparing a list of potential sources (your working bibliography—see Chapter 3), study each entry carefully and copy all needed and useful information, including:

1. *Call number.* This is necessary to locate the book in the library.
2. *Author, title, and facts of publication.* This information is essential for correct documentation of all sources.
3. *Paging.* The length of the book will help you gauge the extent of coverage and plan your study time.
4. *Special notes.* Always check here to see if the book contains a bibliography, another list of potential sources for your research project.
5. *Tracing information.* Note the subject headings under which you will find an entry for this book and check them in the catalog for additional books on your topic.

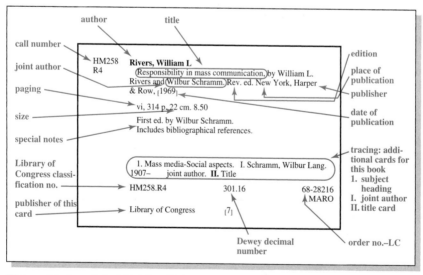

Figure 12 Annotated Catalog Entry.

Online Catalogs

When using OPAC, you will obtain the same information, but it will appear on the screen in a different format. Remember that access points remain the same: You can type in an author's name, a title, or a subject, in addition to a keyword search. If you want a list of all the library's works by Hemingway, for example, type in the author's name. If you want a particular novel, type in the title (excluding initial articles). If you are seeking books on a specific topic, use an LC subject heading or a keyword. Figure 13 illustrates such a screen display from one online catalog. Notice that the sample screen is labeled "Long View." Sometimes you will need a second command to move from a short-view screen that does not contain complete bibliographic information or circulating information to the long (or full) screen that gives you such important information. With the long screen for this particular book, you do not have to check the stacks or the circulation desk to determine the book's status. Here you learn that the book is in the general collection (circulating) and that the three copies should all be on the shelf. Also observe that you are given subject headings under which to look for additional books useful to your study. Finally, the screen provides you with the book's call number and the bibliographic information needed for documentation. Copy *all* of this information into your working bibliography.

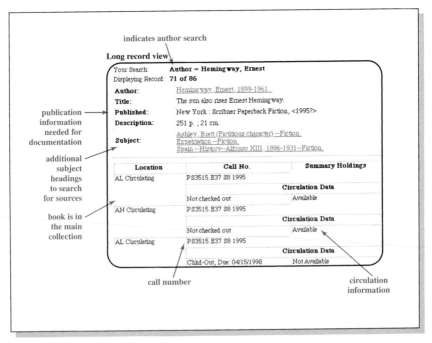

Figure 13 Online Book Entry.

Classification Systems

Books are shelved in libraries according to either the Dewey decimal system or the Library of Congress classification system, two standardized codes combining numbers and letters that classify books by subject.

The Dewey Decimal System

The Dewey decimal system is named for its creator (Melvil Dewey) and for the classification of subjects by divisions of 10. Figure 14 shows the system's classification of knowledge from 000 to 990 in divisions of 10. These sections are further divided, even to the addition of a decimal number, for example, 940.56 for Helen Andrews's *New Insights on World War II*. This system can include a second number, the author number, created from the first letter of the author's last name, a code number given to that author, and the first letter of the book title (excluding *A, An,* and *The*). Thus the complete call number for Andrews's book is 940.56/A566n. Many small libraries using Dewey add only the first letter of the author's last name after the primary classification number.

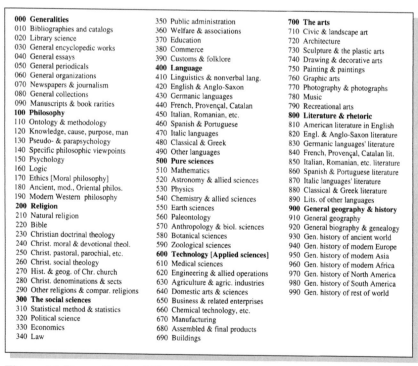

000 Generalities	350 Public administration	**700 The arts**
010 Bibliographies and catalogs	360 Welfare & associations	710 Civic & landscape art
020 Library science	370 Education	720 Architecture
030 General encyclopedic works	380 Commerce	730 Sculpture & the plastic arts
040 General essays	390 Customs & folklore	740 Drawing & decorative arts
050 General periodicals	**400 Language**	750 Painting & paintings
060 General organizations	410 Linguistics & nonverbal lang.	760 Graphic arts
070 Newspapers & journalism	420 English & Anglo-Saxon	770 Photography & photographs
080 General collections	430 Germanic languages	780 Music
090 Manuscripts & book rarities	440 French, Provençal, Catalan	790 Recreational arts
100 Philosophy	450 Italian, Romanian, etc.	**800 Literature & rhetoric**
110 Ontology & methodology	460 Spanish & Portuguese	810 American literature in English
120 Knowledge, cause, purpose, man	470 Italic languages	820 Engl. & Anglo-Saxon literature
130 Pseudo- & parapsychology	480 Classical & Greek	830 Germanic languages' literature
140 Specific philosophic viewpoints	490 Other languages	840 French, Provençal, Catalan lit.
150 Psychology	**500 Pure sciences**	850 Italian, Romanian, etc. literature
160 Logic	510 Mathematics	860 Spanish & Portuguese literature
170 Ethics [Moral philosophy]	520 Astronomy & allied sciences	870 Italic languages' literature
180 Ancient, mod., Oriental philos.	530 Physics	880 Classical & Greek literature
190 Modern Western philosophy	540 Chemistry & allied sciences	890 Lits. of other languages
200 Religion	550 Earth sciences	**900 General geography & history**
210 Natural religion	560 Paleontology	910 General geography
220 Bible	570 Anthropology & biol. sciences	920 General biography & genealogy
230 Christian doctrinal theology	580 Botanical sciences	930 Gen. history of ancient world
240 Christ. moral & devotional theol.	590 Zoological sciences	940 Gen. history of modern Europe
250 Christ. pastoral, parochial, etc.	**600 Technology [Applied sciences]**	950 Gen. history of modern Asia
260 Christ. social theology	610 Medical sciences	960 Gen. history of modern Africa
270 Hist. & geog. of Chr. church	620 Engineering & allied operations	970 Gen. history of North America
280 Christ. denominations & sects	630 Agriculture & agric. industries	980 Gen. history of South America
290 Other religions & compar. religions	640 Domestic arts & sciences	990 Gen. history of rest of world
300 The social sciences	650 Business & related enterprises	
310 Statistical method & statistics	660 Chemical technology, etc.	
320 Political science	670 Manufacturing	
330 Economics	680 Assembled & final products	
340 Law	690 Buildings	

Figure 14 Dewey Decimal Classifications (the 100 Main Divisions).

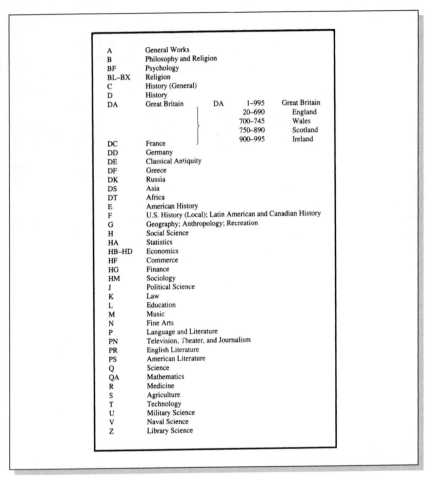

Figure 15 Library of Congress Classification System.

The Library of Congress Classification System

The Library of Congress (LC) system, now used in most college libraries, provides a more complete and logical system of classifying books and gives every book its unique call number. It begins with 21, rather than 10, broad categories, each designated by a letter. These broad categories are then divided by adding a second letter. Numbers are used to further subdivide a subject area. Figure 15 lists the 21 initial categories, includes second-letter categories for many subject areas, and shows how the numbers divide one category, the history of Great Britain. Finally, a third line is used to designate a specific book by a particular author. For example, a specific history text—George M. Trevelyan's *The English Revolution, 1688–1689*—would have the following LC number:

Using Reference Sources:
Sources:
Identifying
Advantages of
Indexes
in Different
Formats

Paper:

- Never "goes off-line"
- Indexes sources before 1980
- Can be faster for locating a few items

CD-ROM:

- Often accompanied by full texts of articles
- More current than print indexes

Online:

- Contains the most current indexes
- Allows search of all years at once
- Especially good for government information and statistical data

DA (history of Great Britain)

452 (history in the period of James II, 1685–1688)

.T7 (author designation combining the first letter of the last name and a code number for the second letter of the last name)

Arrangement of Books on the Shelf

Whichever system your library uses, you will need the complete call number of a book to locate it on the shelf. Each book's call number is provided in the catalog entry and on the spine of the book. LC call numbers arrange books on shelves in the order illustrated in Figure 16. Note that the third line is a decimal number: .K214 precedes .K26.

As you search for sources, use every available opportunity to add to your working bibliography. If you use subject headings or keyword searches on your topic, make a bibliography card or entry in your PC file for every book that might prove useful. Make a special note of books having bibliographies and examine those pages as soon as you locate each book. When in the stacks to pick up books on your topic, take a few minutes to look at those near the books you are seeking, for those nearby will be in the same subject category. If a book you want is not in its proper place on the shelf, look above and below—even behind other books—to see if the one you need is lurking in the wrong place. You might even check the carts of books awaiting reshelving before becoming convinced that the book is not available. Serious researchers need to develop a "nose for books."

USING THE REFERENCE COLLECTION

Doing research often begins with the reference collection. As you have seen, reference materials can be used first to suggest and narrow topics, then to provide background information and an overview of a topic, and finally to supply particular facts or, through indexes, access to needed sources. In

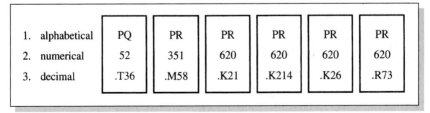

1. alphabetical	PQ	PR	PR	PR	PR	PR
2. numerical	52	351	620	620	620	620
3. decimal	.T36	.M58	.K21	.K214	.K26	.R73

Figure 16 Model of Shelf Order for Books.

addition to dictionaries, encyclopedias, and handbooks of all kinds, the reference collection includes such important research tools as bibliographies and indexes to articles.

Not surprisingly, many tools in the reference collection once only in print form are now also on CD-ROM or online. Some are now only online—so, to have access to all possible useful sources, you will have to join the revolution and get online. On the other hand, online is not always the way to go. Let's consider some of the advantages of each of the formats.

Advantages of the Print Reference Collection

1. The reference tool is only in print—use it.
2. The print form covers the period you are studying. (CD-ROM and online bibliographies, indexes, and abstracts cover only recent years. The printed form of the *New York Times Index*, for example, goes back to the nineteenth century.)
3. You do not have to spell perfectly or get commands exactly right to find what you are looking for in a book. In a book, with a little scanning of pages, you can usually find what you are looking for.
4. If you know the best reference source to use and are looking for only a few items, the print source can be faster.
5. All computer terminals are in use—walk to the print index and get to work!
6. The computers are down—open a book.

Advantages of Reference Materials on CD-ROM

1. CD-ROM indexes are usually easy to use.
2. Some CD-ROM indexes come with full text of articles that can be printed out or downloaded for your use.
3. CD-ROM indexes are usually more current than print materials—although less current than online sources.
4. Your library may "subscribe" to periodicals only on CD-ROM, not in print, so this is your best access to articles in those periodicals. Also, there is no charge for each use.
5. Unlike print indexes, you can usually search all years covered at once, rather than year by year in most print indexes. (However, most indexes and full-text articles on CD-ROM cover only back to 1980, if that far.)

Advantages of the Online Reference Collection

1. Online databases are likely to provide the most up-to-date information. (Some information online is updated daily.)

2. You can search more than one year at a time.

3. Full texts (with graphics) are sometimes available, as well as indexes with detailed summaries of articles. Both can be printed, downloaded, and sometimes e-mailed.

4. Through links to the Internet, you have access to an amazing amount of material. (Unless you focus your keyword search, however, you may be overwhelmed.)

Of course no research guide can begin to explain the wealth of reference materials available to researchers, but we can examine some of the most commonly used. In addition, you need to become acquainted with the key sources in your particular field of study. You can begin by examining the list of works in your discipline listed in Appendix B, browsing through your library's reference collection in the section related to your field of study, and seeking guidance from reference librarians. Before using any reference work, take a few minutes to check the work's date (some information becomes outdated quickly), purpose, and organization. Before using the computer terminals, look for information about the various databases available; this information is usually found in folders or notebooks near the terminals. Additionally, some online databases come with a brief tutorial explaining how best to use the database; take time to go through the tutorial. In these ways you can supplement the following discussion and develop your skills with reference materials.

The Reference Librarian's Guides and Bibliographies

Serious researchers are smart to become familiar with the reference tools relied on by librarians: the trade and general bibliographies. One of the most important, *Books in Print* (1948 to date) lists—by author, title, and subject—all books currently in print that are available from publishers or distributors in the United States. You can check here to see if a book is still in print, to obtain bibliographic information, to find a publisher's address (if you want to order a book directly from the publisher), and, by using the subject listing, to locate books not in your library but perhaps available on interlibrary loan. Your library may have the author and title volumes in print, CD-ROM, or online, but from 1998 on, the subject listing will be online only. Figure 17 shows only some of the many books on noise pollution listed in the *Subject Guide to Books in Print*. Other trade bibliographies to know include:

Cumulative Book Index. 1900 to date, published monthly. (Print, CD-ROM, and online.) Lists all books published in the English language, not just those in print.

Publishers Weekly. 1872 to date. A good source of information on new books.

Ulrich's International Periodicals Directory. (Print—5 vols, CD-ROM, and online.) Here you will find information needed for ordering reprints of articles and locating foreign periodicals.

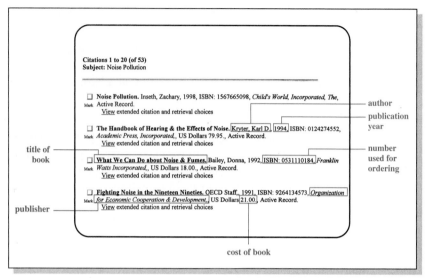

Figure 17 Excerpt from *Subject Guide to Books in Print.*

Union List of Serials in Libraries of the United States and Canada. 3rd ed. New York: Wilson, 1965. Supplements: *New Serials Titles*, Washington, DC: Library of Congress, 1953 to date. Use this work to find a library subscribing to a needed periodical not held by your library.

General bibliographies and guides to reference works can be useful to researchers as well as to librarians. These bibliographies and guides direct you to reference works, bibliographies, or indexes in various subject areas. In other words, these works guide you to other works that contain bibliographies. One example is *Bibliographic Index: A Cumulative Bibliography of Bibliographies* (1938 to date). *Bibliographic Index* indexes, by both author and subject, books and articles that contain bibliographies. The excerpt shown in Figure 18 provides an example. Here are additional guides worth knowing:

A World Bibliography of Bibliographies. (Theodore Besterman)

Guide to the Use of Books and Libraries. (Jean Key Gates)

Guide to Reference Books. (Robert Balay, 11th ed.)

Basic Reference Tools

When most of us think of the reference collection, we picture dictionaries, handbooks, and encyclopedias providing information and factual details in a condensed format. The following discussion reviews some basic reference tools. Some can be used to locate sources. Most are the works you turn to

- for the background information you need to understand your subject or sources

- for facts (or to check facts in your sources) to support your research

Be aware of the support that your library can provide and turn to these works as you need to in the process of your study and writing.

Dictionaries

If you need the spelling of a word not included in your personal computer's spell check, or if you need current definitions of a word, use a good desk dictionary. For specialized words, consult the appropriate subject dictionary, for foreign words, the appropriate foreign language dictionary. If you want to learn about a word's origin or definitions at an earlier time, the place to go is one of the unabridged or specialized dictionaries in your library. Here are three to know:

The Oxford English Dictionary. 20 vols. in print; also on CD-ROM and online. Known as the *OED.* A storehouse of information on English language use and word origins. (The art student studying Chagall can check here for the first use of the term *surrealism.*)

The Random House Dictionary of the English Language.

Webster's Unabridged Dictionary of the English Language.

General Encyclopedias

Two multivolume encyclopedias found in most college libraries are the *Encyclopedia Americana* and the *Encyclopaedia Britannica.* See pages 14–17 for a detailed discussion of the *Encyclopaedia Britannica's* format (and its potential use by the student studying Prohibition). *Britannica, World Book,* and other encyclopedias—and dictionaries—are now available online.

Atlases

Atlases should not be overlooked, for they provide much more than simple maps showing capital cities and the names of rivers. Historical atlases show,

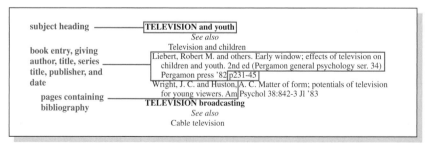

Figure 18 From *Bibliographic Index.*

through maps and other graphics, changes in political geography and economic and cultural changes as well. Topographical atlases support studies in the earth sciences and provide information essential to many contemporary environmental issues. Just a few of the many good atlases are listed here.

Historical Atlas of the United States. National Geographic Society, 1988.

National Geographic Atlas of the World. 6th ed. National Geographic Society, 1995.

The Times Atlas of the World. 9th comprehensive ed. 1992.

Also check to see if your library has one or more atlases on CD-ROM.

Quotations, Mythology, and Folklore

The following works are useful for understanding references or allusions unfamiliar to you in your reading. "To err is human; to forgive divine" may seem too well known to be identified by the author of a book you are reading, but if you do not recognize the quotation, you must look it up. Similarly, if you do not know who Apollo or Orpheus was, you need to refer to a book on mythology. Some standard works include

Familiar Quotations. (John Bartlett, 1992.)

Funk and Wagnall's Standard Dictionary of Folklore, Mythology, and Legend. (1984)

The Golden Bough. (Sir James G. Frazer, 12 vols., 1907–1915; New York: St. Martin's, 1955.) An exhaustive study of myths. A one-volume condensed version is available.

The Home Book of Quotations. (Burton Stevenson, 1984.)

Mythology. (Edith Hamilton, 1971.)

Almanacs and Yearbooks

The following sources answer all kinds of questions about current events and provide statistical information on just about anything: how your congressional representative voted on a key bill, the number of college students in a given year, income distribution in the United States, the size of the largest watermelon. This is a partial list, to give you an idea of what is available. Many of these works—and other factual sources—are now available on CD-ROM and/or online. Check to see which format your library offers.

Congressional Record. 1873 to date. Detailed information about activities of Congress. Issued daily during sessions. (Online as well as in print.)

Facts on File. 1940 to date. Digest of important news events. Issued weekly.

Guinness Book of World Records. 1955 to date.

Information Please Almanac. 1947 to date.

Statesman's Year Book. 1864 to date. Political and economic information of international scope. Issued every two years.

Statistical Abstract of the United States. 1878 to date. (Online by subscription.) Annual publication of the Bureau of the Census, providing information on American institutions and demographics. Much of this is free on the Internet.

World Almanac and Book of Facts. 1868 to date.

Indexes to Biographical Dictionaries

Indexes tell researchers where to look for needed information. Biographical indexes direct you to appropriate biographical dictionaries. Here are two standard indexes:

Author Biography Master Index. This index, arranged alphabetically by author, tells you in which biographical dictionaries to look up entries for both living and deceased authors.

Biography and Genealogy Master Index. (Paper, CD, and online; updated regularly.) This work indexes entries in 350 contemporary biographical reference sources. It is a good place to begin if you need to locate a biographical source for a person whose occupation or reason for fame is unknown to you.

Biographical Dictionaries

Most libraries have an array of biographical dictionaries, some providing brief entries, others specializing by country or profession, still others offering full essays analyzing the life and contributions of famous people. Use biographical dictionaries to check on the credentials of authors you do not know. Read a biographical essay of a person important to your study when you do not need to read a book-length biography. (The student doing a paper on characters in two Hemingway novels may want to read a biographical essay on Hemingway. Her main focus is on the literature, not the author's life; still, a sense of Hemingway's life and the times during which he wrote the novels can provide a good context for her literary analysis.) The following are important research tools:

Universal

Contemporary Authors. 1962 to date. Provides a biographical and bibliographic guide to current fiction and nonfiction writers and their books.

Current Biography. 1940 to date. Includes articles on living persons of significance in a variety of fields throughout the world. Each volume contains a list of persons included, classified by profession.

International Who's Who. 1935 to date. Contains brief biographies of important persons from almost every country. Each new edition both updates existing biographies and adds new ones.

Webster's New Biographical Dictionary. A one-volume biographical reference, worldwide in scope, this dictionary has been enlarged with each new edition since its beginning in 1943.

American

American Men and Women of Science (formerly *American Men of Science*). Provides brief sketches of more than 150,000 scientists. Lists degrees held and field of specialization. Regularly updated.

Dictionary of American Biography. 20 vols. 1928–1937. Supplementary volumes issued in 1944 and 1958. Contains reliable biographical and critical essays on important Americans no longer living.

Who Was Who in America. Contains brief biographical sketches of Americans no longer living.

Who's Who in America. 1899 to date. Offers brief biographical sketches of living Americans. Continually updated.

Who's Who in American Women. 1958 to date. Contains brief articles on more than 24,000 women.

British

Dictionary of National Biography. 63 vols. 1885–1901. Reprinted in 22 vols., 1908–1909. Supplements to 1960. Supplies authoritative biographies of important English men and women no longer living.

Who's Who. 1849 to date. Offers biographical information on living English men and women.

Essay and General Literature Index

Begun in 1900, this index to a broad range of subject areas is published twice a year; a hardcover, permanent cumulation is then issued every five years. In this author and subject index, you are directed to essays that have appeared in books. Without checking the *Essay and General Literature Index*, you might otherwise overlook a book as a possible source of information on your topic. As Figure 19 reveals, several essays that may be useful to the student's exploration of Brett Ashley and Catherine Barkley as Hemingway heroes can be located by using the *Essay and General Literature Index*.

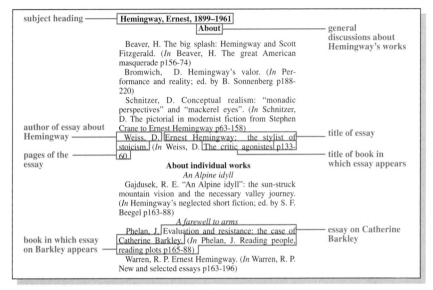

Figure 19 From *Essay and General Literature Index.*

USING INDEXES TO PERIODICALS

Periodicals (magazines, journals, and newspapers) provide good sources for research projects. Some of the most important, most up-to-date, studies of topics are found in journal articles, and recent issues of newspapers and magazines offer information and opinions on current events. Mirroring the changes in book catalogs, periodical indexes are now on CD-ROM and online databases as well as in paper, and the articles themselves may be included with the CD-ROM and online indexes.

Magazines and journals in print are generally shelved alphabetically by title on shelves in a separate area of your library. Back issues of journals are bound in hardcover volumes or placed on microfiche or microfilm. (Readers will be available in the periodicals area.) Current issues are often shelved separately for easy browsing. Current issues of newspapers may be shelved with current magazines. Back issues of newspapers are usually on microfilm or microfiche. Lists of the library's periodicals collection are usually located at the circulation desk or reference desk and may be included in the OPAC as well.

The most efficient way to locate articles on your particular topic is to use one or more of the periodicals indexes. But to be efficient, you need to select the most useful indexes for your particular project. Taking the time to read about the indexes discussed here will speed your search in the library because you will know the best indexes to search for a given topic. Some indexes catalog articles from hundreds of popular magazines covering many subject areas. Others index newspaper articles. Still others are more specialized, indexing articles in scholarly journals in a more specific area of study, such as business or psychology. In several popular indexes, the distinctions among popular magazines, scholarly journals, and newspapers have become blurred. These indexes include serious journals with more popular magazines, and perhaps the *New York Times* as well. Still, there are differences you need to learn so that you do not miss good sources or become overwhelmed with many articles that really are not what you can best use.

Many of the most popular indexes—in print, on CD-ROM, and online—including those that are full text, are described and illustrated below. Your library may have all or some of these, or several others not listed here but organized much the same way.

Indexes to Magazines

The Reader's Guide to Periodical Literature

Probably the most used index prior to the technology revolution, *The Reader's Guide to Periodical Literature* (1900 to date) combines author and subject headings that guide the reader to about 200 popular magazines. Many of those indexed here, including *American Scholar*, *Psychology Today*, and *Science*, have articles of value to undergraduate research. The *Reader's Guide* is a cumulative print index, issued twice monthly (except monthly in July and August) and bound in hardcover volumes annually. When a person is both author and subject, articles *by* the person are given first, followed by articles *about* him or her. Note in the sample entries in Figure 20 that information is heavily abbreviated. Study the explanation provided and, when using the index, check the list of periodicals found in the front of each volume for the complete title of each magazine.

> ✔ Remember: All entries in the various periodicals indexes *must* be rearranged into the correct documentation format for citation in your paper—and for your instructor if you are required to hand in a working bibliography. See Chapter 3 for guidelines.

The *Reader's Guide* remains the most important print index to popular magazines. Note that it goes back to 1900. If you want to sample attitudes toward Prohibition during the 1920s, you will need to use this Index. (If your library does not have the magazines from such an early period, it can probably obtain the articles you want from another library.)

Many students doing research on a current topic find *Magazine Index/Plus* (*Magazine Index* on CD-ROM—usually referred to as *InfoTrac*—and online

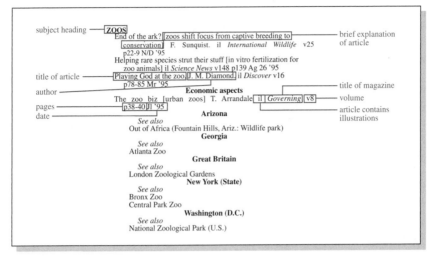

Figure 20 From *The Reader's Guide to Periodical Literature*.

through SearchBank) convenient alternatives to the *Reader's Guide*. You may already have used *InfoTrac* in your search for a topic. See pages 18–19 for a discussion of this index.

SIRS Researcher

SIRS first appeared in notebooks of reprinted articles from many magazines, journals, and newspapers covering current issues such as AIDS or date rape. It is still available in print and on microfiche, but now is also a CD-ROM database. SIRS can be used as an index to survey the number and type of articles (summaries accompany each article) on a given topic, but it also provides full texts of each article. The convenience of a full-text database is obvious: you do not experience the frustration of locating good-sounding articles in indexes only to discover that your library does not subscribe to that periodical. The disadvantages of SIRS are two: (1) The initial response to your keyword search is a list of titles only, no authors or titles of the periodicals. So, you have to go to a second screen for each title that seems useful to obtain the article's full bibliographic information. (2) The articles selected for SIRS may not be current and tend to be fairly simple. Some will not be appropriate for college research projects.

ProQuest

One of the first CD-ROM databases, *ProQuest* is an index to articles in a range of general-interest magazines published from the 1980s on. But *ProQuest's* more than 1100 periodicals provide a greater range than those covered in *Info-Trac* or SIRS, including more scholarly journals. (The online version, *ProQuest*

Direct, covers 4000 titles.) Further, for each article indexed a brief abstract is included, helpful in judging the work's usefulness for your research. In addition, articles in over 200 of the journals indexed are available in full text that can be reproduced on the accompanying printer. *ProQuest* may be accessed on the same terminals as other databases, including the book catalog, or it may be found at a separate station, surrounded by the tiers of CD-ROMs containing the articles for printing. **Note**: Be sure to print a copy of the record for each article before printing the complete article. The index record will contain the information needed for your bibliography; the facsimile pages of the article may not provide all needed bibliographic information.

For this and most of the CD-ROM or online indexes, you will need to find the right keywords to narrow the list of articles to those directly related to your topic. For example, if you type in only "dinosaurs," you will be overwhelmed by the number of "hits," computer talk for the number of articles with the word "dinosaur" in the title or the abstract. For the years from January 1996 to March 1997, a keyword search for "dinosaurs AND extinction" produced 34 hits. You can read the bibliographic information and brief abstracts for 34 articles and either print the information or make bibliography cards for the sources that sound most promising. You may reduce the number to, let's say, 15–20 possible sources and find that full texts are available for 10 of the articles. You can find three more in your library's periodicals collection. These 13 articles, when added to several recent books located in the book collection, will give you a good working bibliography on the topic of dinosaur extinction.

SearchBank

Another index to magazines, SearchBank is actually many indexes. Among the most popular are *Expanded Academic ASAP* and *Business Index*. These CD-ROM and online indexes are updated frequently, provide full texts of many of the articles, include an abstract of each article written by the author of the article, not someone preparing the index, and cover many serious journals in addition to magazines.

The indexes are user-friendly; just follow the directions on the screen to complete a search and locate possibly useful articles. The indexes can also help you narrow a search if you find the number of potential articles to be overwhelming. For example, in May 1997, a keyword search for the word *deforestation* resulted in 73 "hits." You are also informed that there are 28 subdivisions and 5 related topics. Another click provides the list of subdivisions of the topic. Nine articles, six of which are shown in Figure 21, are found under the subdivision "Control." At this stage, you are provided with needed bibliographic information for each article and icons that, when clicked on, allow you to view the particular article or to mark it for later printing—or downloading onto your disk or e-mailing to your PC, if these options are available in your library. Before selecting articles for printing, you may want to view an article's abstract to get a better sense of its use to your research project.

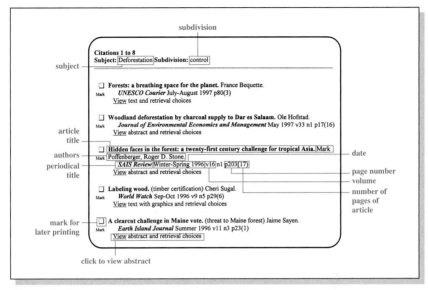

Figure 21 From *Expanded Academic ASAP Index.*

✓ Articles obtained from a CD-ROM or online database require additional bibliographic information in the documentation of your paper. You must indicate that you obtained the article from a specific database. *If* you take any information or ideas from an abstract, you must also document the abstract— and the database from which you obtained it. *Do not attribute information in abstracts to the article author(s) unless the abstract was written by the author(s). If you use any abstracts written by index compilers, you must cite the database as the author.* See Chapter 3 for citation formats.

Indexes to Newspapers

Newspapers are a good source of information about contemporary topics and about the events and issues of a previous period. Since it is one of the most thorough and respected newspapers, the *New York Times* is available in most libraries. Become familiar with the *New York Times Index*, for it can guide you to articles as far back as the mid-nineteenth century. (Back issues are on microfilm.) The print index is a subject index issued twice each month and cumulated annually, with articles arranged chronologically under each subject heading. The *Index* provides a brief summary of each article. Figure 22 explains sample entries in the index's print format. The *Index* is

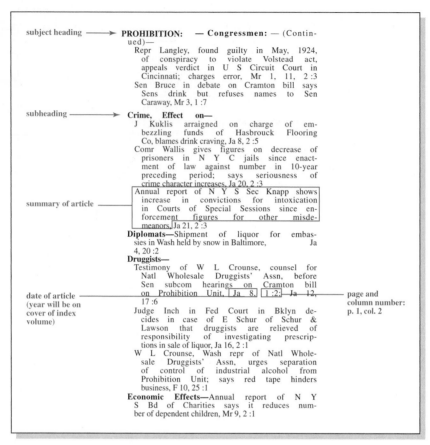

subject heading ⟶ **PROHIBITION:** — **Congressmen:** — (Continued)—
Repr Langley, found guilty in May, 1924, of conspiracy to violate Volstead act, appeals verdict in U S Circuit Court in Cincinnati; charges error, Mr 1, 11, 2 :3
Sen Bruce in debate on Cramton bill says Sens drink but refuses names to Sen Caraway, Mr 3, 1 :7

subheading ⟶ **Crime, Effect on—**
J Kuklis arraigned on charge of embezzling funds of Hasbrouck Flooring Co, blames drink craving, Ja 8, 2 :5
Comr Wallis gives figures on decrease of prisoners in N Y C jails since enactment of law against number in 10-year preceding period; says seriousness of crime character increases, Ja 20, 2 :3

summary of article ⟶ Annual report of N Y S Sec Knapp shows increase in convictions for intoxication in Courts of Special Sessions since enforcement figures for other misdemeanors, Ja 21, 2 :3
Diplomats—Shipment of liquor for embassies in Wash held by snow in Baltimore, Ja 4, 20 :2
Druggists—
Testimony of W L Crounse, counsel for Natl Wholesale Druggists' Assn, before Sen subcom hearings on Cramton bill

date of article ⟶ on Prohibition Unit, Ja 8, 1 :2; Ja 12, ⟶ page and
(year will be on 17 :6 column number:
cover of index Judge Inch in Fed Court in Bklyn decides in case of E Schur of Schur & p. 1, col. 2
volume) Lawson that druggists are relieved of responsibility of investigating prescriptions in sale of liquor, Ja 16, 2 :1
W L Crounse, Wash repr of Natl Wholesale Druggists' Assn, urges separation of control of industrial alcohol from Prohibition Unit; says red tape hinders business, F 10, 25 :1
Economic Effects—Annual report of N Y S Bd of Charities says it reduces number of dependent children, Mr 9, 2 :1

Figure 22 From the *New York Times Index* for 1925.

also on CD-ROM and online, with full texts provided for printing. Your library may have this index in one or more formats.

Your library may also have an index, with full text of articles, to another major newspaper, such as the *Washington Post* or the *Wall Street Journal*. Alternatively, your library may subscribe to *Proquest Newspaper Abstracts*, a CD-ROM database that is a combined index to five major newspapers: *New York Times, Wall Street Journal, Christian Science Monitor, Washington Post,* and *Los Angeles Times. Newspaper Abstracts* has the advantage of covering more sources but the disadvantage of covering only recent years and not providing full text. The combined index is your best choice if you are studying a current issue and your library has the newspapers on microfilm; the *New York Times Index* is the better choice if you need articles from the past and if it is the only newspaper your library has on microfilm. Remember the abstracts (brief summaries) of the articles in *Newspaper Abstracts* are *not* the articles themselves; do not cite them as if they are the same thing. For example, if you were studying the role of zoos in maintaining wildlife, you would locate an article in the *Los Angeles Times* on zoos. But, the article is actually a review of a book by Vicki Croke on zoos. The abstract in *Newspaper Abstracts* is about the review. It is neither the review—written by a journalist—nor the book itself—written by Croke.

Another type of newspaper index is *NewsBank*, an index to and full text of articles from many (sometimes small-town) newspapers and wire services. If your library subscribes to *NewsBank* but not to *Newspaper Abstracts*, then the former index may be worth exploring for some short articles on a current topic. Just remember that it is not a complete index but rather a selection of articles and that it draws, perhaps too heavily, from newspapers other than the "big" five covered by *Newspaper Abstracts*. On the other hand, you will read coverage of your topic from several geographical areas.

Indexes to Academic Journals

The indexes to magazines and newspapers just reviewed provide many good articles for some undergraduate research topics. For other research topics, particularly those for papers in upper-level courses, you will be expected to rely primarily on the work of scholars. You have already learned that databases such as *ProQuest* and *Expanded Academic Index* index many current scholarly journals as well as popular magazines. Other indexes focus almost exclusively on scholarly journals. Some, such as *Social Sciences Index*, cover a range of related areas of study; others, such as *Art Index*, are more narrow in focus. And of course, some of these indexes began as print resources but are now on CD-ROM or online. The most important specialized indexes are listed, by discipline, in Appendix B. Here is a sampling of some of the most widely used indexes by undergraduate researchers. Depending on your field of study, you may use one or more of these reference tools each time you are assigned a research project.

Social Sciences Index and Humanities Index

Originally print indexes, these two began as one combined index but have been divided since 1974. (Both are now online, available through First-Search.) The *Social Sciences Index* covers articles on political science, psychology, economics, law, medical science, and related subjects. The *Humanities Index* covers articles on art, literature, philosophy, folklore, history, and related subjects. The student investigating Marc Chagall as a surrealist painter can use *Humanities Index*, looking up both *surrealism* and *Marc Chagall* as subject headings. The excerpt from *Humanities Index* (in print) shown in Figure 23 reveals a list of additional subject headings to check. Note the journals included in the excerpt; you will not find *Artforum* included in *The Reader's Guide*.

Surrealism
  See also
  Dadaism
  Fantasy in art
  Magic realism (Literature)
  Pop art
The antipodes of surrealism: Salvador Dalí and Remedios
  Varo. G. Duran. il *Symposium* 42:297–311 Wint '89
A cinema of cruelty: Antonin Artaud. S. Barber. *Artforum*
  28:163–6 O '89
Enrico Donati: Manhattan transfer. C. Ratcliff. il *Art Am*
  77:175–80 My '89
A land of myth and dreams. N. Barrett. il *Aperture*
  no115:50–5 '89
Memory palaces. W. Christenberry. il *Aperture* no115:46–9
  Summ '89
The methodology of the marvelous. G. F. Orenstein. il
  Symposium 42:329–39 Wint '89
Purity. D. Cotton. *Crit Inq* 16:173–98 Aut '89
Toyen: toward a revolutionary art in Prague and Paris. W.
  Chadwick. *Symposium* 42:277–95 Wint '89

Figure 23 Excerpt from *Humanities Index.*

ScienceSource

The CD-ROM database NewsBank *ScienceSource* indexes articles that cover a range of scientific topics and issues. (The online *General Science Index*, available through FirstSearch, is an alternative.) The student interested in the problem of rain forest destruction will find articles through either one of these databases, articles such as Norman Myers's "The World's Forests: Need for a Policy Appraisal," published in the journal *Science*. A student exploring the issue of dinosaur extinction will locate the *New Scientist* article "Did Acid Rain Kill the Dinosaurs?" A portion of the entry for this article is shown in Figure 24. Observe that *ScienceSource* provides fairly lengthy digests of each article indexed. Keep in mind that digests are not the same as full texts of the articles. Use *ScienceSource* as an index; go to the journal to read the complete article. If you cite the digest, you must credit *Biology Digest*, not the author of the article. If you rely heavily on summaries, abstracts, or digests found in indexes, rather than reading the complete articles, your instructor may question your interest in the topic and your commitment to research.

Other indexes, available online through FirstSearch, that cover a range of academic fields include *Arts and Humanities Search, Applied Science & Technology Index, Social Sciences Index,* and *Wilson Business Abstracts.* We cannot survey all of the specialized indexes here (they are listed in Appendix B), but here are a few that are commonly used.

MLA International Bibliography

Students in literature and language courses may have occasion to use the *MLA International Bibliography.* In the print format, the index is an annual

```
┌─────────────────────────────────────────────────────────────────────┐
│                                                                       │
│     **NewsBank ScienceSource Collection**        Record **18** of **21** │
│    ─────────────────────────────────────────────────────────────     │
│                                                                       │
│    Abstract by Biology Digest, Volume 15, Issue 2                     │
│                                                                       │
│    Article appeared in: New Scientist, Volume 117, Issue 1600, February 18 1988 │
│    Page: 32                                                           │
│                                                                       │
│    Title: Primeval Acid Rain Could Have Killed Off Dinosaurs          │
│                                                                       │
│    Topics:                                                            │
│    **dinosaurs**                                                      │
│    **extinction** and extinct species                                │
│    acid rain                                                          │
│    theory                                                            │
│                                                                       │
│    Estimated printed pages: 2                                         │
│                                                                       │
│    Abstract Text:                                                     │
│    New measurements support a theory that acid rain wiped out dinosaurs and many other life forms │
│    65 million years ago, at the end of the Cretaceous period. These measurements show a sudden │
│    variation in the ratio of two isotopes of strontium in sediments deposited at that period. │
│                                                                       │
│    Ronald Prinn of the Massachusetts Institute of Technology had predicted such a variation in his │
│    attempt to explain how the impact of a giant meteor at the end of the Cretaceous could have caused │
│    mass extinctions. He suggests that the energy given off by the impact would have heated the │
│    atmosphere, thereby causing nitrogen and oxygen to combine. These would then form nitrogen │
│    oxides which, Prinn argues, combined with atmospheric water and oxygen to form nitric acid and │
│    hence acid rain....                                                │
│                                                                       │
└─────────────────────────────────────────────────────────────────────┘
```

Figure 24 From *ScienceSource* Database.

listing of books, articles, and dissertations in the field. It comes in two volumes, *Classified Listings with Author Index* and *Subject Index*. In the first volume, entries are organized first geographically (French literature; American literature), next by period (1800–1899; 1900–1999), and then by individual author (Ernest Hemingway). If you know the author you are interested in but not the period, start with the *Author Index*. If you want to put together a list of utopian novels, for example, look for "utopian novel" in the *Subject Index*. In the online format, updated 10 times each year, you will generate a list of possible sources, as you would with any of the databases we have examined, by typing in your keyword or phrase. The student interested in Hemingway will find (as Figure 25 shows) articles on the character Brett Ashley that may prove helpful to the student's study of Brett and Catherine Barkley.

ERIC Indexes

The Educational Resources Information Center (ERIC), a federally funded organization, provides two (print) indexes to sources on educational issues. Many undergraduate researchers can find useful materials here to support the study of a wide range of topics. In its print format, there are two sections,

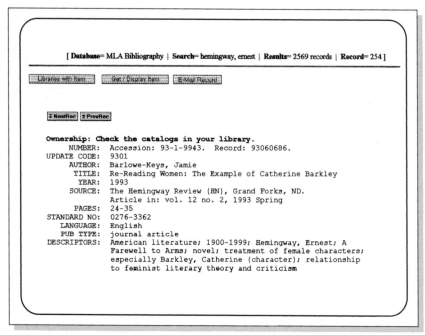

Figure 25 From *MLA International Bibliography*—Online Format.

Current Index to Journals in Education (CIJE) and *Resources in Education*, a collection of unpublished reports on educational issues. If you wanted to find articles on student cheating, for example, you would start with a subject index, looking up "cheating," and then be directed to the main-entry section. Many libraries have *RIE*–documents on microfiche. Now, of course, ERIC indexes are online, covering from 1966 to date and updated monthly. If you are exploring an educational topic, ask a reference librarian about the ERIC format in your library.

Dissertation Abstracts International (DAI)

You have observed that many CD-ROM and online indexes provide some discussion of each article, ranging from a brief summary to a fairly lengthy digest. In many cases, these are not written by the author of the article. In some indexes authors have written the abstracts, or, to put it more accurately, the authors' abstracts, originally published with their articles, have been included in the indexes. In others, the author of the abstract is identified, at least by initials. A number of indexes with abstracts (for example, *Psychological Abstracts, Chemical Abstracts*) serve a particular discipline. One important abstracts collection serves all researchers: *Dissertation Abstracts International*. In its print form, it is a monthly publication of University Microfilms International. (It is also online.) Each complete dissertation is avail-

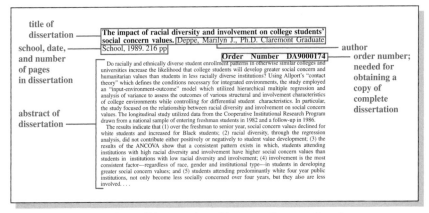

Figure 26 Excerpt from *Dissertation Abstracts International.*

able from University Microfilms in paper and on microform. If you cite information from the abstract (see Figure 26), you must document the abstract. See page 106 for the proper form of citation; note that the university is given as part of the documentation, so be certain to include that information in your working bibliography.

Citation Indexes

The citation indexes (*Arts and Humanities Citation Index, Science Citation Index,* and *Social Sciences Citation Index*) have still another look—quite literally—but these rather complex research tools can be helpful to your projects. The name—using *Science Citation Index* as our example—highlights one of four interrelated parts found in each yearly cumulation. The *Citation Index* leads you to recent journal articles that have cited (referred to) an earlier work on a given topic. So, if you know one work on your subject, you can look it up under the author's name to find other authors who have cited that work. The idea is that articles referring to a source for your study will probably also be relevant to your study.

Another part of *Science Citation Index* is the *Corporate Index,* a list of members of specific organizations and institutions who have published in a given year. Scientists with the U.S. Geological Survey can be expected to publish studies on, for example, earthquake prediction problems. Undergraduate researchers are more likely to begin with the *Permuterm Subject Index,* a list of key terms that becomes a subject index. As Figure 27 illustrates, you can look up "Dinosaurs" and find a long list, organized by subtopics, of authors who have published on this topic.

These three parts of *Science Citation Index* all provide access to the fourth part, the *Source Index,* the volumes that supply a full bibliographic listing of specific articles. The *Source Index* is an alphabetic-by-author listing, so

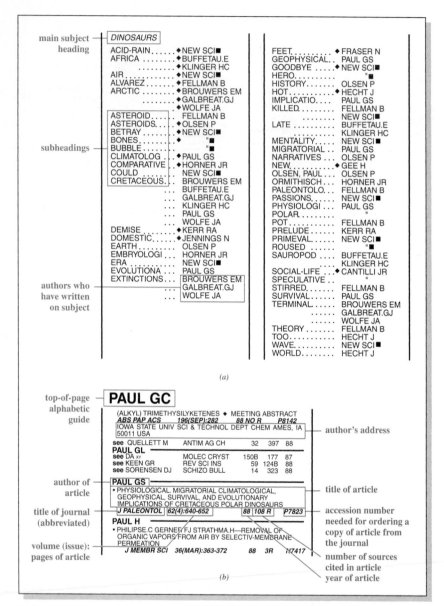

Figure 27 Excerpts from *Science Citation Index*. *(a)* From *Permuterm Subject Index*; *(b)* from *Source Index*.

for researchers who do not already know authors on their subject, checking one of the other three parts is a necessary first step to locating articles. After finding writers on the subject of dinosaur extinction, the researcher can find needed bibliographic information on each article written by those writers. The *Source Index*'s listing of G. S. Paul's article is shown in Figure 27. After studying the explanation, look again at the *Permuterm Subject Index* excerpt. Notice that "G. S. Paul" appears several times—in one year. There are also other names appearing more than once. These heavily published scholars are likely to be experts on your topic; read and consider their works. Further, when you locate the first two writers on dinosaur extinction, you will learn that their articles are letters, responses to a previous article, in one issue of *Science* magazine. These letters, and the original article, probably offer insight into the debate over dinosaur extinction. Specialized indexes do more than help you prepare a working bibliography on your topic. They also help you understand the field of research you are exploring.

LOCATING GOVERNMENT DOCUMENTS AND RELATED PUBLICATIONS

The federal government is, among others things, one of the country's largest publishing houses, each year printing tens of thousands of documents ranging from pamphlets to maps to multivolume reports. Some government documents are free; others are for sale; many are now available on the Internet. Most libraries subscribe to two kinds of indexes to government documents:

Monthly Catalog of U.S. Government Publications. Each monthly issue lists between 1,500 and 3,000 new entries, organized into four indexes: author, title, subject, and series report. For each document, the catalog provides sales and bibliographic information.

The GPO Publications Reference File or *GPO Access* (on the Web). The former, a total sales catalog issued on microfiche, has been replaced by the regularly updated index on the Internet. You can reach *GPO Access* at this Web address: http://www.access.gpo.gov/su_docs.

Via the Internet, you have access to the *Congressional Record*, an index to the National Archives, the current Federal budget, and information on various department and agency Home Pages, to list only a few of the possibilities. Figure 28 shows part of the first screen to appear. You can click on any one of the items listed. A click on the first item leads to a screen that lists many databases which can be searched in the usual way of typing in your search terms. A student exploring problems in immigration can examine, for example, recently passed or pending legislation on immigration.

Free Access to Electronic Government Information Products

The *Federal Register, Congressional Record, Congressional Bills* and other Federal Government information are available online via *GPO Access*, a service of the U.S. Government Printing Office (GPO). Public access is available through the Federal Depository Library, or directly from GPO.

- Search and Retrieve Full Text Online via *GPO Access* from Over 70 Databases
- Specialized Search Pages to Help Make A Search More Specific
- Federal Agency Files via the *GPO Access* Federal Bulletin Board
- Agency for Health Care Policy and Research
- Bureau of Land Management Publications
- Budget of the United States Government, Fiscal Year 1998
- CBDNet (Commerce Business Daily)
- Congress of the United States
- Congressional Pictorial Directory (105th Congress)
- Department of Interior Office of Inspector General
- Food and Drug Administration
- General Accounting Office
- National Archives and Records Administration's Office of the Federal Register
- Office of Technology Assessment
- The Plum Book (Committee on Government Reform and Oversight)

Figure 28 Some of the Materials Available from the GPO Online.

Another reference source that indexes government documents and related materials on public affairs and public policy issues is the *Public Affairs Information Service Bulletin (PAIS)*. The *PAIS Bulletin*, in print, extends back to 1915 and covers periodicals, books, pamphlets, proceedings, and government documents. *PAIS* is also online, covering the years from 1980 to the present and updated monthly. The bulletin is international in scope and emphasizes works that are strong on facts and statistics.

SEARCHING THE INTERNET

You have already seen just how many standard reference tools have switched from print to CD-ROM or online formats, or have added online to an ongoing use of the print format. These reference tools are available at terminals in the library because the library has purchased the databases, just as it has, in the past, purchased the print form. In addition to finding sources online from purchased databases, you can also search the Internet directly for the information that is free to all who have paid for access to the Internet. So, you can reach *GPO Access* (for example) in the library but also on your own PC. If you have been surfing the Net for years, you already understand the difference between accessing databases through your library's software and doing your own search. If you are new to online searching, you will need to spend a little time reading directions next to the terminals—and practicing—until you grasp the search process and learn how to tailor searches to find what you can use. Alternatively, read what follows, work through one of the tutorials on the Web, and ask librarians or a knowledgeable friend to help you get started.

Some Basics about the Internet

When you have access to the Internet, either from your own PC or on one of your library's terminals, you can use a number of sources or functions to obtain information useful to a research project. Here are the most common:

- E-mail
- Mailing Lists (Listserves)
- Newsgroups
- the World Wide Web (usually called simply the Web)

E-mail

As discussed on page 68, you can e-mail a request for information instead of writing to a government agency or company. You may also send a request for information or a query to an individual, some expert on your topic, providing you can obtain that person's e-mail address. If you have a PC but have not yet established your own e-mail address, you should do that now so that you can use this Internet function. (As already noted, in many libraries, you can send citations of sources or full texts of articles from your library to yourself—at your own e-mail address—and then download into your research-project file or print copies for study.)

Mailing Lists (Listserves)

Once you have your e-mail in place, you can receive what can best be described as continually updated bulletin boards on a particular subject. In other words, listserves are organized mailing lists on various topics. If you find one relevant to your research project, you can subscribe for awhile and unsubscribe when you are no longer interested in getting e-mail on that topic.

Note that some mailing lists are moderated by someone who selects the messages that go to everyone, but others are not moderated so that every message submitted by every subscriber is sent to every other subscriber. Remember: You subscribe (and unsubscribe) at one Internet address and put your messages on the bulletin board at another address. Do not confuse them. Other subscribers will not want to read your request to unsubscribe via their e-mail—and your message to the wrong address will result in your continuing to be a subscriber and getting a "ton" of information.

Newsgroups

Newsgroups differ from mailing lists in that the discussions and exchanges are collected for you to retrieve; they are not sent to your e-mail address. Otherwise, they are much the same; newsgroups are discussion groups, people carrying on a conversation about a specific topic. Figure 29 shows a partial list of exchanges, organized by topic, available through *All Politics* (a good source of current news and analysis). The arrangement by topics on this bulletin board allows you to select only those messages that may be useful to a particular research topic. To find newsgroups on a specific topic, you can use Dejanews Research Service (http://www. dejanews. com), a research tool that surveys all newsgroups. Other ways to access newsgroups or listserves include

Indiana University's List of Mailing Lists
   http://scwww.ucs.indiana.edu/mlarchive/

Listserve Home Page
   http://www.tile.net/tile/listserv/index.html

> ✓ Note: Anyone with access can post a message on a listserve or
> newsgroup. Some may be experts communicating with other experts.
> You are allowed to "tune in" to their discussion and learn from them. Most are
> not experts. Unless you choose carefully, you can waste time—with regard to
> your research. And, you *must* evaluate everything you read online, and then
> document any information and opinions you take from the Internet.

World Wide Web

For most researchers, the Web will provide more useful information than the bulletin boards. Still, your task remains the same: To wade through an enormous amount of material, much of which is not helpful, to find what you can use. Get in the habit of Bookmarking sites you visit frequently, because you cannot hope to remember many complicated Internet addresses. Some addresses useful to researchers are listed in Appendix B under the appropriate subject heading.

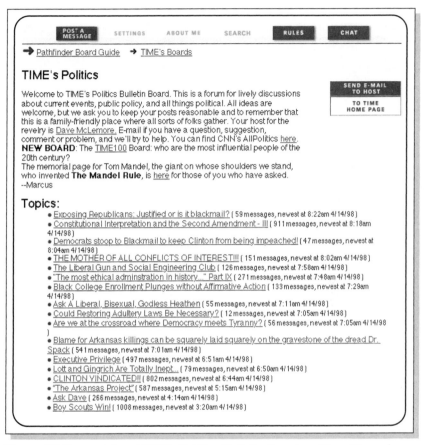

Figure 29 Excerpt from TIME's Politics Bulletin Board on Time Warner's Pathfinder Network, http://pathfinder.com. (Reprinted by permission. Copyright © 1998 Time Inc. New Media. All rights reserved. Reproduction in whole or in part without permission is prohibited. Pathfinder is a registered trademark of Time Inc. New Media.)

The Internet has its own language, much of which you do not need to know to do searches on the Web. But do keep in mind that the browser is the program that allows you to move around the Web. (As Figure 30 shows, my browser is Netscape Navigator.) To search the Web for material on a specific topic, you need either to type in the Web "address" (the URL—uniform resource locator) if you know it or to select a search engine or web guide. (When I connect to the Internet, my first screen, shown in Figure 30, gives me the choice of many search engines. All I have to do is click on the one I want to use.)

As you can see, there are quite a few search engines; as you might guess, people differ in their views as to which are the best. (Also keep in mind that

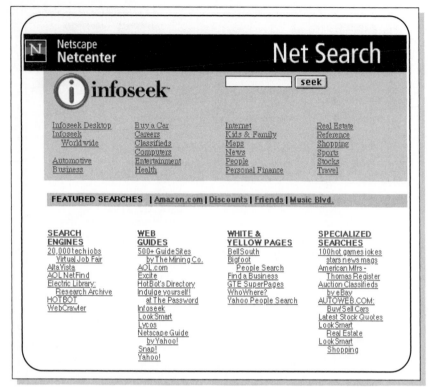

Figure 30 Netscape Net Search Screen Showing Many Popular Search Engines. (Copyright © 1998 Netscape Communications Corp. All Rights Reserved. This page may not be reprinted or copied without the express written permission of Netscape.)

any description of the Internet today may be invalid tomorrow. The Internet is ever changing.) Here are brief comments about some popular search engines. *Alta Vista* is currently the largest Web-search database; it will probably give you the most wide ranging results. To use it without being overwhelmed with thousands of hits, you need to learn how to limit your search terms with connectors AND, NOT, and BUT. (These are known as Boolean operators. They help to narrow a search by limiting keywords. For example, if you type in "wildlife preservation AND zoos," you will be given only those materials that contain both terms.) Some people think that *InfoSeek* is the best all round engine. You can type in a complex query without Boolean operators and *InfoSeek* will find relevant sites. *Excite* provides services other than just searching, including current news and reviews of Web sites. *Lycos* is good if you are looking for sites that include images and sound. You may want to try several of the search engines and then teach yourself how to do complex searching on just one.

It is just as easy to waste time visiting useless Web sites as it is to waste time reading useless mailing lists. You may have fun surfing without advancing your research. So, try to keep focused on your research needs and the time you have to complete your project. Also, remember what the Web is best for: current information and government documents. We have already covered *GPO Access*. Other good sources for current news, legislative information, historical documents, and the *Congressional Record* include *All Politics*, mentioned above, and *Thomas* (http://thomas.loc.gov/). If you are interested in the problem of balancing preservation of whales and the whaling industry, for example, you can explore Congressional committee activity to see if relevant bills are under discussion, or see what has happened on the floor of Congress. Figure 31 includes part of a speech by Representative Metcalf from Washington State on the subject of whaling and whale populations.

The Web can yield useful information on a variety of topics. The student interested in the role of zoos in wildlife preservation used *Excite* and typed in the keywords "wildlife preservation." The result: over 200,000 hits. He narrowed his search to "wildlife preservation and zoos" and still found many sites to review, several of which are shown in Figure 32. One item listed was the Nature Conservancy, a well-respected organization committed to wildlife preservation. A visit to its home page provided a list of publications, including the article "State of the Nation's Species" that discusses the major causes for species at risk of extinction. But look again at Figure 32. The "World Wide Raccoon Web" is not going to help the student develop his topic. Visit the National Wildlife Federation home page but ignore the other hits shown.

Here are some guidelines for searching the Web:

- Make your search as precise as possible to avoid getting overwhelmed with hits.

- Learn to use Boolean connectors to make your search more precise.

- If you are not successful with one search engine, try a different one.

- If you are not getting any hits with the second search engine, check your spelling. Search engines cannot guess what you mean, as readers can. Spelling must be exact.

- Bookmark sites you expect to use frequently.

- Be certain to complete a bibliography card—including the date you accessed the information and the complete address (URL)—for each separate site from which you take information.

THIS SEARCH	*THIS DOCUMENT*	*THIS CR ISSUE*	*GO TO*
Next Hit	Forward	Next Document	New Search
Prev Hit	Back	Prev Document	HomePage
Hit List	Best Sections	Daily Digest	Help
	Doc Contents	House Contents	CR Issues by Date

Congressional Record entry 53 of 100

WHALING AND WHALE POPULATIONS (House of Representatives - April 16, 1997)

[Page: H1602]

The SPEAKER pro tempore. Under a previous order of the House, the gentleman from Washington [Mr. **Metcalf**] is recognized for 5 minutes.

Mr. METCALF. Mr. Speaker, I rise today to oppose yet another proposal to hunt and kill gray whales along the coast of Washington State and Canada. It has recently come to my attention that the Nuu-Chah-Nulth tribe of British Columbia is planning to hunt whales for the first time in 70 years. Last year tribes from Washington State proposed a whale hunt off the Washington coast, but their petition was denied by the International Whaling Commission after they were notified of a resolution in opposition passed unanimously by the House Resources Committee. The human and economic effects as well as the impacts on whales need to be seriously considered before anyone decides to reopen commercial whaling off the west coast of the United States and Canada.

My district includes the San Juan Islands, and that borders Canada and Vancouver Island near where the proposed Canadian hunt is to take place. The whale watching industry and tourism are among the main economic forces in this area, and they generate between

$15 and $20 million per year in revenue. Now this is not insignificant, the whale watching. The thousands who come to our region to visit and see the whales each year should be able to enjoy these animals, and the people of this region, many of whom are my constituents, should be allowed to operate their businesses and thrive on the presence of these unique creatures.

These whales have become like pets. Lots and lots of boats go out to see them. They are not afraid of boats, they are used to boats. They are very trusting. They are very smart animals. And once commercial whaling, hunting of gray whales, begins, their demeanor will soon change, and they will not allow a boat to get anywhere near them. Thus a $15 to $20 million whale watching business will be decimated just for the personal profit of a few tribes.

Figure 31 From the *Congressional Record* Online.

✔️ Remember: All sources you use in your research essay must be documented. Make complete citations for all possible sources to build your working bibliography. Guidelines for documenting Internet sources are included in Chapter 3. Chapter 4 discusses the researcher's important role of evaluating sources. You must be especially careful to evaluate all information you take off the Internet.

```
Documents  11-20                              View Titles only  View by Web Site

78% NATIONAL WILDLIFE FEDERATION  [More Like This]
URL: http://www.nwf.org/nwf/
Summary: NWF's National Conference on Habitat Conservation Plans (May 17-18) Ranger Rick
Articulos en español NWF Seeks Supporters for Collaborative Computing Project! Now Is a Great Time
to Start A Backyard Wildlife Habitat Serving Up Conservation: McDonalds Helps NWF bring Habitat
Lesson to Millions NATURE'S WEB: COMMUNITIES & CONSERVATION.

78% GORP - Birding  [More Like This]
URL: http://www.gorp.com/gorp/activity/birding.htm
Summary: The areas in and around the US National Parks, US National Forests, US Wilderness Areas
and US National Wildlife Refuges offer some great opportunities for birdwatching! Arctic Treks - A
premier outfitter for 17 years in Alaska's Brooks Range offering ecotourism trips into the best wildlife
viewing and birding areas of the Arctic National Wildlife Refuge and Gates of the Arctic National Park.

77% The World Wide Raccoon Web  [More Like This]
URL: http://www.loomcom.com/raccoons/
Summary: So, Welcome to the WORLD WIDE RACCOON WEB, where I pay tribute to The Raccoon,
my favorite creature, my favorite companion, and one of my greatest inspirations. [Skip Prev] [Prev]
[Next] [Skip Next] [Random] [Next 5] [List Sites].

76% Adam's Fox Box II  [More Like This]
URL: http://tavi.acomp.usf.edu/foxbox/
Summary: foxes newsgroup / Net comic: Nicky the Fox / Grey fox: information.
```

Figure 32 From an Online Search.

LOCATING SOURCES OUTSIDE THE LIBRARY

The books and articles found in libraries or information retrieved through the Internet are the essential tools for most research projects, but there are other kinds of sources that can enrich many projects and should not be overlooked. Students developing experiments or doing fieldwork in various science and social science disciplines will use library sources as background for their unique projects. Students in many humanities, social science, and business or technical courses who usually rely primarily on the library to develop research topics can often make their projects unique by using sources outside the library. Here are some suggestions.

Federal, State, and Local Government Documents

In addition to searching the *PAIS Bulletin* and *GPO Access*, when appropriate to your topic, consider the potential use of materials in the National Archives Building in Washington, DC, or one of the regional branches. To discover materials that may be useful explore the *Guide to the National Archives of the United States* and *Select List of Publications of the National Archives and Records Service.*

Additionally, consider state and county archives, maps, and other published materials. Your school library or a nearby public library may have a "state room," an area devoted entirely to materials relevant to state history and government. Instead of selecting a global topic for a history or government course, consider examining the debates over a controversial bill introduced in your state legislature. Use periodicals from the period preserved in the state room and interview legislators and journalists who participated in or covered the debates or served on committees that worked with the bill.

You can also request specific documents from appropriate state or county agencies and nonprofit organizations. One student, given the assignment of examining solutions to any ecological problem, decided to study the local problem of preserving Chesapeake Bay. She obtained issues of the Chesapeake Bay Foundation newsletter and brochures prepared by the CBF advising homeowners about hazardous household waste materials that end up in the Bay. Reading these sources led to a decision to focus on ways that northern Virginia homeowners and builders can preserve the land and the local streams that feed into the Bay. Added to her sources were U.S. Department of Agriculture bulletins on soil conservation, Virginia Department of Conservation brochures on soil and water conservation, and Fairfax County bulletins on landscaping tips for improving the area's water quality. (Local telephone directories, available in your library, will give you the addresses and phone numbers of state and local government agencies and local organizations interested in the topic you are researching. Alternatively, visit their home pages on the Web for information and for ways to contact the agencies or organizations.) Local problems can lead to interesting research topics because they are current and relevant to you and because they involve uncovering different kinds of source materials.

Correspondence

Business and government officials are usually willing to respond to written requests for information. Make your letter brief and well written. Either include a self-addressed, stamped envelope for the person's convenience or e-mail your letter. To be obliging, you may invite the person to call you, but only if you have an answering machine or can specify times that you are available. If you are not e-mailing, write as soon as you discover the need for information and be prepared to wait several weeks for a reply. It is appropriate to indicate your deadline and ask for a timely response. Three guidelines you should keep in mind include:

1. Explain precisely what information you need. Avoid writing a general "please send me anything you have on this topic" kind of letter. Busy professionals are more likely to respond to requests that are specific and reveal a control of the topic.

2. Do not request information that can be found in your library's reference collection. See Appendix B under "Business and Economics" for sources that provide information about companies.

3. Explain how you plan to use the information. Businesses are understandably concerned with their public images and will be disinclined to provide information that you intend to use as a means of attacking them. (For example, a chemical company is not likely to tell you how many times the Environmental Protection Agency has cited it for dumping toxic waste into a nearby stream. You will have to uncover this information from other sources, perhaps the EPA or local newspapers.)

Use reference guides to companies and government agencies to obtain addresses and the person to whom your letter should be addressed. For companies, address your request to the public information officer. For e-mail addresses, check the organization's home page.

Interviews

Some experts are available for personal interviews. Call or write for an appointment as soon as you recognize the value of an interview. Remember that interviews are more likely to be scheduled with state and local officials than with the president of General Motors. If you are studying a local issue, also consider leaders of the civic associations with an interest in the issue. In many communities, the local historian or a librarian will be a storehouse of information about the community's customs or past or its famous citizens. Professors or former teachers and principals can be interviewed for papers on a current issue in education. Interviews with doctors or nurses can add a special dimension to papers on various contemporary medical issues—on passive euthanasia for severely deformed newborns, for example. The student interested in the role of zoos in wildlife preservation could interview city zoo officials.

If an interview is appropriate for your topic, follow these guidelines:

1. Prepare specific questions in advance.

2. Arrive on time, properly dressed, and behave in a polite, professional manner throughout the interview.

3. Take notes, asking the interviewee to repeat key statements so that your notes are accurate.

4. Take a tape recorder with you but ask for permission to use it before beginning to tape the conversation.

5. If you quote any statements in your papers, quote accurately, eliminating only such minor speech habits as "you know's" and "uhm's." Make certain that the interviewee knows that you may quote or paraphrase portions of the interview. (See p. 108 for the proper documentation pattern for interviews.)

6. Direct the interview with your prepared questions but also give the interviewee the chance to approach the topic in his or her own way. You may obtain information or views that had not occurred to you.

7. Do not get into a debate with the interviewee. You are there to obtain information and ideas, not to do all the talking or to convince the interviewee to change some opinions.

Lectures

Check the appropriate information sources at your school to keep informed of visiting speakers. On most college campuses speakers appear frequently, lecturing on a wide range of topics. If you are fortunate enough to attend a lecture relevant to a current research project, take careful, detailed notes during the lecture. (See p. 108 for documenting information for a lecture.)

Films, Tapes, Television

Your library will have audiovisual materials that provide good sources for some kinds of topics; in the collection will also be professors' lectures. Many videotapes, films, and television programs are also valuable resources. If you are studying *Death of a Salesman,* view the videotaped version of the play starring Dustin Hoffman. Mel Gibson's (or Kenneth Branagh's) version of *Hamlet* can be contrasted with earlier film versions—or with the play as you have read and studied it. *My Fair Lady* makes an interesting comparison to Shaw's *Pygmalion,* the play upon which the musical and its film version were based.

Also pay attention to documentaries on public television and to the many news and political "talk shows" on both public and commercial channels. In many cases transcripts of shows can be obtained from the television station. Usually a transcript is free but must be requested in writing. Take good notes while watching a program and then request a transcript if you want to quote from it. Alternatively, tape the program while watching it so that you can view it several times. The documentation format for such nonprint sources is illustrated on pages 109–10.

Surveys, Questionnaires, and Original Research

Depending on your paper, you may want to take a simple survey or write and administer a questionnaire. Surveys can be used for many campus and local issues, for topics on behavior and attitudes of college students and/or faculty, and for topics on consumer habits. You could, for example, enrich a study of voter apathy in the United States by conducting a survey of voting habits among students and faculty. Prepare a list of questions (Are you registered to vote? If so, did you vote in the 1998 congressional election? Do you vote in local elections?) with space for answers. You may want to ask for each respondent's age and sex (if you want to compare voting habits by these factors), even party affiliation or preference—whatever variables you think might make for interesting comparisons. You can reach faculty through their campus mailboxes. Include a cover letter with your survey that explains your project and requests return by a specific date. You can reach students by polling personally in several dorms or by asking your instructors for a few minutes of class time to poll students in your classes. Use the discussion of preparing tables (see Chapter 5) as guidelines for presenting the results of your survey.

Complicated questionnaires requiring control for bias and random sampling need skillful preparation. Instructors in upper-level courses in the social sciences approving projects based on questionnaires will advise you on appropriate wording and sampling strategies. Without reaching for those standards of statistical validity, however, you can effectively engage in simple but useful surveys, and your efforts will be rewarded with original evidence to analyze and present along with your reading on a topic. To give other examples, if you are studying the Depression, see if you can question several people who lived during the 1930s and incorporate their experiences into your paper. If you are examining the role of zoos in preserving wildlife, do a questionnaire of attitudes toward zoos. Do most people think that zoos are good for, or bad for, animals?

When writing questions, keep these guidelines in mind:

- Use simple, clear language.

- Devise a series of short questions rather than only a few that have several parts to them. (You want to separate information for better analysis.)

- Phrase questions to avoid bias (wording that seeks to control the answer). For example, do *not* ask: How did you survive the *horrors* of the Depression? Do *not* write: Did you perform your civic duty by voting in the last election? These are loaded questions that prejudge the respondent's answers.

In addition to adding the results of surveys and questionnaires to your research essay, you can incorporate some original research. As you read sources on your topic, be alert to reports of studies that you could redo and update in part or on a smaller scale. Many topics on advertising and television give opportunities for your own analysis. Examine, for example, the evening new programs. How much time is given to commercials and announcements of what's coming? How much time is devoted to each news story? What kinds of events get the most—and most frequent—coverage? Tape a week's programs and do your own analysis.

Local-issue topics may provide good opportunities for gathering information on your own, not just from your reading. One student, examining the controversy over a proposed new mall on part of the Manassas Battlefield, made the argument that the shopping mall served no practical need in the community. He supported his assertion by describing the existing malls in the area, including the number and types of stores each contained and the number of miles each was from the proposed new mall. How did he obtain this information? He drove around the area, counting miles and stores. Sometimes a seemingly unglamorous approach to a topic turns out to be an imaginative one.

Preparing a
Working
Bibliography

- Know your documentation style and use it each time—do not "mix and match."
- Take down <u>all</u> needed information—going back to the library isn't fun!
- Try to understand the logic of documentation—you are giving readers information they need to locate each source.

Bibliographic information for a book:

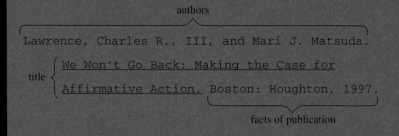

authors

Lawrence, Charles R., III, and Mari J. Matsuda.

title We Won't Go Back: Making the Case for Affirmative Action. Boston: Houghton, 1997.

facts of publication

Bibliographic information for an electronic database:

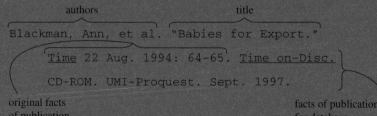

authors   title

Blackman, Ann, et al. "Babies for Export."

Time 22 Aug. 1994: 64-65. Time on-Disc.

CD-ROM. UMI-Proquest. Sept. 1997.

original facts of publication

facts of publication for database used: title of database, format, name of vendor, date last updated

3

PREPARING A BIBLIOGRAPHY

C hapters 2 and 3 together provide the information and guidance you need to go forward with your research project, once you have selected your topic and completed your research proposal. In fact, the text's first three chapters illustrate the overlapping and recursive nature of the research process. For example, you may have explored your library and used some of its reference materials as an aid to selecting and narrowing your topic, the first stage of research. Similarly, you cannot usefully gather sources—the second stage of research—without deciding on your method for recording potential sources and a format for documentation. To make these decisions and have the information to continue, you need this chapter. You will need to return to this chapter when preparing your completed paper to double-check the accuracy of your bibliographic citations, but you will find the final stages of completing your paper easier and less prone to error if you study the opening pages and then skim the rest of Chapter 3 now.

As you search for sources, you want to take down the necessary bibliographic information about each potential source in a systematic and thorough way—to prepare a preliminary or *working bibliography*. To be systematic and thorough, you need to select a recording method and a specific documentation format.

GUIDELINES FOR PREPARING A WORKING BIBLIOGRAPHY

The list you compile is only a working bibliography because you do not yet know exactly which possible sources you will use in your paper. (Your final bibliography will include only those sources you cite—actually refer to—in your paper.) Your working bibliography serves three purposes:

1. It becomes a survey of your proposed topic, helping you decide if there are adequate sources for completing your paper.

2. It becomes a list of specific sources with information for locating the sources for study and note taking.

3. It contains the information needed to prepare proper documentation for your paper.

There are several guidelines for preparing a working bibliography, procedures you are wise to follow for the best reason of all: they work. These guidelines used to begin with the assertion to use 3 × 5 index cards. Today, though, with many writers composing at their personal computers, we need to consider a second possible method: using a separate file in your PC in which to list potential sources as you find them. *If you have a PC and know how to combine files—and you are not required to turn in bibliography cards—you may want to develop your working bibliography as a list stored in your PC*. Note that there are several "Ifs" here. If you do not own a PC, if you are not sure how to merge files, if you cannot download bibliographic information directly from online indexes to your PC file, this method is not for you. If you have the computer and the skills, but your instructor requires cards, the PC method is also not for you at this time.

The following six guidelines direct you to a working bibliography on cards. If you are using the PC method, follow guidelines 3 through 6.

1. Use 3×5 index cards. (Do *not* use a legal pad, notebook paper, or the backs of envelopes!)

2. Put only *one* source on a card. (Never write on the back of a card; you might overlook the information on the back.)

3. Check *all* reasonable catalogs and indexes for possible sources. (Do *not* use only one reference source—*InfoTrac* on CD-ROM, for example—even if that reference tool provides enough titles to meet your assignment's requirements. You are looking for the best sources, not just the first eight you find.)

4. Complete a card—or make an entry—for *every* relevant source listed in catalogs, indexes, and other reference sources.

5. Copy *all* information needed to complete a bibliographic citation and locate the source. (When using an index that does not give all needed information, leave space on the card—or in your PC list—to be filled in when you read the work itself.)

6. Put bibliographic information in the *correct format* for every source.

Over time these guidelines have acquired the force of rules for several good reasons. First, cards offer flexibility. You can easily add to your stack while keeping the cards alphabetized, or organized in the sequence in which you plan to read the sources, or arranged by location if you are using more than one library. Eventually, cards for sources not used can be eliminated, and the remaining cards alphabetized in preparation for typing your final list of works cited.

Alternatively, the PC method offers speed for those who type fast, who will compose their paper at the computer, and who will be using many online indexes from which they can print lists of potential sources directly onto discs. If you print bibliographic information directly onto a disc, you avoid the possibility of copying incorrectly—or incompletely. On the other hand, the format of citations from indexes will not be correct for your completed paper, so you will have to revise your list of sources to conform to the expected documentation method. (See example on page 80.) Also, be sure to have some index cards with you when searching for sources; not all sources will be found in online databases.

The third guideline is a reminder that we do research to learn about a topic, not to meet minimum requirements for an assignment. Although you are not expected to compile an exhaustive list of sources on a topic, still you will need an adequate number of reliable sources on the subject. Use your course texts, your instructor, and reference tools to find out who the experts are on the topic and to locate the best sources for study.

> ✓ The research of college students cannot be based on encyclopedias or exclusively on articles from popular magazines. For articles on dinosaurs, for example, turn to *Natural History* or *Scientific American* or *Science*, not *Time* or *Newsweek*.

The final three guidelines focus on using time efficiently, on looking ahead to the next stages of the research process. It is faster to prepare cards (or a file) for all potential sources and to copy all needed information the first time around than to return to the library to find additional sources or complete a citation. Also, you want to compile a list of more sources than you can reasonably study. You will find that some sources will turn out to be of little use or to repeat what other sources have already provided. Additionally, if you copy information thoroughly and correctly, you will save time, reduce the potential for error, and avoid frustration when preparing your completed paper. Do not think that you can write first and then "put in" the documentation later or piece together a correct Works Cited page the night before the paper is due. Remember, too, that some instructors will ask to see a working bibliography early in the research process. They expect to see (and will grade you on) citations that are complete and in correct format.

> ✓ **Note:** Sources found on CD-ROM or online databases, or on the Internet, require additional information about the medium used. Also, for databases, you will need the latest date on the database. You may find the date at the top of your terminal screen or, quite often, at the bottom of the first screen. Take a minute to scroll down to the bottom of the database's "title page" to find the required date. For Internet sources, you will need the date you accessed the material. Be sure to include that date in your working bibliography. Study the models of bibliographic citations on pages 101–05 to become familiar with the information you will need for these types of sources.

WRITING BIBLIOGRAPHY CARDS FOR YOUR FIELD OF STUDY

All works—books, articles, interviews, Internet materials—used in a research project are presented to readers at the end of the research paper in a list, usually alphabetized and labeled "Works Cited" or "References," depending on the documentation format. These bibliographic citations include, regardless of the type of source or the documentation format followed, the source's *author*, *title*, and *publication information*. Since these are the facts you will need to complete your paper, these are the facts you want to record in your working bibliography. All researchers, regardless of field of study, need these basic facts about a source, but not all fields of research follow the same conventions for presenting the information. Many researchers in the humanities follow the style established by the Modern Language Association (MLA), and this is the style usually expected in college composition courses. Researchers in the social sciences follow, for the most part, the style established by the American Psychological Association (APA). Researchers in the sciences follow a greater variety of styles depending on the specific discipline.

Illustrated below are models of MLA, APA, and (to represent the sciences) American Chemical Society styles. Observe that these patterns for books, although similar, are sufficiently varied to demand careful attention to each style's guidelines. (Citations of articles vary even more among the three styles.)

The sample bibliography cards and detailed patterns of citations in this chapter show you the correct format according to the Modern Language Association. If you are using a citation pattern other than MLA, turn to Chapter 7 for the format required in your field of study.

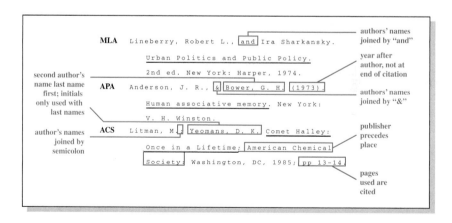

Do *not* try to mix or blend styles. Select the style used in your field or requested by your instructor and follow it *exactly*. You will be graded in part on the accuracy of your documentation.

WRITING BIBLIOGRAPHY CARDS: MLA STYLE

Basic Form for Books

As Figure 33 illustrates, the basic bibliographic form for books requires the following information, in this pattern:

1. The author's full name, last name first
2. The title (and subtitle, if there is one) of the book, underlined
3. The facts of publication: the city of publication (followed by a colon), the publisher (followed by a comma), and the date of publication

Observe: Periods are placed after the author's name, after the title, and at the end of the citation. Other information necessary to some books (e.g., the name of an editor, the number of volumes) is added in appropriate places to the basic pattern. These variations are illustrated in the many sample citations that follow in the second part of this chapter.

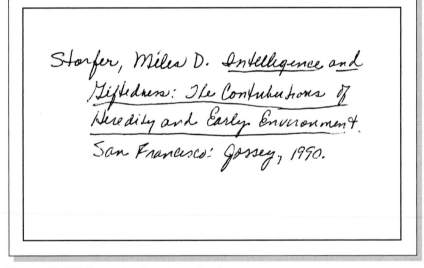

Figure 33 Bibliography Card for a Book.

Basic Form for Periodicals

Figure 34 illustrates the simplest form for journal, magazine, and newspaper articles. Periodicals citations require the following information, in this order:

1. The author's full name, last name first
2. The title of the article, in quotation marks
3. The facts of publication: the title of the periodical (underlined), the volume number (if the article is in a scholarly journal), the date (followed by a colon), and inclusive page numbers

   Observe: Periods are placed after the author's name, after the article's title, and at the end of the citation. **But,** there is no period after the title of the periodical.

Turning Information into Citations

In your search for sources, you will discover that bibliographic information does not usually come in the required MLA format. Information given in most

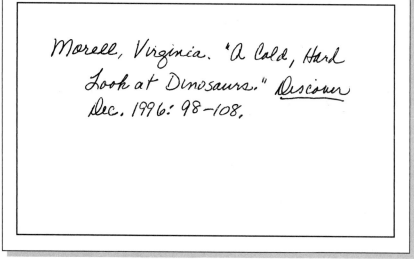

Figure 34 Bibliography Card for an Article.

periodical indexes will have to be arranged on your card (or PC list) into the format needed for documenting in MLA style. Here, for example, is a source on dinosaurs found in *InfoTrac* (*Magazine Index Plus*—CD-ROM):

A piece of the dinosaur killer found? (possible remnant of asteroid found that collided with Earth 65 million years ago) Richard A. Kerr. <u>Science</u>, March 29, 1996, v271 n5257 p1806(1).

To turn this information into a correct bibliographic citation, you need to:

- rearrange the information to put the author first
- eliminate bold type and place the article title in quotation marks
- eliminate such information as the brief summary
- present the volume, date, and page number in MLA form

Figure 35 illustrates a correct citation for this source, as it would appear in your PC bibliography file.

The same procedure will be needed with the following source, obtained from a list of references in a geology text:

KENNEDY, V. S., ed. 1980, Estuarine Perspectives. Academic Press, Inc., New York. 533 pp.

Kerr, Richard A. "A Piece of the Dinosaur Killer Found?" <u>Science</u> 271 (1996): 1806.

Figure 35 Correct MLA Format for a Source—Shown in PC File.

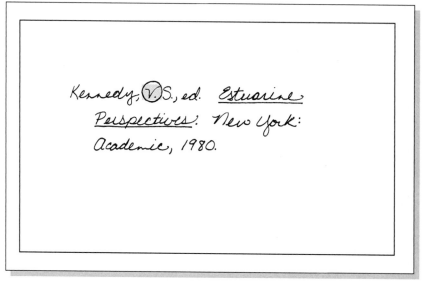

Figure 36 Bibliography Card for a Book Listed in a Textbook's List of References.

On your card, put the facts of publication in the right order and format, underline the book's title, and circle the author's first initial as a reminder to get the full name from the title page when you read the book. (See Figure 36.)

Once you get used to the fact that titles are rarely underlined or put in quotation marks in the periodical indexes and become familiar with the order of information you need for MLA documentation, you will find that getting your working bibliography completed accurately is not too difficult—most of the time. Some sources are unusual and require rather complicated citations. Always be sure to look carefully at each source when you read it to make certain that you have a full and accurate citation. Consider, for example, the title and copyright pages illustrated in Figure 37. Your bibliography card, shown in Figure 38, must include the original publication date, the publisher's imprint (Harper Torchbooks), and the publication date of the Torchbook edition, the one used for your research.

These and other variations of the basic MLA citation format are illustrated and explained in the latter part of this chapter. Study the general conventions of citation on pages 89–110 and then take this handbook with you as you put together your working bibliography.

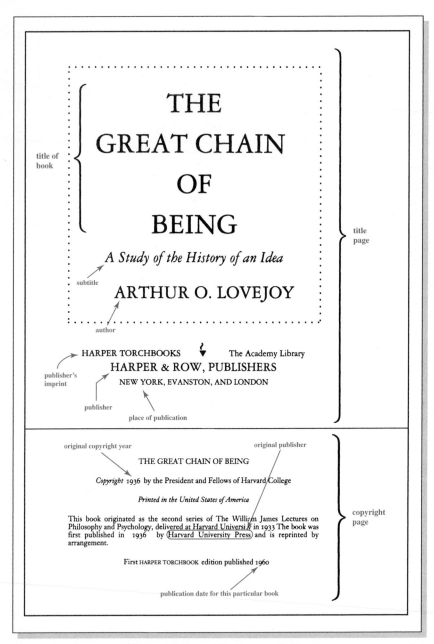

Figure 37 Annotated Title and Copyright Pages of a Book.

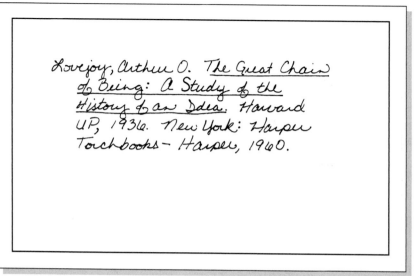

Figure 38 Bibliography Card for a Book Shown in Figure 37.

Working with Bibliography Cards

In addition to getting all needed information in the correct format on your cards—or PC list—you should include additional information that will help you locate and use the sources you have listed. If you are using more than one library, for instance, indicate the source's location. When checking OPAC for books, copy onto your cards or list the full call number for each book you might use. Make a note of all books containing a bibliography, a good place to look for additional sources on your topic. When you begin skimming sources, you may also want to note the contents of a work and how you may use it. See Figure 39 for a sample card that works for the researcher.

CONVENTIONS OF BIBLIOGRAPHIC FORM

The following summary of the conventions of citation will guide you in preparing a working bibliography and, later, your Works Cited page. After the rules come many examples to serve as models. Strive to complete each citation correctly so that you learn the right form and avoid introducing errors that may be transferred to your completed paper.

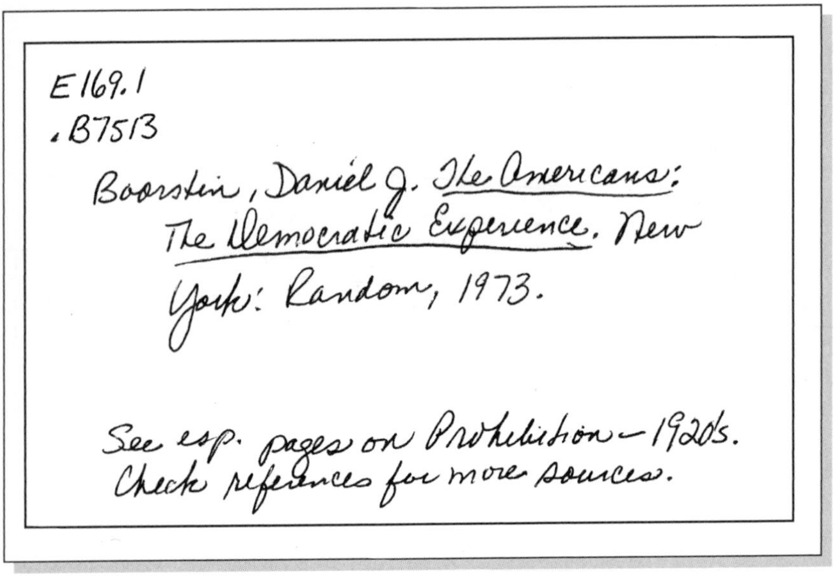

E169.1
.B7513

Boorstin, Daniel J. The Americans: The Democratic Experience. New York: Random, 1973.

See esp. pages on Prohibition—1920's.
Check references for more sources.

Figure 39 Bibliography Card with Student's Notes.

Warning: *Always* compare citations in your working bibliography with each actual source when you start to read it. *Never* assume that someone else's list of sources contains accurate information. It is your paper, not the reference source, that gets a grade!

Bibliographic Citations—General

1. **Present each citation with hanging indentation**. The first line of each citation begins at the left margin. Second and subsequent lines are indented five spaces from the left margin. The appearance is the reverse of paragraphing. Use hanging indentation when copying information on bibliography cards or PC lists, so that you remember to use this pattern on your Works Cited page.

2. **Place a period after each of the three main parts of a citation: author, title, facts of publication**. Leave two spaces after each period, just as you space between sentences. However, if the author's name ends with a middle initial, the one period after the initial is sufficient. If the title ends

in a question mark or exclamation point, do not add a period after it. In general: Do not use two forms of end punctuation together.

3. **Supply information about books, as appropriate, in the following order:**
author*
chapter or part of book
title of book*
editor or translator
number or type of edition
number of volumes
name of the series
place of publication*
publisher*
date of publication*
Items marked with an asterisk are required in each citation. Other items may be needed for some books.

4. **Supply information about periodicals, as appropriate, in the following order:**
author*
title of the article*
name of the periodical*
volume, issue
date*
page numbers of article*
Items marked with an asterisk are required. Volume and issue numbers are needed for scholarly journals. (Section letter or number and edition may be needed for newspapers.)

5. **Do *not* number citations in a Works Cited list.**

6. **Alphabetize Works Cited by author last name. If there is no author, alphabetize by the title, excluding articles (*A, An,* or *The*).**

Conventions for Authors

1. **Give the author's full name as it appears with the work.** If you use an index that gives only initials, complete the author's name when you obtain the work.

   Example: J. A. Lee (from <u>Reader's Guide</u>) becomes Lee, John A.

2. **For a work by two or three authors, cite all names but give only the first author's name with the last name first.** The second (or third) name should appear in signature order.

   Example: Gove, Walter R., Michael Hughes, and Michael R. Geerken.

3. **If a work has four or more authors, give only the first name listed, followed by a comma and the Latin abbreviation** *et al.* **(for "and others").**

Example: Baugh, Albert C., et al.

Conventions for Titles

1. **Underline titles of books, magazines, newspapers, plays, movies, works of art, and computer software.** Long poems, published in book form, are underlined. Pamphlet titles are underlined because, regardless of length, pamphlets are separate publications. **Note:** MLA style requires underlining, not the use of *italics.*

2. **The Bible and books of the Bible are not underlined.** Unless you specify a particular version, readers assume that you have cited the King James Version of the Bible.

3. **Place quotation marks around titles of articles, essays, newspaper articles, lectures, poems, short stories, chapter titles, TV or radio episodes in a series, songs, and speeches.** Place the period ending the title part of the citation before the final quotation mark.

Example: "The Palestinian Tug-of-War."

4. **Capitalize the first and last words of a title and all the other words except articles (***a, an, the***), conjunctions (***and, or, but, for, nor, yet, so***), and prepositions of fewer than six letters (e.g.,** *for, to, with,* **but** *Between***).** Follow this rule even if the title is not capitalized in the periodicals index or other source used.

5. **Include a work's subtitle as part of the title, also underlined and preceded by a colon, even if there is no colon on the title page or in the reference source used.** The first word of the subtitle is capitalized.

Example: Children & Television: Images in a Changing Sociocultural World

6. **Indicate a work in its second or later edition, or in a revised edition, by adding the appropriate information after the title.**

Example: The Growth of American Thought. 3rd ed.

Conventions for Publication Information—Books

1. **Give the city of publication (followed by a colon), the publisher's name (followed by a comma), and the date of publication (followed**

by a period). Confirm information taken from a reference source by checking the book's title and copyright pages.

Example: Englewood Cliffs: Prentice, 1997.

2. **Cite only the city of publication, not the state**. Add the country, abbreviated, for books published abroad, *if* the city may be unfamiliar to readers.

   Example: Manchester, Eng. *But not:* London, Eng.

3. **Give only the first city listed on the book's title page,** even if several cities are listed.

4. **If no place or no date appears in a book, write *n.p.* or *n.d.* in the appropriate place in the citation**.

5. **Give the most recent copyright date provided on the copyright page**. Do *not* cite a printing date for the copyright date.

6. **Use the shortened forms of publishers' names. Follow these guidelines**:

   - Omit business abbreviations (*Co.*, *Inc.*) and descriptive terms (*Press, House, Publishers*).

Full Name	**Citation Form**
Macmillan Publishing Co., Inc.	Macmillan
The Free Press	Free
Basic Books	Basic

   - If the publisher's name includes several surnames, cite only the first name.

Farrar, Straus, and Giroux, Inc.	Farrar
Appleton-Century-Crofts	Appleton
Prentice-Hall	Prentice

   - If the publisher's name is one person's name, cite only the surname.

Harry N. Abrams, Inc.	Abrams
George Allen and Unwin Publishers, Inc.	Allen
Alfred A. Knopf, Inc.	Knopf

   - Shorten university press names thus:

Harvard University Press	Harvard UP
The Johns Hopkins University Press	Johns Hopkins UP
University of Chicago Press	U of Chicago P

- Use standard abbreviations of publishing organizations that will be known to your readers.

The National Education Association	NEA
The Modern Language Association	MLA
Government Printing Office	GPO

Conventions for Publication Information—Periodicals

1. **For popular magazines, cite the following information: title of the magazine (underlined), date of publication (followed by a colon), and the page numbers of the article. Do _not_ put any punctuation after the magazine title.**

   Examples: Scientific American Nov. 1991: 48–54. Time 21 Oct. 1996: 94.

2. **Most scholarly journals are paged consecutively throughout all the issues in one year. For journals paged annually, cite the following publication information: title of the journal, volume number (an arabic numeral), the year of publication in parentheses (followed by a colon), and the page numbers of the article.** (See some variations on page 97.)

   Example: Modern Drama 8 (1966): 347–61.

3. **Abbreviate months of the year except May, June, and July.** Put a period at the end of the abbreviation. (See 1 above.)

4. **For magazines published weekly, cite the full date in the order of day, month, year.** (See 1 above.)

5. **Provide inclusive page numbers for articles printed on successive pages. For articles that are interrupted with other material, provide the first page number followed, without spacing, by a "+."**

   Examples: Scientific American Nov. 1991: 48–54. New Republic 13 Jan. 1979: 12+.

6. **For articles appearing on page 100 or higher, cite inclusive page numbers without repeating the first digit of the three-digit number.**

   Example: 347–61 or 122–34. _BUT:_ 397–412.

7. **For newspapers, cite the following publication information: name of the paper (underlined); the day, month, and year of publication (followed by a colon); and the page(s) on which the article appeared.**

   Example: Christian Science Monitor 15 Jan. 1991: 18.

8. **If the newspaper has lettered sections, add the appropriate letter before the page number, without a space.**

   Example: Washington Post 10 May 1997: A20.

MLA Citations
for the Works
Cited Page

Always compare your source information with the appropriate model to transfer information into MLA form.

1. *From a psychology textbook bibliography:*

   ```
   Rotter, J.B. (1971, June). External
        control and internal control.
        Psychology Today, pp. 37-42,
        58-59.
   ```

   In MLA form:

   ```
   Rotter, Julian B. "External Control
        and Internal Control." Psychology
        Today June 1971: 37+.
   ```

2. *From an online database:*

   ```
   New Scientist, April 27, 1996
        v150n2027 p36(4) Demon farmers
        and other myths. Kate de
        Selincourt.
   ```

   In MLA form:

   ```
   de Selincourt, Kate. "Demon Farmers
        and Other Myths." New Scientist
        27 Apr., 1996: 36-40.
   ```

9. **If the newspaper has numbered sections, provide the section number, with the abbreviation "sec.," after the date.**

   Example: <u>Los Angeles Times</u> 1 Apr. 1996, sec. 2: 9.

10. **If the newspaper appears in more than one edition each day, include the edition used after the date.**

    Example: <u>Wall Street Journal</u> 10 Feb. 1988, eastern ed.: 23.

11. **When citing the name of the newspaper, omit the initial article, even though it is on the paper's masthead.** Thus, *The New York Times* is cited as <u>New York Times</u>.

12. **If the city is not part of the newspaper's name as it appears on the masthead, give it in square brackets—unless the paper is published nationally, such as the Wall Street Journal.**

    Example: <u>Plain Dealer</u> [Cleveland]

PREPARING MLA CITATIONS FOR THE "WORKS CITED" PAGE

If you have developed a thorough and accurate working bibliography during your search for sources, the correct documenting (acknowledging) of sources in your paper should not be a problem. One part of the required documentation—the in-text citing of author and page—is explained and illustrated in Chapter 5. These in-text citations are supported, or completed, by the final page (or pages) of your paper: the "Works Cited" page. To prepare your Works Cited, all you need to do is alphabetize, by author last name, the cards (or list) of all sources you actually refer to (cite) in your paper and then type each source's citation according to the conventions explained above and illustrated in the following pages. (Guidelines for formatting the entire Works Cited page(s) are found on pages 222–23.)

Forms for Books: Citing the Complete Book

A Book by a Single Author

Fisher, David E. <u>Fire & Ice: The Greenhouse Effect,</u>

  <u>Ozone Depletion and Nuclear Winter</u>. New York:

  Harper, 1990.

The subtitle is included, preceded by a colon, even if there is no colon on the book's title page.

A Book by Two or Three Authors

Yergin, Daniel, and Thane Gustafson. <u>Russia 2010: And</u>

<u>What It Means for the World</u>. New York: Random,

1993.

Second (and third) authors' names appear in signature form.

A Book with More Than Three Authors

Baker, Susan P., et al. <u>The Injury Fact Book</u>. Oxford:

Oxford UP, 1992.

Use the name of the first author listed on the title page. The English "and others" may be used instead of "et al."

Two or More Works by the Same Author

Allen, Frederick Lewis. <u>The Big Change</u>. New York:

Harper, 1952.

---. <u>Only Yesterday: An Informal History of the</u>

<u>Nineteen-Twenties</u>. New York: Harper, 1931.

Give the author's full name with the first entry. For the second (and additional works), begin the citation with three hyphens followed by a period. Alphabetize the entries by the books' titles.

A Book Written under a Pseudonym with Name Supplied

Wrighter, Carl P. [Paul Stevens]. <u>I Can Sell You</u>

<u>Anything</u>. New York: Ballantine, 1972.

Supply the author's name in square brackets.

An Anonymous Book

<u>Beowulf</u>. Trans. E. Talbot Donaldson. New York: Norton,

1966.

Do not use "anon." Alphabetize by the book's title.

An Edited Book

Hamilton, Alexander, James Madison, and John Jay. <u>The</u>

  <u>Federalist Papers</u>. Ed. Isaac Kramnick. New York:

  Viking-Penguin, 1987.

Lynn, Kenneth S., ed. Huckleberry Finn: <u>Text, Sources,</u>

  <u>and Criticism</u>. New York: Harcourt, 1961.

If you cite the author's work, put the author's name first and the editor's name after the title, preceded by "Ed." If you cite the editor's work (an introduction or notes), then place the editor's name first, followed by a comma and "ed."

A Translation

Kundera, Milan. <u>The Farewell Party</u>. Trans. Peter

  Kussi. New York: Viking-Penguin, 1977.

Cornford, Francis MacDonald, trans. <u>The Republic of</u>

  <u>Plato</u>. New York: Oxford UP, 1945.

If the author's work is being cited, place the author's name first and the translator's name after the title, preceded by "Trans." If the translator's work is the important element, place the translator's name first, as in the second example above. If the author's name does not appear in the title, give it after the title. For example: by Plato.

A Book in Two or More Volumes

Spielvogel, Jackson J. <u>Western Civilization</u>. 2 vols.

  Minneapolis: West, 1991.

A Book in Its Second or Subsequent Edition

O'Brien, David M. <u>Storm Center: The Supreme Court in</u>

  <u>American Politics</u>. 2nd ed. New York: Norton,

  1990.

Sundquist, James L. <u>Dynamics of the Party System</u>. Rev.

  ed. Washington: Brookings, 1983.

Always include the number of the edition you have used, abbreviated as shown, if it is not the first edition.

A Book in a Series

Maclean, Hugh, ed. <u>Edmund Spenser's Poetry</u>. A Norton
     Critical Edition. New York: Norton, 1968.

Waggoner, Hyatt H. <u>Nathaniel Hawthorne</u>. University of
     Minnesota Pamphlets on American Writers, No. 23.
     Minneapolis: U of Minnesota P, 1962.

The series title—and number, if there is one—follows the book's title but is not underlined.

A Reprint of an Earlier Work

Cuppy, Will. <u>How to Become Extinct</u>. 1941. Chicago: U
     of Chicago P, 1983.

Twain, Mark. <u>Adventures of Huckleberry Finn</u>. 1885.
     Centennial Facsimile Edition. Intro. Hamlin Hill.
     New York: Harper, 1962.

Faulkner, William. <u>As I Lay Dying</u>. 1930. New York:
     Vintage-Random, 1964.

Since the date of a work is often important, cite the original date of publication as well as the facts of publication for the reprinted version. Indicate any new material that is part of the reprinted book, as in the second example. The third example shows how to cite a book reprinted, by the same publisher, in a paperback version. (Vintage is a paperback imprint of the publisher Random House.)

A Book with Two or More Publishers

Green, Mark J., James M. Fallows, and David R. Zwick.
     <u>Who Runs Congress?</u> Ralph Nader Congress Project.
     New York: Bantam; New York: Grossman, 1972.

If the title page lists two or more publishers, give all as part of the facts of publication, placing a semicolon between them, as illustrated above.

A Corporate or Governmental Author

California State Department of Education. <u>American</u>

   <u>Indian Education Handbook</u>. Sacramento: California

   State Department of Education, Indian Education

   Unit, 1991.

Hispanic Market Connections. <u>The National Hispanic</u>

   <u>Database: A Los Angeles Preview</u>. Los Altos, CA:

   Hispanic Market Connections, 1992.

   List the institution as the author even when it is also the publisher.

A Book in a Foreign Language

Blanchard, Gerard. <u>Images de la musique au cinéma</u>.

   Paris: Edilig, 1984.

Gnüg, Hiltrud, ed. <u>Literarische Utopie-Entwürfe</u>.

   Frankfurt: Suhrkamp, 1982.

   Capitalize only the first word of titles and subtitles and words normally capitalized in that language, e.g., proper nouns in French, all nouns in German. A translation in square brackets may be provided. Check your work carefully for spelling and accent marks.

The Bible

The Bible. [Always refers to the King James Version.]

The Bible. Revised Standard Version.

The Reader's Bible: A Narrative. Ed. with Intro.

   Roland Mushat Frye. Princeton: Princeton UP,

   1965.

   Do not underline the title. Indicate the version if it is not the King James Version. Provide facts of publication for versions not well known.

A Book with a Title in Its Title

Piper, Henry Dan, ed. <u>Fitzgerald's</u> The Great Gatsby:

    <u>The Novel, the Critics, the Background</u>. Scribner

    Research Anthologies. Gen. Ed. Martin Steinmann,

    Jr. New York: Scribner's, 1970.

If a book's title contains a title normally placed in quotation marks, retain the quotation marks, but if it contains a title normally underlined, do not underline that title, as illustrated above.

Forms for Books: Citing Part of a Book

A Preface, Introduction, Foreword, or Afterword

Sagan, Carl. Introduction. <u>The Red Limit: The Search</u>

    <u>for the Edge of the Universe</u>. By Timothy Ferris.

    New York: Morrow, 1977. 13-16.

Use this form if you are citing the author of the preface, etc. Provide the appropriate identifying word after the author's name and give inclusive page numbers for the part of the book by that author at the end of the citation. The author of the book itself goes after the title, as illustrated.

An Encyclopedia Article

Ostrom, John H. "Dinosaurs." <u>McGraw-Hill Encyclopedia</u>

    <u>of Science and Technology</u>. 1987 ed.

"Prohibition." <u>New Encyclopaedia Britannica:</u>

    <u>Micropaedia</u>. 1988 ed.

When articles are signed or initialed, give the author's name. Complete the name of the author of an initialed article thus: K[enney], E[dward] J. Identify well-known encyclopedias and dictionaries by the year of the edition only. Give the complete facts of publication for less well-known works or those in only one edition: "Benjamin Franklin." <u>Concise Dictionary of American Biography</u>. Mgr. Ed. Joseph G. E. Hopkins. New York: Scribner's, 1964.

One or More Volumes in a Multivolume Work

James, Henry. <u>The Portrait of a Lady</u>. Vols. 3 and 4 of

    <u>The Novels and Tales of Henry James</u>. 26 vols. New

    York: Scribner's, 1908.

When using a complete work that makes up one or more volumes of a multivolume work, cite the title and volume number(s) of that work followed by the title, editor (if appropriate), total number of volumes, and facts of publication for the multivolume work.

A Work Within One Volume of a Multivolume Work

Shaw, Bernard. <u>Pygmalion</u>. Vol. 1. <u>The Complete Plays</u>

    <u>with Prefaces</u>. New York: Dodd, 1963. 197–281.

    6 vols.

Cite the author, title of the single work used, the volume number in which it appears, and then the title and facts of publication for the multivolume work. Then give the inclusive page numbers for the specific work followed by the total number of volumes.

A Work in an Anthology or Collection

Hurston, Zora Neale. <u>The First One</u>. <u>Black Female</u>

    <u>Playwrights: An Anthology of Plays before 1950</u>.

    Ed. Kathy A. Perkins. Bloomington: Indiana UP,

    1989. 80–88.

Comstock, George. "The Medium and the Society: The

    Role of Television in American Life." <u>Children</u>

    <u>and Television: Images in a Changing</u>

    <u>Sociocultural World</u>. Eds. Gordon L. Berry and Joy

    Keiko Asamen. Newbury Park, CA: Sage, 1993.

    117–31.

Cite the author and title of the work you have used. Then give the title, the editor(s), and the facts of publication of the anthology or collection. Conclude by providing inclusive page numbers for the work used.

An Article in a Collection, Casebook, or Sourcebook

Welsch, Roger. "The Cornstalk Fiddle." Journal of

American Folklore 77 (1964): 262-63. Rpt. in

Readings in American Folklore. Ed. Jan Harold

Brunvand. New York: Norton, 1979. 106-07.

MacKenzie, James J. "The Decline of Nuclear Power."

engage/social April 1986. Rpt. as "America Does

Not Need More Nuclear Power Plants" in The

Environmental Crisis: Opposing Viewpoints. Eds.

Julie S. Bach and Lynn Hall. Opposing Viewpoints

Series. Ser. Eds. David L. Bender and Bruno

Leone. St Paul: Greenhaven, 1986. 136-41.

Most articles in collections have been previously published, so a complete citation needs to include the original facts of publication (excluding page numbers if they are unavailable) as well as the facts of publication for the collection. The original facts of publication can be found at the bottom of the first page of the article or on an acknowledgments page in the front or back of the casebook. End the citation with inclusive page numbers for the article used.

Cross-References

If you are citing several articles from one collection, you can cite the collection and then provide only the author and title of specific articles used, with a cross-reference to the editor(s) of the collection:

Head, Suzanne, and Robert Heinzman, eds. Lessons of

the Rainforest. San Francisco: Sierra Club, 1990.

Bandyopadhyay, J., and Vandana Shiva. "Asia's Forests,

Asia's Cultures." Head and Heinzman 66-77.

Head, Suzanne. "The Consumer Connection: Psychology

and Politics." Head and Heinzman 156-67.

Forms for Periodicals: Articles in Journals

Article in a Journal with Continuous Paging Throughout the Issues of Each Year

Truman, Dana M., David M. Tokar, and Ann R. Fischer.

"Dimensions of Masculinity: Relations to Date

Rape, Supportive Attitudes, and Sexual Aggression

in Dating Situations." Journal of Counseling and

Development 76 (1996): 555-62.

Give the volume number followed by the year only, in parentheses, followed by a colon and inclusive page numbers. Neither issue number nor month (or season) is necessary to locate the article.

Article in a Journal with Separate Paging for Each Issue

Lewis, Kevin. "Superstardom and Transcendence." Arete:

The Journal of Sport Literature 2.2 (1985):

47-54.

When each issue of a journal begins with a new page 1, volume and year are not sufficient to locate the article, so give the issue number, immediately following the volume number, separated by a period.

Article in a Journal That Uses Issue Numbers Only

Keen, Ralph. "Thomas More and Geometry." Moreana 86

(1985): 151-66.

If the journal uses only issue numbers, not volume numbers, treat the issue number as a volume number.

Article in a Journal with More Than One Series

Payne, Samuel B., Jr. "The Iroquois League, the

Articles of Confederation, and the Constitution."

William and Mary Quarterly 3rd ser. 53 (1996):

605-20.

Provide the series number and the abbreviation "ser." immediately after the journal title. To indicate a new or original series of a journal, use the abbreviation "ns" or "os" immediately after the journal title, without any punctuation.

Forms for Periodicals: Articles in Magazines

Article in a Monthly Magazine

Zimring, Franklin E. "Firearms, Violence and Public

   Policy." <u>Scientific American</u> Nov. 1991: 48-54.

Blankenship, Jane, and Janette Kenner. "Images of

   Tomorrow: How Advertisers Sell the Future."

   <u>Futurist</u> May-June 1986:19-20.

   Articles in popular magazines are best identified by date, not volume number, so do not use volume or issue number, even if the magazine gives them. Instead, cite the month(s) and year after the title, followed by a colon and inclusive page numbers.

Article in a Weekly Magazine

Mestel, Rosie. "Cold-Blooded Dinosaurs Ahead by a

   Nose." <u>New Scientist</u> 18 Mar. 1995: 6.

   Provide the complete date, after the magazine title, using the order of day, month, and year, followed by a colon and inclusive page numbers.

An Anonymous Article

"Death of Perestroika." <u>Economist</u> 2 Feb. 1991: 12-13.

   The order is the same for any article. The missing name indicates that the article is anonymous. This citation would be alphabetized under D.

A Published Interview

Angier, Natalie. "Ernst Mayr at 93." Interview.

   <u>Natural History</u> May 1997: 8-11.

   Follow the pattern for a published article, but add the identifying word "Interview" (followed by a period) after the article's title.

A Review

Beardsley, Tim. "Eliciting Science's Best." Rev. of

   <u>Frontiers of Illusion: Science, Technology, and</u>

   <u>the Politics of Progress</u>, by Daniel Sarewitz.

   <u>Scientific American</u> June 1997: 142.

```
Shales, Tom. "'The Odyssey' Mything Persons." Rev. of

     the movie The Odyssey. NBC, 18 May 1997.

     Washington Post 18 May 1997: G1.

"Briefly Noted." Rev. of The Scientific 100: A Ranking

     of the Most Influential Scientists, Past and

     Present, by John Simmons. Scientific American

     March 1997: 125.
```

If the review is signed, begin with the author's name, then the title of the review article. Since review titles rarely make clear the work being reviewed, give the title of the work being reviewed and its author, preceded by "Rev. of." Alphabetize unsigned reviews by the title of the review. For reviews of art shows, videos, or computer software, provide place and date or descriptive label to make the citation clear.

An Article with a Quotation in the Title

```
Greenfield, Meg. "'Colorizing' the News." Newsweek 18

     Feb. 1991: 76.
```

Use single quotation marks around quoted words or phrases, or a quoted title, in the title of the article you are citing.

Forms for Periodicals: Newspapers

An Article from a Newspaper

```
Arguilla, John. "What Deep Blue Taught Kasparov—and

     Us." Christian Science Monitor 16 May 1997: 18.
```

Newspapers are cited much the same as articles in weekly magazines, except for some additional information illustrated in the examples below. A newspaper's title should be cited as it appears on the masthead, excluding any initial article; thus, New York Times, not The New York Times.

An Article from a Newspaper with Lettered Sections

```
Fiss, Owen M. "Affirmative Action: Beyond Diversity."

     Washington Post 7 May 1997: A21.
```

Place the section letter immediately before the page number, without any spacing.

An Article from a Newspaper with Numbered Sections

Roberts, Sam. "Another Kind of Middle-Class Squeeze."

New York Times 18 May 1997, sec. 4:1+.

Place the section number after the date, preceded by a comma and the abbreviation "sec."

An Article from a Newspaper with a Designated Edition

Pereira, Joseph. "Women Allege Sexist Atmosphere in

Offices Constitutes Harassment." Wall Street

Journal 10 Feb. 1988, eastern ed.: 23.

If a newspaper is published in more than one edition each day, the edition used is cited after the date.

An Editorial

"Where Welfare Stands." Editorial. New York Times 18

May 1997, sec. 4:16.

Add the descriptive label "Editorial" after the article title. Alphabetize by the title.

A Letter to the Editor

Wiles, Yoko A. "Thoughts of a New Citizen." Letter.

Washington Post 27 Dec. 1995: A22.

If the letter is titled, add the descriptive word "Letter" after the title. If the letter is untitled, place "Letter" after the author's name.

An Article from a Microform Collection Such as NewsBank

Birch, Doug. "Congress Acts to Save More Land for

Historic Antietam." Sun [Baltimore] 25 Sept.

1988. NewsBank: Housing and Land Development

(1988) fiche 89, grid E9.

Give the facts of publication for the article and then the facts needed to locate the article in the NewsBank collection—your source of the article.

Forms for Electronic Sources

Computer technology now offers information in many forms other than the traditional print medium. Patterns for documenting electronic sources are still evolving, in part because the technology continues to evolve. As you study the following models, keep in mind that you are (1) still providing author, title, and the facts of publication and (2) the formats are based on those for books and articles and then varied to accommodate the different media. For electronic sources, the "facts of publication" will differ. Within the category of electronic sources, we can distinguish among those works published in print that are also available electronically, and those works available only electronically. We also document CD-ROM and online sources differently.

Citing CD-ROMs, Diskettes, or Magnetic Tapes

An Article Published Both in Print and on CD-ROM (or Diskette, etc.)

Sheridan, Mary Beth. "Americans Fuel Tejuana Drugstore

  Boom." <u>Los Angeles Times</u> 5 July 1996: A1.

  <u>CDNewsBank</u>. CD-ROM. NewsBank. April 1997.

Detweiler, Richard A. "Democracy and Decency on the

  Internet." <u>Chronicle of Higher Education</u> 28 June

  1996: A40. <u>General Periodicals Ondisc</u>. CD-ROM.

  UMI-ProQuest. April 1997.

For works published in print that you have obtained on CD-ROM, first cite the article in the standard format. Then add the following:

title of the database, underlined

the publication medium (CD-ROM, diskette, etc., because the work may be available in more than one medium but may not be exactly the same in each.)

name of the vendor (because leased information may vary among vendors.)

electronic publication date (the latest date on the disk).

(Note: NewsBank is on both microfiche—see above—and CD-ROM; compare the different citation patterns.)

A Work or a Part of a Work on CD-ROM, Diskette, or Magnetic Tape

"Surrealism." <u>Oxford English Dictionary</u>. 2nd ed. CD-

  ROM. New York: Oxford UP, 1992.

Eseilonis, Karyn. "Georgio de Chirico's <u>Mysterious</u>

    <u>Bathers</u>." <u>A Passion for Art: Renoir, Cezanne,</u>

    <u>Matisse and Dr. Barnes</u>. CD-ROM. Corbis

    Productions. 1995.

Barclay, Donald. <u>Teaching Electronic Information</u>

    <u>Literacy</u>. Diskette. New York: Neal-Schuman, 1995.

Cite, in quotation marks, the portion of the "book" you have used, as you would with a print dictionary or encyclopedia. Give the publication medium before the facts of publication. If you cannot locate all information, give what you can find. You may need to ask a librarian to look on the CD-ROM itself, or the box it came in, to locate the work's producer or date, for example. In the second example, each brief essay on one of the paintings in the Barnes collection concludes with the author's initials. The authors' full names are given at the end of the work, similar to movie credits at the end of a film.

Abstracts of Books or Articles in CD-ROM Indexes

Many of the CD-ROM databases provide abstracts, or even rather long digests, of the works indexed in the database. In most cases, the abstract is not written by the author but by employees of the company creating the database. *Never attribute these abstracts to the author. Never quote directly from these abstracts. Always try to find and study the compete article.* If you cannot locate the article and must paraphrase some facts from the abstract, *always indicate that you have used the abstract, not the original article.* Cite as follows.

Cowen, Ron. "The Day the Dinosaurs Died." <u>Astronomy</u>

    Apr. 1996: 34-42. Abstract. <u>InfoTrac:Expanded</u>

    <u>Academic Index</u>. CD-ROM. Information Access. Dec.

    1997.

Citing Online Sources

MLA's updated guidelines for citing online sources show, in some cases, many pieces of information that may be included to identify a specific source. Actually, few, if any require more than four of the following items, and most of these you are already familiar with. As always, begin with the author (or editor or translator, as appropriate), the title of a short work (within quotation marks), the title of a book (or journal, as appropriate), and the publication information for a work that has a print version. Then provide the title of the project, database, periodical, or site (e.g., Home page); the editor (if relevant);

any identifying number (if relevant); the date of electronic publication, latest update, or posting; the number of pages, paragraphs, or sections; the name of any institution sponsoring the site; the date you accessed the information; and the electronic address (URL) in angle brackets.

If you cannot find all needed information, cite what you do have. The easiest way to be sure to have the electronic address is to download each source. This also provides you with a copy for verification should your instructor want to see the source. (Remember: material disappears off the Internet.) The following examples illustrate some common sources and patterns of documentation.

A Source from a Database of Previously Published Articles

"Breaking the Glass Ceiling." Editorial. The Economist

10 Aug. 1996: 13. General Business File ASAP. Jan.

1998. 12 Jan. 1998 <http://sbweb2.med.iacnet.com/

infotrac/session/460/259/2012624/

131xrn_39&bkm_13>.

If a URL must be divided, break it only after a slash. Do *not* add a hyphen at the break.

Moffat, Anne Simon. "Resurgent Forests Can Be

Greenhouse Gas Sponges." Science 18 July 1997:

315-16. SIRS Researcher on the Web. 1997.

24 Jan 1998 <http://library2.cc.va.us>.

Although the SIRS database is sold nationally, it is usually installed locally or regionally. The result is an address (URL) that is specific to a particular library or consortium of libraries. Your instructor can check your work, but you cannot locate SIRS with the above address.

Article from a Reference Database

"McGraw-Hill Five Year Financial Summary." Dow Jones

News Service. 1998. 3 pars. 10 Jan. 1998

<telnet://telnet.exlibris.uls.vcu.edu>.

"Prohibition." Britannica Online. Vers. 98.1.1. Jan.

1998. Encyclopaedia Britannica. 24 Jan. 1998

<http://www.eb.com:180>.

Poem from a Scholarly Project

Keats, John. "Ode to a Nightingale." <u>Poetical Works</u>.

    1884. <u>Project Bartleby</u>. Columbia U. 15 Jan. 1998

    <http://www.columbia.edu/acis/bartleby/

    keats53.html>.

Book or Pamphlet for a Scholarly Project

Butler, Josephine E. <u>The Education and Employment of</u>

    <u>Women</u>. Liverpool, 1868. <u>Victorian Women Writers</u>

    <u>Project</u>. Ed. Perry Willett. Indiana U. Sept.

    1997. 30 Apr. 1998 <http://www.indiana.edu/

    ~letrs/vwwp/butler/educ.html>.

Provide author and title of work followed by original publication informa-tion. List the title of the project or database, underlined, followed by an editor if one is identified, followed by the sponsoring institution and the latest up-dating information. Conclude with the access date and URL.

Online News Source

Associated Press. "Three African Nations Launch Bid to

    Resume Trade in Elephant Ivory." <u>CNN Interactive</u>.

    9 June 1997. 10 June 1997 <http://www.cnn.com>.

Article in an Online Magazine

Saletan, William. "Roe vs. Wade." <u>Slate</u> 23 Jan. 1998.

    6 pars. 24 Jan. 1998 http://www.slate.com/

    framegame/98-01-23/ framegame.asp>.

Information from a Government or Professional Site

U.S. Department of Health and Human Services. "The HHS
    Poverty Guidelines." 21 Jan. 1998. 23 Jan 1998
    <http://aspe.os.dhhs.gov/poverty/97/
    poverty.htm>.

Lewis, R. W. B. "The Women in the Life of Henry
    James." Lecture delivered at the Mercantile
    Library of New York. 14 April 1993. 15 June 1997
    <http://www.bookpage.com/the merc/
    womeninthelife.html>.

E-Mail

Monaco, Pamela. "Summary of Conference." E-mail. 14
    June 1997.

Other Sources

The materials in this section, although often important to research projects,
do not always lend themselves to documentation by the forms illustrated
above. Follow the basic order of author, title, facts of publication as much as
possible and add whatever information is needed to make the citation clear
and useful to a reader.

A Bulletin

Krasnowiecki, Jan, and others. <u>Legal Aspects of
    Planned Unit Residential Development,</u> with
    <u>Suggested Legislation</u>. Technical Bulletin No. 52.
    Washington: Urban Land Institute, 1965.

Cartoons and Advertisements

Schulz, Charles M. "Peanuts." Cartoon. <u>Washington Post</u>
    10 Dec. 1985: D8.

    Give the cartoon title, if there is one; add the descriptive label "Cartoon";
then give the facts of publication. The pattern is similar for advertisements:

Halleyscope. "Halleyscopes Are for Night Owls."

    Advertisement. <u>Natural History</u> Dec. 1985:15.

Computer Software

Eysenck, H. J. <u>Know Your Own I.Q.</u> Computer software.

    Bantam Software, 1985. Commodore 64, disk.

    Give author, title, descriptive label, distributor, and year of issue. The computer the software is designed for and the form can also be given.

Dissertation—Unpublished

Deepe, Marilyn J. "The Impact of Racial Diversity and

    Involvement on College Students' Social Concern

    Values." Diss. Claremont Grad. Sch., 1989.

Dissertation—Abtract from *Dissertation Abstracts*

Deepe, Marilyn J. "The Impact of Racial Diversity and

    Involvement on College Students' Social Concern

    Values." Diss. Claremont Grad. Sch., 1989. <u>DIA</u> 50

    (1990): 2397A.

    Use this citation form when you cite *only* the abstract, not the dissertation itself. Include the appropriate letter following the page number to designate the volume from which the source comes (A—Humanities and Social Sciences, B—Sciences and Engineering, C—Worldwide dissertations).

    For the online version, use this form of citation:

Sieger, Thomas Martin. "Global Citizenship: A Model

    for Student Inquiry and Decision-Making." 1996.

    <u>Dissertation Abstracts Online</u>. Feb./Mar. 1998.

    30 Apr. 1998 <http://medusa.prod.oclc.org:3054/

    FETCH:next=html/fsrecord.htm:recno=6:resultset=3:

    format=M:numrecs=1:%3Asessionid=2958713:5:/

    fsrec5.txt>.

Government Documents

U.S. President. <u>Public Papers of the Presidents of the</u>
<u>United States</u>. Washington: Office of the Federal
Register, 1961.

United States. Senate. Committee on Energy and Natural
Resources. Subcommittee on Energy Research and
Development. <u>Advanced Reactor Development</u>
<u>Program: Hearing, May 24, 1988</u>. Washington: GPO,
1988.

---. Environmental Protection Agency. <u>The Challenge of</u>
<u>the Environment: A Primer on EPA's Statutory</u>
<u>Authority</u>. Washington: GPO, 1972.

Observe the pattern illustrated here. If the author of the document is not
given, cite the name of the government first followed by the name of the department or agency. If you cite more than one document published by the U.S.
government, do not repeat the name but use the standard three hyphens followed by a period instead. If you cite a second document prepared by the Environmental Protection Agency, use the following pattern:

United States. Senate. . .

---. Environmental Protection Agency. . .

---. ---. [second source from EPA]

If the author is known, follow this pattern:

Geller, William. <u>Deadly Force</u>. U.S. Dept. of Justice
National Institute of Justice Crime File Study
Guide. Washington: U.S. Dept. of Justice, n.d.

If the document contains no date, use the abbreviation "n.d."

Hays, W. W., ed. <u>Facing Geologic and Hydrologic</u>
<u>Hazards</u>. Geological Survey Professional Paper
1240-B. Washington: GPO, 1981.

Abbreviate the U.S. Government Printing Office thus: GPO.

An Interview

Plum, Kenneth. Personal Interview. 5 Mar. 1995.

Alternative descriptive labels include "Interview" and "Telephone interview."

A Lecture

Bateson, Mary Catherine. "Crazy Mixed-Up Families."

  Lecture delivered at Northern Virginia Community

  College. 26 Apr. 1997.

Legal Documents

U.S. Const. Art. 1, sec. 3.

The Constitution is referred to by article and section. Abbreviations are used; do not underline.

Turner v. Arkansas. 407 U.S. 336. 1972.

In citing a court case, give the name of the case (the plaintiff and defendant); the volume, name, and page of the report cited; and the date. The name of the court case is underlined in the text but not in the Works Cited.

Federal Highway Act, as amended. 23 U.S. Code. Sec.

  109. 1970.

Labor Management Relations Act (Taft-Harley Act).

  Statutes at Large. 61. 1947. 34 U.S. Code. 1952.

Citing laws is complicated, and lawyers use many abbreviations that may not be clear to nonexperts. Bills that become law are published annually in *Statutes at Large* and later in the *U.S. Code.* Provide the title of the bill and the source, volume, and year. References to both *Statutes at Large* and the *U.S. Code* can be given as a convenience to readers.

An Unpublished Letter

McCulley, Cecil M. Letter to the author. 5 June 1968.

Treat a published letter as a work in a collection.

Maps and Charts

<u>Hampshire and Dorset</u>. Map. Kent, Eng.: Geographers'

A-Z Map, n.d.

The format is similar to that for an anonymous book, but add the appropriate descriptive label.

Mimeographed or Photocopied Material

Burns, Gerald. "How to Say Some Interesting Things

about Poems." Dittoed essay. 1972.

Give credit to instructors for any class handout that you use.

Plays or Concerts

<u>Mourning Becomes Electra</u>. By Eugene O'Neill.

Shakespeare Theater. Washington DC. 16 May 1997.

Include title, author, theater, city, and date of performance. Principal actors, singers, musicians, and/or the director can be added as appropriate.

Recordings

Stein, Joseph. <u>Fiddler on the Roof</u>. Jerry Bock,

composer. Original-Cast Recording with Zero

Mostel. RCA, LSO-1093, 1964.

The conductor and/or performers help identify a specific recording. Also include manufacturer, catalog number, and date of issue.

A Report

<u>Environment and Development: Breaking the Ideological

Deadlock</u>. Report of the Twenty-first United

Nations Issues Conference, 23-25 Feb. 1990.

Muscatine, Iowa: Stanley Foundation, n.d.

Television or Radio Program

"Breakthrough: Television's Journal of Science and
Medicine." PBS series hosted by Ron Hendren. 10
June 1997.

A Videocassette

The Killing Screens: Media and the Culture of
Violence. Sut Jhally, exec. prod. and dir.
Videocassette. Northampton, MA: Media Education
Foundation, 1994.

4

UNDERSTANDING
SOURCES AND
TAKING NOTES

Now that you have selected and focused a topic and have gathered sources on that topic in a systematic way, preparing an accurate working bibliography, you are ready to dig in to your sources: to read, to learn about your subject, and to take notes on the material you need to develop an interesting paper that fulfills its purpose.

YOUR RELATIONSHIP TO SOURCES

At this stage of your project, you will become well aware of the recursive nature of research. To select a topic, you may have done some reading, *exploring* reference sources for topic ideas. To prepare a working bibliography, you may have done additional reading, *skimming* articles and books to identify useful sources. Now you need to read again, *studying* in depth this time to learn about your topic, while continually *rethinking* your purpose and approach. Of all the stages in the research process, this fourth stage is the longest, most complex, and probably most important one in determining the quality of your project. The following chart suggests both the complexity of Stage 4 and the researcher's relationship to sources throughout the first four stages of research.

Stages in Research	*Using Sources*
1. Select and limit topic.	**Explore** reference sources to find topic ideas.
2. Focus and plan.	**Explore** reference sources to focus topic.
3. Gather sources, preparing a working bibliography.	**Use** reference works to find potential sources. **Skim** sources to find additional sources.
4. Begin study of sources: Read primary sources first. Read general works before specific ones for background.	**Flip and skim** to judge reliability and usefulness; take summary notes.
Expand research proposal into preliminary outline.	Begin preliminary **reading** of sources.
Study sources in depth.	**Take detailed notes.**

The chart reveals that using sources is an *interactive process*, not a mechanical copying activity. Observe that the guidelines for actually taking notes are placed near the end of this chapter.

Reasons for Using Sources

Your work with sources will be more profitable if you keep in mind why you need sources and what different sources have to offer the researcher. The way you work with sources will vary somewhat depending on your writing purpose, the knowledge you bring to the project, and the expectations for the research assignment. Let's consider four research projects:

1. A current problem and possible solutions: The role of zoos in supporting wildlife preservation.
2. The effects of a law on a particular period: The effects of Prohibition on the 1920s.
3. A literary analysis: Are Catherine Barkley and Brett Ashley Hemingway heroes?
4. An examination of an unresolved debate: Were dinosaurs warm-blooded?

1. If you have already decided that zoos offer an important solution to the problem of wildlife preservation, you may approach your sources primarily to obtain evidence to support your views. You need facts and expert opinion to demonstrate that many species are endangered and that the work of zoos provides at least a partial solution. Should you scan sources quickly, looking just for the evidence to support your position? That approach is probably too hasty. Remember that good arguments are built on a knowledge of counterarguments. You are wise to study sources offering a variety of attitudes on the issue so that you can develop a sound challenge to opposing views. Remember that most problems—and their solutions—are complex. For example, some people believe that keeping wild animals in cages is always cruel and therefore wrong.

2. Remember that the Prohibition topic, as presented in Chapters 1 and 2, was selected by a student because of his interest in the 1920s, not because he already possessed knowledge and a position to develop. This student will be turning to sources to learn about a relatively new subject for him. He will need to read widely, beginning with sources presenting an overview before moving on to more specialized works. As he reads, he will be looking not just for information but for ways to focus his topic, for discussions that will develop or challenge the idea of differing effects on different classes and parts of the country.

3. The student selecting the Hemingway study has been introduced to the concept of the Hemingway hero in class and decides to explore two of Hemingway's novels, *The Sun Also Rises* (read for class) and *A Farewell to Arms*, to see if the lead female characters also fit the hero concept. What sources will she need? First, she will need to read *A Farewell to Arms* and to reexamine key passages in *The Sun Also Rises* that feature Brett Ashley.

Second, the student will need to read the chief studies that explain and debate the concept of the Hemingway hero. Third, she may want to read some analyses of the two novels, especially those that focus on Brett and Catherine. The first two steps are essential to develop the topic. The third type of source may be studied briefly or in depth, depending on the expectations of the assignment. For a short paper in a sophomore or junior course, few sources in the third category will be expected. The emphasis should be on the student's application of the concept to her understanding of the characters. In advanced courses, especially in a seminar course requiring a lengthy study, the student will be expected to know the major studies of the novels.

4. This assignment calls for a review of the literature, of the critical debate, on an unresolved issue. The student will need to read widely on the issue of dinosaur warm-bloodedness, study the theories of the key scientists, and then develop a clear and organized account of the debate. In response to this assignment, students are expected to show an understanding of the issue but not to argue for one theory, even though students often learn so much about their topic that they frequently become strong supporters of a particular position. The report of such a study usually takes the form of either an annotated bibliography (a summary of each source studied) or an essay that explains the various theories. (Both an annotated bibliography and a review-of-the-literature essay are illustrated in this chapter; see pages 140–152.)

These four research assignments differ in purpose and thus in the researcher's use of sources. Still, each *re-search* task shares a special relationship to what has already been written on a topic. Remember that doing research is a way of participating in the academic community, in the ongoing examination of the body of knowledge and issues that concern people in a given field. Individual scholars do not operate independently of previous work. They build on existing knowledge, ideas, and strategies or models for examining the material. It is the responsibility of scholars to know what work has already been done, to acknowledge that work, and then to qualify, challenge, or build on that work. Undergraduates are expected to do more than "write something" on a topic. They are expected to learn this process of surveying the information and ideas already presented and to place their contribution in the context of an ongoing discussion and debate among experts. These expectations apply to the argumentative research essay as well as to the review of literature.

> ✓ Students need to understand how their work fits into the ongoing discussion of a topic and to acknowledge indebtedness to those sources that have provided an approach or information or ideas.

Avoiding Plagiarism

!WARNING! *Each one of the following strategies results in a form of plagiarism!*

- Downloading a paper from the Internet

- "Borrowing" a friend's paper from last semester

- Turning in a paper without any documentation

- Turning in a paper with in-text citations but no Works Cited page—or the other way around

- Copying passages from a source without putting the passages within quotation marks

- Documenting only quoted material but not documenting paraphrased material

- Retaining too much of the wording and style of the original in paraphrasing

- Placing in-text citations at the end of long passages without making clear how much of the passage is from the source

Documenting Sources to Avoid Plagiarism

Your relationship to sources is made clear to readers by the formal pattern of documentation you use. The pattern you select depends on your field of study, but the need to document accurately and fully applies to all researchers. Proper documentation shows readers the breadth of your research and distinguishes between the work of others and your contribution to the understanding of a topic.

Improper documentation of sources—plagiarism—is both unethical and illegal. To fail to document sources used is to lose your credibility and reputation. Ideas, new information, and wording belong to their author. To borrow them without acknowledgment is against the law and has led to many celebrated lawsuits. Clearly, paying for a paper from a service and submitting a friend's paper are examples of plagiarism. More often, however, students plagiarize unintentionally because they do not understand the researcher's relationship to sources and the requirements of documentation. Be certain that you know what constitutes appropriate documentation.

MLA documentation requires that precise page references be given for all ideas, opinions, and information taken from sources—except for common knowledge. Author and page references provided in the text are supported by complete bibliographic citations on the Works Cited page. In sum, you are required to document the following:

- Direct quotations from sources
- Paraphrased ideas and opinions from sources
- Summaries of ideas from sources
- Factual information, except common knowledge, from sources

Understand that putting an author's ideas in your own words in a paraphrase or summary does not eliminate the requirement of documentation. To illustrate, consider the following excerpt from Thomas R. Schueler's report *Controlling Urban Runoff* (Washington Metropolitan Water Resources Planning Board, 1987: 3–4) and a student paragraph based on the report.

Source

The aquatic ecosystems in urban headwater streams are particularly susceptible to the impacts of urbanization. . . . Dietemann (1975), Ragan and Dietemann (1976), Klein (1979), and WMCOG (1982) have all tracked trends in fish diversity and abundance over time in local urbanizing streams. Each of the studies has shown that fish communities become less diverse and are composed of more tolerant species after the surrounding watershed is developed. Sensitive fish species either disappear or occur very rarely. In most cases, the total number of fish in urbanizing streams may also decline.

Similar trends have been noted among aquatic insects which are the major food resource for fish. . . . Higher postdevelopment sediment and trace metals can interfere in their efforts to gather food. Changes in water temperature, oxygen levels, and substrate composition can further reduce the species diversity and abundance of the aquatic insect community.

Student Paragraph

Studies have shown that fish communities become less diverse as the amount of runoff increases. Sensitive fish species either disappear or occur very rarely and, in most cases, the total number of fish declines. Aquatic insects, a major source of food for fish, also decline because sediment and trace metals interfere with their food-gathering efforts. Increased water temperature and lower oxygen levels can further reduce the species diversity and abundance of the aquatic insect community.

The student's opening words establish a reader's expectation that the student has taken information from a source, as indeed the student has. But where is the documentation? The student's paraphrase is a good example of plagiarism: an unacknowledged paraphrase of borrowed information that even collapses into copying the source's exact wording in two places. For MLA style, the author's name and the precise page numbers are needed (as illustrated in Chapter 5) for proper documentation. Additionally, most of the first sentence and the final phrase must be put into the student's own words or be placed within quotation marks. The following revised paragraph shows an appropriate acknowledgment of the source used.

Revised Student Paragraph

In Controlling Urban Runoff, Thomas Schueler explains that studies have shown "that fish communities become less diverse as the amount of runoff increases" (3). Sensitive fish species either disappear or occur very rarely and, in most cases, the total number of fish declines. Aquatic insects, a major source of food for

```
fish, also decline because sediment and trace metals
interfere with their food-gathering efforts. Increased
water temperature and lower oxygen levels, Schueler
concludes, "can further reduce the species diversity
and abundance of the aquatic insect community" (4).
```

Students are often uncertain about what is considered common knowledge and wonder if most of their sentences will need documentation. In general, common knowledge includes:

* Undisputed dates
* Well-known facts
* Generally known facts, terms, and concepts in a field of study

So, even if you had to check a reference source for the exact dates of the American Revolution or learn from several biographies that Benjamin Franklin experimented with electricity, you would not document the sources used because such information is readily available in many reference works and is known by many readers.

You also would not cite sources for the concept of character conflict in literature or the superego in psychology. On the other hand, you must acknowledge a historian who analyzes the causes for England's loss to the Colonists, a scientist who evaluates Franklin's contribution to the study of electricity, or a critic who explains Hemingway's concept of a hero. *Opinions* about well-known facts must be documented. *Discussions* of debatable dates, terms, or concepts must be documented. The more you learn about a field of study the more comfortable you will become deciding when to document. If, after studying your sources to judge what most writers accept as common knowledge, using common sense, and checking with your instructor, you are still uncertain, defend your integrity by documenting the information. Understanding your appropriate relationship to sources will guide your note taking. In Chapter 5, additional guidelines will help you turn notes into passages in your paper that are free from unintentional plagiarizing.

UNDERSTANDING THE ROLES OF PRIMARY AND SECONDARY SOURCES

Knowing when primary sources are needed in addition to secondary sources is part of understanding your relationship to sources. To be successful you need to ask yourself what information your study requires and what sources should be reviewed. What is the difference between primary and secondary sources? When do you need to use both?

Primary sources have the most immediate or direct relationship to the subject; they are firsthand works. *Secondary sources* are studies and interpretations of primary sources; they are secondhand. The following partial list, by subject area, will help you distinguish between the two.

Subject Area	Primary Sources	Secondary Sources
History and government	State papers Legislation Letters, diaries	Histories Biographies
Literary studies	Novels, plays, short stories, poems, letters, early drafts	Analyses and interpretations Biographies
Social sciences	Findings from questionnaires, interviews, case studies, tests, experiments	Evaluations in books and articles of data found in primary sources
Sciences	Experiments, discoveries, testing methods, theoretical models	Discussions in books and articles of test results, discoveries, and experiments
Business	Market research, computer data, technical reports, designs	Articles and books on business and management

Rarely are research projects based solely on primary sources. Reports of experiments or discoveries in the sciences and social sciences are usually accompanied by both analyses and interpretation of the results and reference to previous relevant research. Some kinds of research topics, such as a study of zoos and wildlife preservation, can be developed from secondary sources only, although a student selecting this topic may be expected to be familiar with zoos and perhaps to have interviewed a zoologist. A review of the theories of dinosaur warm-bloodedness would be one kind of project based only on secondary sources.

Many research projects call for a combination of primary and secondary sources. This combination is valuable because primary sources provide a check against inaccuracies that may exist in secondary sources. Also, secondary sources present the opinions of their authors. When you study relevant primary sources, you can develop your own ideas and analyses. You would never attempt, for example, a study of Hemingway's Catherine Barkley based only on critical studies of his novels. You must first read *A Farewell to Arms* and think about the character for yourself. Similarly, you would not write a paper on Marc Chagall as a surrealist painter just from reading without ever looking at his paintings. If you want to study the effect of television advertising on children, you should spend a number of mornings in front of the television watching and taking notes during children's programs. There are important differences between the entire text of a president's speech, a news article about the speech (even "straight" news has a particular point of view), and an editorial reacting to the speech. If the speech is a vital part of your project, you must know it thoroughly. Every other source you may choose to read is of secondary importance.

EVALUATING SOURCES

When you use facts and opinions from sources, you are saying to readers that the facts are accurate and the ideas are credible. If you do not evaluate your sources before using them, you risk losing your credibility as a writer.

> ✓ Remember: The first 10 sources you locate may not be the best 10 for your research project. Check more than one source to verify information. Judge the credibility of potential sources. The success of your project is on the line!

Assessing the reliability as well as the usefulness of potential sources has always been an essential part of the research process. Today, with access to so much material on the Internet, the need to evaluate sources is even more critical. Here are some strategies for judging reliability of sources.

Use the Best Authors and Works

To produce the best understanding of your topic you need to find accurate, authoritative works. You want to select writers with credentials and works produced by credible publishers. This means, for example, that you will use the *New York Times*, not the *National Enquirer*, as a newspaper source. Other major city newspapers also have excellent reputations, but the tabloids at grocery-store checkout counters are not credible sources. Beyond these obvious distinctions, how do you decide which sources are credible?

Locate an Author's Credentials

A writer's degrees, current position, and other publications are often provided with an article or on a book jacket. If no brief biography is provided, try to find an article on the writer in a biographical dictionary such as *Contemporary*

Authors or *American Men and Women of Science.* If these strategies fail, ask your instructor if he or she has heard of the author. With regard to the World Wide Web, remember that anyone can create a Web Page. There are no editors making selections and no publishers with a reputation to consider. *Never* use material from a Web source that does not identify the author or the organization responsible for the material.

Find Reviews of the Work

Examine the *Book Review Digest* (in paper and online) for a book's publication year to learn how reviewers evaluated the book. Several thousand books are reviewed in each yearly print volume. As Figure 40 illustrates, the *Book Review Digest* includes a summary and one or more reviews of each book. *The Booklist,* a source primarily for librarians that researchers can also use, reviews new books in a monthly magazine format.

Use the Appropriate *Citation Index* to Locate the Books and Articles Most Frequently Cited in Other Works

The various parts of the *Citation Indexes* (for the arts and humanities, the social sciences, and the sciences) and the methods for using them are explained in Chapter 2. Remember that the *Citation Index* lists sources that are cited by other writers. We can conclude that the works frequently cited by others writing on the subject are key works on that subject. Another part of each *Citation Index,* the *Permuterm Subject Index,* lists authors who have written on a given subject. Writers who are listed several times, who have published frequently on a subject, are probably experts whose works should be included in your study.

Pay Attention to Authors Whose Works Are Included in Your Text's References and Who Appear Frequently in the Bibliographies Found in the Sources You Have Already Found

The concept here is the same as with *Citation Index.* Writers who have written several works on your topic and have been acknowledged by other writers are among the experts you need to study. Consider, for example, the partial list of references, shown in Figure 41, from an article on children and television. Clearly, Rubinstein is an important researcher on this topic; so are Comstock and Gerbner.

Select Properly Documented Sources

Consider a work's use of documentation when judging its credibility. Scholarly works cite sources. Well-researched and reliable pieces intended for a less specialized audience will also make clear the source of any statistics used or the credentials of any authority who is quoted. One good rule: Never use undocumented statistical information presented in a secondary source. Keep this rule in mind when surfing the Web. In general, stick to information

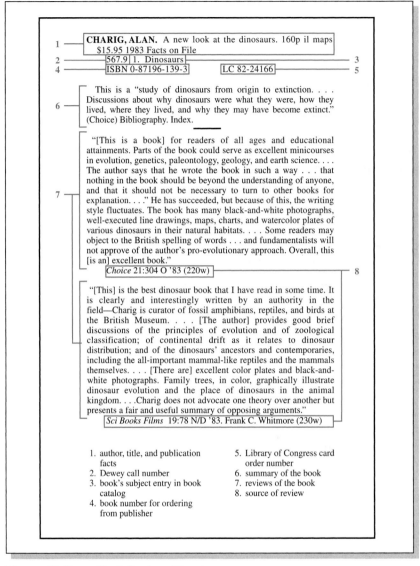

Figure 40 From *Book Review Digest.*

from an "edu" (educational institution) site or from an organization with a reliable reputation that you can verify.

Select Recent Secondary Sources

Some studies published years ago remain classic works in their field, but many older works become outdated because new information is available to

REFERENCES

McCombs, and D. Roberts. 1978. *Television and Human Behavior.* Columbia University Press.

Comstock, G., and M. Fisher. 1975. *Television and Human Behavior: A Guide to the Pertinent Scientific Literature.* Santa Monica, CA: Rand Corporation.

Comstock, G., and G. Lindsey. 1975. *Television and Human Behavior: The Research Horizon, Future and Present.* Santa Monica, CA: Rand Corporation.

Consumers Union. 1976. *The Six Billion Dollar Sell.* Mount Vernon, NY.

Cook, T. D., H. Appleton, R. F. Conner, A. Shaffer, G. Tomkin, and S. J. Weber. 1975. *Sesame Street Revisited.* New York: Russell Sage Foundation.

Dienstbier, R. A. 1977. Sex and violence: Can research have it both ways? *J. Communication* 27:176-88.

Fernandez-Collado, C., and B. S. Greenberg. 1977. *Substance Use and Sexual Intimacy on Commercial Television.* Report #5, Mich. State Univ.

Feshbach, S. 1961. The stimulating versus cathartic effects of a vicarious aggressive activity. *J. Abnormal and Soc. Psych.* 63:381-85.

Ford Foundation. 1976. *Television and Children: Priorities for Research.* New York.

Franzblau, S., J. N. Sprafkin, and E. A. Rubinstein. 1977. Sex on TV: A content analysis. *J. Communication* 27:164-70.

Frueh, T., and P. E. McGhee. 1975. Traditional sex-role development and amount of time spent watching television. *Devel. Psych.* 11:109.

Gerbner, G. 1972. Violence in television drama: Trends and symbolic functions. In *Television and Social Behavior,* vol. 1. *Media Content and Control,* ed. G. A. Comstock and E. A. Rubinstein. U. S. Government Printing Office.

Gerbner, G., L. Gross, M. Jackson-Beeck, A. Jeffries-Fox, and N. Signorielli. 1978. *Violence Profile No. 9.* Univ. of Pennsylvania Press.

Kochnower, J. M., J. F. Fracchia, E. A. Rubinstein, and J. N. Sprafkin. 1978. *Television Viewing Behaviors of Emotionally Disturbed Children: An Interview Study.* New York: Brookdale International Institute.

Lefkowitz, M. M., L. D. Eron, L. O. Walder, and L. R. Huesmann. 1972. Television violence and child agression: A follow-up study. In *Television and Social Behavior,* vol. 3. *Television and Adolescent Aggressiveness,* ed. G. A. Comstock and E. A. Rubinstein. U. S. Gov. Printing Office.

Lesser, G. S. 1974. *Children and Television: Lessons from "Sesame Street."* Random House.

Liebert, D. E., R. M. Liebert, J. N. Sprafkin, and E. A. Rubinstein. 1977. Effects of television commercial disclaimers on the product expectations of children. *J. Communication* 27:118-24.

Lyle, J., and H. Hoffman. 1972. Children's use of television and other media. In *Television and Social Behavior,* vol. 5. *Television in Day-to-Day Life: Patterns of Use,* ed. E. A. Rubinstein, G. A. Comstock, and J. P. Murray. U. S. Government Printing Office.

Ratner, E. M., et al. 1978. FTC *Staff Report on Television Advertising to Children.* Washington, DC: Federal Trade Commission.

Robertson, T. S., and J. R. Rossiter. 1974. Children and commercial persuasion: An attribution theory analysis. *J. Consumer Research* 1:13-20.

Rubinstein, E. A. 1975. Social science and media policy. *J. Communication* 25:194-200.

———. 1976. Warning: The Surgeon General's research program may be dangerous to preconceived notions. *J. Soc. Issues* 32:18-34.

Rubinstein, E. A., J. F. Fracchia, J. M. Kochnower, and J. N. Sprafkin. 1977. *Television Viewing Behaviors of Mental Patients: A survey of Psychiatric Centers in New York State.* New York: Brookdale International Institute.

Rubinstein, E. A., R. M. Liebert, J. M. Neale, and R. W. Poulos. 1974. *Assessing Television's Influence on Children's Prosocial Behavior.* New York: Brookdale International Institute.

Figure 41 Partial List of References from "Television and the Young Viewer."

today's scholars. In scientific and technical fields, the "information revolution" has outdated works of only five or ten years ago. For example, studies based on statistics from the 1980 Census are no longer current, and those based on the 1990 Census may not be reliable either. Studies of Saturn that fail to consider new knowledge from Voyager II are no longer up-to-date. The classic studies in any field (Freud's *Interpretation of Dreams;* Darwin's *On the Origin of Species*) have acquired the status of "primary" sources; read them to learn about your field of study. But pass over old, now undistinguished secondary sources in favor of current studies. Studies of the dinosaurs, for instance, that describe them all as slow and dim-witted are themselves fossils.

Use Credible Sources at the Appropriate Level

Consider a writer's intended audience and purpose in writing as part of your evaluation and selection of sources. For articles, think about the readers of the journal or magazine that published the article. You want to avoid articles that are too specialized for you at this point, but you also need to pass up articles that are too general or elementary for college study. If you are examining a current issue in the news, select articles from the *New York Times* or *Wall Street Journal* rather than a small-town paper. Although freshmen may want to pass on articles in the *Journal of Cell Biology* or *Psychological Bulletin,* they should also pass on typical articles in the newsmagazines as too general and elementary. In between these extremes are many sources you can use: *Natural History Magazine, Psychology Today, Scientific American, Journal of Communication, Journalism Quarterly,* and *Harvard Business Review* are just a few possibilities of periodicals containing well-researched articles that you do not have to be an expert to understand. For books, in addition to reading reviews, study the language as a guide to the author's intended audience. If skimming a book reveals short sentences and a simple vocabulary, the book may be too elementary for your research project.

A writer's purpose needs consideration, too. Often articles in popular magazines, although easier to read, may lack the balanced, objective approach of a scholarly work. (Remember that articles in scholarly periodicals have been peer-reviewed. That is, a group of specialists have read and approved the manuscript for publication.) The goal of a popular article may be to persuade rather than to analyze and inform. Be especially cautious with works designed to reinforce biases already shared by the intended audience—the publications of the National Rifle Association or Planned Parenthood are examples. When on the Internet, ask yourself why this person decided to have a Web Page or contribute to a newsgroup. Stick to works that have some authority—the authority of an author or publisher with credentials and respect. (Remember that you can still disagree with the ideas of respected writers, but you are likely to get credible, documented information from them.)

Examine Sources for Relevance

Judging the usefulness of sources can also be a problem for beginning researchers. But if you can learn to make a good decision about usefulness without having to read an entire work, you will become a more efficient researcher—and save money copying many pages of works that turn out to be unhelpful. Here are some guidelines for judging a work's potential value to your project.

Guidelines for Judging the Usefulness of Articles

1. Consider the intended audience and purpose of the periodical. How much information can you expect the article to have? That is, how detailed and complex will the treatment be for that intended audience and purpose?

2. When articles are accompanied by an abstract, read that first to get an overview of the article.

3. Flip through the article to note headings and subheadings and graphics to see what is covered.

4. Read the first two or three paragraphs quickly to judge coverage and the author's level of writing.

Guidelines for Judging the Usefulness of Books

1. Think about both the title and subtitle. Sometimes titles that might be misleading are clarified by their subtitles. Cynthia Russett's title *Darwin in America* becomes clear when we read the subtitle: *The Intellectual Response 1865–1912*.

2. Read the *Preface* or *Introduction*. Here the author establishes the book's focus and scope, and perhaps some key ideas that underlie his or her approach to the subject.

3. Skim the *Table of Contents* to get a better idea of specific topics covered in the book. You may find that only one chapter is useful to you, but that one turns out to be extremely valuable for your research.

4. Look over any *Appendices*, where you may find charts and graphs presenting statistical information of use to you.

5. If there are *reference notes* or a *bibliography*, these will guide you to other sources on your topic. They also mark the scholarly nature of the book.

6. Study the *Index* for the quickest view of the most specific topics covered in the book.

The student studying Prohibition applied these guidelines to judge a book he found while browsing through the American history section of the library stacks. The book, published by a university press, was written by a college professor. The title—*Into the Twenties: The United States from Armistice to*

Normalcy—suggests that the book will examine the years during which the 18th Amendment was passed by Congress and ratified by the states, so it could well have a section on Prohibition. Flipping through the book, the student saw that the text was heavily documented with footnotes and concluded with a 10-page bibliographic essay. The book certainly appeared to have credibility, and if it treated the student's topic at all, it should yield additional sources on the topic. Neither the Preface nor the Table of Contents mentioned Prohibition specifically, but one chapter, "American Society, 1920," showed promise, so the student examined the Index and found the following entry:

> Prohibition, 165, 166; and fundamentalism, 166; and rural-urban conflict, 166–67; and progressivism, 166–67

Although the book gives only three pages to the student's subject, they turned out to be three important pages containing references to a dozen sources and a debate on the extent to which Prohibition represented an "urban-rural, Catholic-Protestant, and immigrant-nativist" dichotomy. In only a few minutes, the student was able to evaluate the source and find the portion of it that was useful to his research.

PREPARING A PRELIMINARY OUTLINE

Reflecting on the kinds of sources your topic needs and skimming sources as you evaluate their potential should help you prepare a preliminary outline to guide reading and note taking. A preliminary outline does not need to be in finished form because it is designed only for you. Still, make it as detailed as possible so that it can guide your reading. Most important: Make it reflect your research purpose.

Review Your Research Purpose

You have used your research purpose as a guide to selecting sources. Now use it to develop your preliminary outline. Let's consider our sample topics once again.

The Role of Zoos in Supporting Wildlife Preservation

The student exploring this issue began by stating a position and then listing elements to be covered.

> Thesis: Although some environmentalists object to zoos because they "cage wild animals," zoos actually help preserve wildlife.

> Items to cover: objections to zoos expressed by some, care animals actually get in modern zoos, breeding activities with endangered species

This student has done some basic thinking about how to develop the thesis but still needs to shape an approach to the topic.

The Effects of Prohibition on the 1920s

From his preliminary reading, the student took the idea of examining the effects on urban and rural areas and on different classes of society. After gathering sources and doing some preliminary reading, the student decided to focus his study on this research question: Why was Prohibition more acceptable to rural areas than to the urban Northeast? He then developed this preliminary guide:

social/cultural demographics
  country
  city
economics of Prohibition
  country
  city
religious values
  country
  city
conclusion: Look past the 1920s to long-range effects of Prohibition.

Catherine Barkley and Brett Ashley as Hemingway Heroes

After thinking about the kinds of sources she would need, reading *A Farewell to Arms*, and developing a bibliography on the Hemingway hero concept, the student decided to limit her topic to better fit the guidelines of a six-page paper. She decided to concentrate on Catherine in *A Farewell to Arms*. She prepared the following research question and preliminary outline:

Does Catherine Barkley show the major traits of Hemingway's male heroes?

Introduction: Establish critical concept of Hemingway hero.

Body: Describe major traits of Hemingway hero.
            Taking one trait at a time, analyze Catherine to see if she has each trait.

Conclusion: Answer the research question.

Dinosaur Warm-bloodedness: A Review of the Debate

The student understands that he is required to produce an organized paper, not a series of summaries of sources loosely "glued" together. When Aaron (whose essay appears on pages 144–52) first started reading, he thought that using chronological order would be the best approach. He would explain the older theories first and then move to more current studies. After further reading, however, Aaron decided that the more useful approach for his particular topic was to organize by key ideas or evidence debated by the experts. Here is his preliminary outline:

Introduction: The debate—How dinosaurs have been viewed and key terms related to the issue of warm-bloodedness.

Body: Body weight
            Bone structure
            The heart's strength
            Leg position
            Respiratory turbinates

Conclusion: Where does the debate stand today?

An annotated bibliography (See the sample on pages 140–43) is organized by the sources studied, but a literature review needs to be organized by ideas. Aaron's outline reflects that understanding of his research purpose.

Review Basic Organizational Strategies

You want to be aware of several basic organizational strategies that researchers frequently use because they correspond to the kinds of questions we ask and approaches we take to studying issues. Knowing these patterns, instructors often give research assignments that will require the use of one of the following strategies.

The "Journal" Report Structure

The expected organization for scholarly journal articles reporting findings in the sciences and social sciences will be appropriate for primary investigations and experiments. The expected pattern is firmly established and should be followed with little variation.

Introduction: states hypothesis or research question

Review of literature: examines previous studies and discussions of the issue

Methods: explains research procedures

Results: presents data obtained from experiment, case studies, interviews, questionnaires, etc.

Discussion: presents an analysis and interpretation of data and the implications of the results

Comparison/Contrast Structure

Research projects often call for a comparison or contrast: of two philosophies, two psychological models, two management strategies, two literary works, two educational theories, and so on. At times you may be expected to give full and equal treatment to both similarities and differences. More often, you will need a thesis that dictates either a comparative study or a contrasting study. If your thesis is "In spite of some obvious similarities, 'A' and 'B' differ in significant ways," then you can begin by noting some similarities, but most of your paper will be organized by differences. If your thesis notes similarities, then the body of your paper will be organized to show similarities. Whether your project is predominantly comparison or contrast, organize by using either the "whole-by-whole" or the "part-by-part" structure, illustrated below.

Whole-by-Whole	*Part-by-Part*
Theory A	Difference 1
Difference 1	Theory A
Difference 2	Theory B
Difference 3	Difference 2
Theory B	Theory A
Difference 1	Theory B
Difference 2	Difference 3
Difference 3	Theory A
	Theory B

Usually the "part-by-part" structure is the better choice because it is a stronger comparison/contrast pattern. It better focuses the reader's attention on similarities or differences, the purpose of your paper. Unless handled carefully, the "whole-by-whole" structure can collapse into two loosely connected summaries.

Test or Apply a Theory, Concept, or Model

A common assignment in many fields is the testing of a theory, concept, or model or the application of a theory, concept, or model to a new situation. In foreign policy analyses, one can test the concept of nation-states acting autonomously. In her psychology paper (see Chapter 7), Mary Adams analyzes or "tests" various theories of the causes of eating disorders. In the study of Catherine as a Hemingway hero, the student is applying a concept about several male Hemingway characters to a female character.

Exactly how such a paper should be developed will depend on the specific topic and the student's field of study, but, in general, follow this pattern:

Introduction: Establish theory, concept, or model.
Review literature on theory, concept, or model.
Introduce test or application to be developed.

Body: Develop test or application of theory, concept, or model.

Conclusion: Draw conclusion about theory, concept, or model, namely, that it is (or is not) sound, that it can (or cannot) be applied to the situation studied.

Problem-Solution Structure

Many argumentative research essays examining public policy issues can be seen as arguments over solutions to problems. There are a number of elements to include in such arguments, depending on the problem you are writing about and your purpose in writing. Some arguments need to concentrate on the nature of the problem, because how a problem is defined has much to do with finding appropriate solutions. (For example, is world hunger an agricultural or political problem?) Other arguments need to convince readers that some situation is a major problem, or convince readers of the causes of the problem. Possibly as many as seven steps may be needed to develop and support a solution or solutions to a problem. When planning, consider each of the following steps and decide which are relevant to your issue. Then discuss each of the relevant steps in the following order.

1. Demonstrate that a situation exists.

   (Cite low test scores in math and science by American students.)

2. Demonstrate that the situation is a problem.

   (Weaker skills in math and science can reduce American scientific and technical competitiveness, and many American citizens—scientifically illiterate—are unable to understand the world they live in.)

3. Explain causes of the problem. If your proposed solution(s) calls for removing the causes, then you must establish the causes.

   (One cause: teenagers' negative attitudes about academic performance.)

4. Present your solution(s).

   (One solution: change students' attitudes; get students to believe that it is cool to learn.)

5. Explain the process for achieving your solution(s).

   (Start a media blitz.)

6. Support the feasibility of your solution(s).

   (TV "ads" can change attitudes over time.)

7. Show that your solution is better than others.

   (If attitudes don't change, then adding courses or extending the school year will not make much difference in students' skills.)

Consider how these steps can be used by the student researching zoos and wildlife preservation to develop a preliminary outline that will be more helpful than what she has to date (see page 125). Since most people understand that animals die, and sometimes entire species become extinct, the student does not need to begin with Step 1. However, the student could usefully take time to remind readers of the seriousness of endangered species, to convince readers that the situation is a serious problem. The student is not interested in exploring the various causes for endangered species and extinction. What she is interested in doing is offering one solution to the problem—greater recognition of and support for the work that zoos do to address the problem. So, she needs to focus primarily on Steps 4 through 7. She can write a better preliminary outline by using the problem/solution structure:

> Thesis: Although some environmentalists object to zoos because they "cage wild animals," zoos actually help preserve wildlife.

Introduction:	Discuss some popular zoo animals who are endangered in their natural habitats—to remind readers that there is a problem needing solutions.
Body:	1. Explain how zoos are one solution to the problem. Discuss care of animals and breeding to keep species from extinction.
	2. Zoos need more support; become a contributor; push for more funding for city zoos.
	3. Give examples of animals bred in captivity to stave off extinction.
	4. Show advantages of support for zoos over other possible solutions; in many cases solutions require international cooperation; zoos are usually local facilities.
Conclusion:	Show how this solution is in the best interests of animals, a concern of environmentalists.

TAKING NOTES

With sources in hand and a preliminary outline to guide your reading and thinking, you are now ready to study sources and take notes. You have two ways to take notes acceptable to most instructors—and a third way that students often use regardless of standard advice. You can take notes using your PC or you can take notes using note cards—or, you can annotate photocopies of sources and work directly from those copies. If you are required to turn in note cards, then the decision of format for note taking has been decided for you. Increasingly now, instructors are letting students with the skills and access to a computer to take keyboarded notes, but they may still ask to see them. If you are required to hand them in, you will have to print out copies of your notes, but you may want to do this anyway (see guidelines below). Instructors requiring notes probably will not accept annotated photocopies of sources. What they want to see is how you have taken material from your sources. If you use note cards, follow these guidelines.

Guidelines for Note Taking: Cards

1. **Use 4 × 6 cards, or half sheets of letter-size paper.** This size gives you more space for writing and also distinguishes clearly between note cards and 3 × 5 bibliography cards.
2. **Write in ink.** Penciled notes will blur with shuffling and rearranging.
3. **Write only one item on each card.** Each card should contain only one idea, piece of information, or group of related facts. The flexibility gained by using cards is lost if you do not adhere to this principle. You want to be able to group cards according to your outline when you are ready to draft the paper.
4. **Write on only one side of each card.** Material on the back may be forgotten when you start drafting your paper. If you must go to the back to finish a long note, write "OVER" at the bottom of the card as a reminder.

Guidelines for Taking Notes: With a Computer

1. **Make one file titled "notes" or make a separate file for each note.** Both strategies work. You need to think about which approach is easier for you to cut and paste and blend notes into a draft of a paper.
2. **Establish clear headings and subheadings for notes so that you can find particular notes easily.**
3. **Some students prefer to print copies of notes and cut them into separate "cards" for shuffling and organizing prior to drafting.** When drafting, do not re-keyboard. Just use your printed notes as a guide to placement in the draft. Use the cut and paste or move strategies of the computer to rearrange notes into the order you want in your draft.

Guidelines for Writing Notes: Cards or Keyboarded

1. **Study first; write notes later.** Avoid rushing into note taking. First, do background reading. Second, skim what appear to be your chief sources. Prepare summary notes or highlight and annotate photocopies of sources. Read to obtain a general knowledge of your topic and to develop a preliminary outline. Learn what the experts consider to be important details and concepts. In this way, you will avoid writing many useless notes, a time-wasting and frustrating activity.

2. Identify the source for each note. *Before writing or typing any note,* place the author's name, a shortened title if necessary to identify the source, and the precise page number from which the note is taken in the upper right-hand corner. *Remember: All borrowed information and ideas must be documented in your paper with precise page numbers, if you are using MLA style—and for all direct quotations if you are using APA style.*

3. Place an identifying word or phrase at the top of each note. Identifying labels will help you sort cards (or find notes) when you are ready to draft. The identifying words or phrases should be selected carefully to correspond to the subsections of your paper according to your preliminary outline.

4. Take down the information itself—accurately and clearly—on a card or in your PC. Record the information in summary or paraphrase form or as a direct quotation, as illustrated below.

5. Distinguish carefully between fact and opinion. A note that records facts does not need labeling, but a note that records opinion should be introduced with a statement such as "Smith believes that," "Smith asserts that," or "Smith concludes that." Alternatively, label the note "opinion."

6. Distinguish clearly between ideas or opinions taken from sources and your own opinions, questions, or reactions to the information you have recorded. Write your reactions so that you do not forget good ideas that come to you as you are reading. Just be certain to avoid confusion either by placing your ideas in separate notes—marked "my notes"—or by drawing (or typing) a line between information from a source and your response.

Figure 42 shows a sample note card written according to these guidelines.

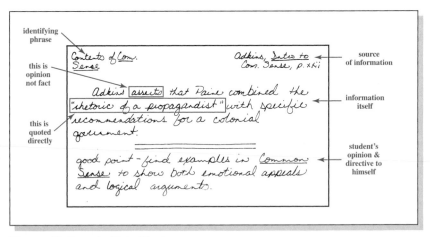

Figure 42 Sample Note Card.

Methods of Note Taking

Writing notes should be mechanical only insofar as you develop the habit of recording all necessary information in a consistent pattern on each card. Notes are actually brief letters to yourself. They need to make sense and help you prepare a paper weeks after they are first written. As you review the following conventions for taking notes, think not only about format but also about when each type of note will best serve your research purpose.

Summary Notes

Summary notes are most useful during the background reading stage. Summary notes will help you decide to which sources to return later for more specific note taking. In addition, when you respond to your reading with written notes, you will remember more of what you have read on your topic.

Summary notes also provide a condensed version, in your own words, of a longer passage of information or ideas. When preparing summary notes, be sure to include the precise page numbers for the passage you have condensed, for you will need to document the information if it is used in your paper. Figure 43 shows a summary note of an article on television news programs. Observe that "shows" is in quotation marks to capture Postman's use of the term as a criticism of network news programs.

Analysis and Judgment of News   Postman, "Television
Shows (Summary Note)   News Narcosis"
                                       pp. 377-79

   Network news programs are "shows." They use music,
have attractive readers, & cover many events briefly
to provide variety—Postman asserts that it is
entertainment. The result is that viewers are not
given the chance to think about the events or respond
to them emotionally. Postman gives a description of a
typical 1/2-hour format.

Figure 43 Summary Keyboard Note.

Paraphrase Notes

A paraphrase is a restatement in your own words of a passage. A paraphrase note differs from a summary note because it is not a condensed version. Paraphrasing can result in about the same number of words as in the original—just different ones. A paraphrase note differs from a direct-quotation note because it uses *your* words. Read and understand the material; then rewrite the passage. *If you change or rearrange a few words only, you will be plagiarizing.*

For example, the student working with Postman's article on news programs wants to take a note on the following passage:

> It is also believed that audiences are captivated by variety and repelled by complexity, which is why, during a typical thirty-minute show, there will be between fifteen and twenty "stories." Discounting time for commercials, promos for stories to come, and news readers' banter, this works out to an average of sixty seconds a story.

Suppose the student were to prepare the following paraphrase note:

```
Because it is believed that audiences like variety and

dislike complexity, a typical thirty-minute show has

between fifteen and twenty "stories." When you

discount time for commercials, promos, and banter,

this works out to about sixty seconds a story.
```

Is this an acceptable paraphrase of the source? No. It relies too heavily on Postman's words and ordering of ideas. Figure 44 presents an acceptable paraphrase of Postman's passage.

Some instructors advise students to take time at the note-taking stage to write fairly polished paraphrases so that these can be inserted into a draft with little revision. Others advise writing rough paraphrases—using fragments, listing points—on the argument that you may have to reword each note anyway, once you see where and how it will be used. Also, rough notes are less likely to pick up the words and style of the original passage; hence, you avoid the risk of plagiarism. Figure 45 provides a good example of a paraphrase note that is simply written, or "rough." The note also makes clear that the statements represent Postman's opinion.

Direct-Quotation Note

Since most of your paper should be in your own words, most of your notes should be paraphrases rather than direct quotations. A paper that is a string of quotations "glued" together with a few transitional sentences is

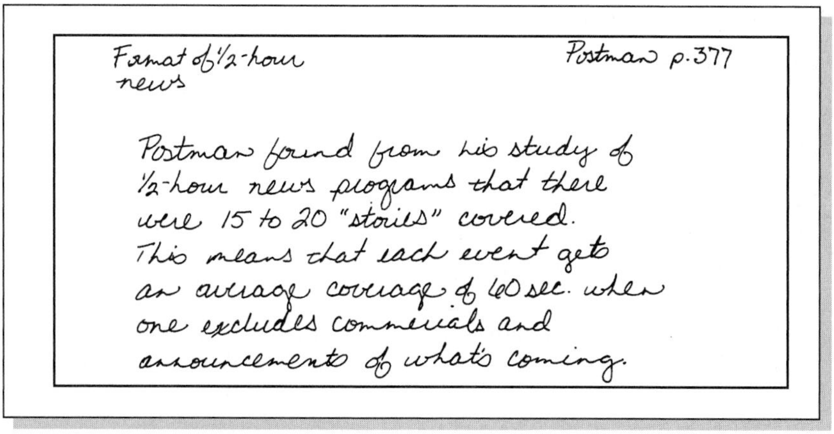

Format of ½-hour   Postman p.377
news

Postman found from his study of
½-hour news programs that there
were 15 to 20 "stories" covered.
This means that each event gets
an average coverage of 60 sec. when
one excludes commercials and
announcements of what's coming.

Figure 44 Paraphrase Note Card.

```
Effect of format on viewers          Postman p.377-78

   Opinion

1. There isn't time to think about each event—causes
   & effects & significance.

2. The format doesn't contribute to feeling deeply
   about the events.
```

Figure 45 Keyboarded Paraphrase Note (Rough Paraphrase).

mere patchwork, not your own paper. One good way to resist using too many quotations is not to take notes that are directly quoted. One argument for taking more direct-quotation notes is that you then have the exact words to contemplate when you draft and that the time to move to paraphrase is at the writing stage. The problem with this thinking is that you are only postponing the task of putting the information in your own words, and, if you are pushed to complete a paper, you may be tempted not to paraphrase at all.

There are four legitimate uses of direct quotations in a research paper:

1. To present statistical information. Paraphrasing a series of statistics without distorting the evidence can be difficult. Also, you may not be sure, at the note-taking stage, how much of the statistical information you will actually use in your paper.

2. To give examples of a writer's ideas or style of writing. When your purpose is to examine a writer's ideas or stylistic techniques, you must give specific examples of those ideas or techniques in direct quotation and then analyze them. For example, the student writing on Thomas Paine's skill as a persuasive writer should take notes from *Common Sense* in direct quotation, as examples of Paine's style.

3. To cite an authoritative opinion. When the opinion of an authority is especially helpful in support of a controversial thesis, it may be important to present that opinion in the authority's exact words. If you intend to challenge an authority's views, you will need to give readers the exact passage that you then dispute.

4. To capture special phrasing. At times a writer's views will be expressed in a phrase or sentence that cannot be paraphrased without changing the meaning or losing the power of the statement. Be careful, though, not to overuse this justification for quoting. Your paper should reflect not only your own thinking but also your own writing style. *If you cannot justify a direct quotation on the basis of these guidelines, paraphrase instead.*

When preparing a direct-quotation note, make sure that you compare your note word for word with the source to ensure accurate spelling and punctuation, as well as completeness. Then place all quoted material within quotation marks or, better yet, within double-angle brackets—<<and>>—so that there is no doubt that you have someone else's words in the note.

Figure 46 illustrates a direct-quotation note.

Photocopying

Photocopying (and downloading to your PC and e-mail) all make possible working at home or in your room with articles and sections of reference works and other source materials that in the past you would have studied in the library. Photocopying provides convenience, but it does not eliminate the need

> ✓ When you have reason to quote, keep in mind that you are lifting a short passage out of a larger context. Be certain that what you quote is faithful to the entire source and does not misrepresent the writer's views on the topic.

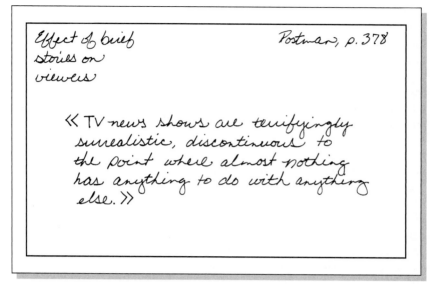

Effect of brief
stories on
viewers

Postman, p. 378

≪ TV news shows are terrifyingly
surealistic, discontinuous to
the point where almost nothing
has anything to do with anything
else. ≫

Figure 46 Direct-quotation Note.

to take from each source only those key points that will advance your paper. Marking passages that you would, without these new strategies, have put in a direct-quotation note, can save time and be a guard against copying errors. But since most of your paper needs to be in your own words, at some point you will have to paraphrase the information in those photo or electronic copies.

Probably some combination of strategies is appropriate. Photocopy (or download or e-mail to yourself) key sources so that you can easily work with them. Mark segments to be quoted and make paraphrase notes for most of the information so that you can synthesize that material with information from other sources.

The Note-Taking Process

The sample notes drawing on Neil Postman's article serve as a good example of the note-taking process. Suppose you have decided to do some primary research on television programming, but have not yet decided on a focused topic. You begin by reading some articles on television, including Postman's "Television News Narcosis." As a part of your preliminary reading, you prepare a summary note on Postman's article, as illustrated in Figure 43.

After reading additional sources on the topic, you decide that you want to update and extend Postman's analysis of television news programs. You set up a plan for analyzing the format and content of evening network news programs. But, since you need to give credit to Postman for the idea of your study and to test some of his conclusions, you take several detailed notes, such as those shown in Figures 44–46. Although you may first record the sentence in Figure 46 as a direct quotation, you will probably include most of it in your paper in a paraphrased form, perhaps quoting only the phrase "terrifyingly surrealistic."

Some sources will be more difficult to work with than Postman's essay because the style of writing is technical or the ideas are complex or unfamiliar. The test of your grasp of complicated sources is your ability to restate key ideas in your own words. Do not rely on quoting as a way around the problem. If you quote passages you do not understand, you may end up with a paper that does not make good sense. (Your instructor may even ask you to explain parts of your paper filled with complex quoted material to see if you did understand what you were including. You will be embarrassed if you cannot explain ideas in your own paper.)

Suppose that you are writing a paper on the characteristics of conservative thought in the United States after the Civil War. In Richard Hofstadter's study of social Darwinism (*Social Darwinism and American Thought*), you read the following paragraph:

[1] As a phase in the history of conservative thought, social Darwinism deserves remark. [2] Insofar as it defended the status quo and gave strength to attack on reformers and on almost all efforts at the conscious and directed change of society, social Darwinism was certainly one of the leading strains in American conservative thought for more than a generation. [3] But it lacked many of the signal characteristics of conservatism as it is usually found. [4] A conservatism that appealed more to the secularist than the pious mentality, it was a conservatism almost without religion. [5] A body of belief whose chief conclusion was that the positive functions of the state should be kept to the barest minimum, it was almost anarchical, and it was devoid of that center of reverence and authority which the state provides in many conservative systems. [6] Finally, and perhaps most important, it was a conservatism that tried to dispense with sentimental or emotional ties.

Hofstadter's sentences are complex and some terms may be unfamiliar, but the paragraph does have a clear structure. It can be divided into the following sections and subsections that clarify his main points:

Sentences 1 and 2	Sentences 3, 4, 5, and 6
Social Darwinism was an important form in American conservatism. Its conservative characteristics were 1. Favoring the status quo 2. Opposing social change (This could lead to one note with the heading "Characteristics of Conservative thought.")	It was unlike other forms of conservatism because 1. It was secular, not religious 2. It did not value governmental authority and wanted governmental functions to be limited. 3. It wanted to get rid of sentimentality. (This could be another note with the heading "Characteristics of social Darwinism.")

Two valuable notes can be obtained by the patient student who takes time to understand the paragraph and take from it the key points. Patience is rewarded: unnecessary direct quoting is avoided; excessive dependence on the author's language (hence plagiarism) is avoided; and the student actually learns about conservative thought.

WRITING ABOUT SOURCES

To introduce students to key scholars and significant issues in a field of study, instructors often assign projects that require students to write about the books and articles they have read on a specific topic. These assignments also prepare students for more advanced projects that must be based on a review of previous works on a topic. Two formats used for writing about sources are the *annotated bibliography* and the *review of literature*. With either format, your purpose is to explain the sources themselves rather than to use them to develop your own thesis.

Preparing an Annotated Bibliography

An *annotation* is a brief note that explains the contents of a specific source. Preparing annotations of sources for a research project can help you evaluate the sources and provide an understanding of the state of scholarly debate on a particular subject. An annotated bibliography also demonstrates your reading and summary skills. Aaron Kingsley's reading on the issue of dinosaur warm-bloodedness led to the following annotated bibliography. Examine it both for the annotations and for correct bibliographic citations.

Dinosaur Metabolism: Is It a Warm
or a Cold Furnace?
Selected Annotated Bibliography
Aaron Kingsley

Bakker, Robert. <u>The Dinosaur Heresies</u>. New York:
    Morrow, 1986. Paleontologist Robert Bakker
    was one of the first scientists to challenge
    the common view that dinosaurs were slow-
    moving, ectothermic reptiles. Rather, he
    argues strongly that most dinosaurs were
    active, endothermic creatures more like
    mammals than reptiles.

Benton, Michael J. <u>Vertebrate Paleontology:</u>
    <u>Biology and Evolution.</u> London: Unwin, 1990.
    Dr. Michael Benton presents the evolution of
    vertebrates, animals with backbones,
    chronologically, starting from early fishes
    and ending with humans. Additionally, he
    includes clear explanations of current
    paleontologic studies related to the
    vertebrates and the analytical methods of
    obtaining this information.

Fischman, Joshua. "Were Dinosaurs Cold-Blooded
    after All? The Nose Knows." <u>Science</u> 270
    (1995): 735-36. Fischman reports on John
    Ruben's research on respiratory turbinates in
    dinosaur fossils and gives background on the
    cold-blooded versus warm-blooded debate.

Fischman explains the role of respiratory
turbinates in warm-blooded animals.

Lampton, Christopher. <u>New Theories on the
Dinosaurs</u>. New York: Watts, 1989. Christopher
Lampton first presents what was the
traditional view of the dinosaur as pea-
brained, slow, and ectothermic. However, he
immediately follows up that view of dinosaurs
with new theories on the dinosaurs' life
style, biology, and extinction.

Lessem, Don. <u>Dinosaurs Rediscovered: New Findings
Which Are Revolutionizing Dinosaur Science</u>.
New York: Simon, 1992. Don Lessem asserts
that paleontology has gained momentum again,
causing new dinosaur discoveries around the
world at an astounding rate of "a new dino
every seven weeks or so." Lessem highlights
thirty scientists who, he believes, are
primarily responsible for these numerous new
discoveries.

McGowan, Christopher. <u>Dinosaurs, Spitfires, and
Sea Dragons</u>. Cambridge: Harvard UP, 1991. In
an interesting manner, Christopher McGowan
addresses most of the major arguments and the
criticisms of those arguments on the most
controversial issues concerning dinosaurs.
These include endothermy vs. ectothermy, the

relationship between dinosaurs and birds, and
the extinction of the dinosaurs.

Mestel, Rosie. "Cold-Blooded Dinosaurs Ahead by a
Nose." New Scientist 18 Mar. 1995:6. The
author writes about the research done by John
Ruben and William Hillenius on respiratory
turbinates in dinosaur fossils. So far, their
research shows no evidence that dinosaurs had
respiratory turbinates and were not warm-
blooded.

Monastersky, Richard. "What Lurks Inside a
Dinosaur's Nose?" Science News 148 (1995):
330. Richard Monastersky reports on the
annual meeting of the Society for Vertebrate
Paleontology. Researchers are trying to
determine if dinosaurs had respiratory
turbinates, found only in warm-blooded
animals.

Norman, David B. Dinosaur! New York: Prentice,
1991. Dr. David B. Norman's book establishes
a good foundation of general knowledge on all
types of dinosaurs. Additionally, he enters
into the debate on dinosaurs as endotherms or
ectotherms, as well as the debate on
dinosaurs' relationship to birds.

Parker, Steve. The Practical Paleontologist. Ed.
Raymond L. Bernor. New York: Simon, 1990.

Steve Parker presents an informative history
of the dinosaur as well as current methods
used to unearth, classify, and reconstruct
the skeletons of the dinosaurs, increasing
our understanding of these fascinating
animals.

Wilford, John Noble. The Riddle of the Dinosaur.
New York: Knopf, 1986. Showing how their work
formed a basis for the modern study of
paleontology, Wilford discusses the lives of
several of the founding paleontologists. He
also presents in great detail the debates on
the dinosaurs' extinction and whether or not
they were endothermic.

Preparing a Review of the Literature on a Topic

An noted previously, a review of the literature presents, in an organized essay, a discussion of the key sources on a specific topic. In this study of key sources, you go beyond the preparation of an annotated bibliography. Now you need to shape your knowledge of individual sources into a discussion of the major issues in the debate on the topic. Individual sources must be grouped in some meaningful way to aid a reader's understanding of the topic's controversial issues. Aaron Kingsley's reading on dinosaur warm-bloodedness has led to the following polished and thoughtful essay on the debate. You can study the essay not only as a review of literature but also as a model for introducing material from sources, blending quoting and paraphrasing, and documenting in MLA style.

Aaron Kingsley

Professor Seyler

English 111

December 5, 1997

Dinosaur Metabolism:

Is It a Warm or a Cold Furnace?

A Selected Review of the Literature

Until the 1960s the traditional view of the
dinosaur was as a cold-blooded, slow, pea-
brained reptile. Since the 1960s, one of the
significant debates in paleontology has been
over dinosaur warm-bloodedness. Three key terms
are important to this debate: ectotherm,
endotherm, and homiotherm. <u>Ectotherm</u> means that
an animal's metabolism holds its body
temperature at air temperature. <u>Endotherm</u> means
that an animal's metabolism remains at a
constant internal temperature regardless of its
surroundings. <u>Homiotherm</u> is a cross between an
endotherm and an ectotherm; a homiotherm is a
creature that has such a large body mass that it
neither gains nor loses heat rapidly. Currently,
the most widely accepted view of dinosaurs is
that probably <u>some</u> of them were endothermic, but
the evidence for this conclusion still generates

controversy. The controversial evidence includes
body weight, bone structure, heart strength, leg
position, and respiratory turbinates.

Dinosaur Body Weight

The body weight of a dinosaur provides one of
the arguments supporting the assertion that some
dinosaurs were endotherms. Don Lessem reports
that one reason for paleontologists' change of
thinking arose in 1964 from Dr. John Ostrom's
discovery of Deinonchyus, "terrible claw," in
central Montana (43). Christopher Lampton argues
that since Deinonchyus had large claws on its
feet, and was only as tall as a human, it must
have been endothermic to remain active enough to
flee from larger predators and to attack its own
prey with its terrible claws (90). Lampton
quotes Ostrom in further support of
Deinonchyus's endothermy: "'It does not surprise
us to see a hawk slash with its talons. . . .
Reptiles are just not capable of such intricate
maneuvers, such delicate balance'" (88-89).
Lampton concludes that Deinonchyus could not
have been ectothermic and still remain an
aggressive predator that actively hunted by
slashing with the claws on its feet (89). The

Kingsley 3

evidence suggests that at least this one
dinosaur was endothermic.

Dinosaur Bone Structure

The structure of the dinosaur's bones can also
indicate to paleontologists if the dinosaur was
endothermic. Dr. Robert Bakker, arguing that all
dinosaurs were endothermic, states that the
presence of Haversian canals, concentric bone
layers characteristic of endotherms, in many
dinosaurs' bones indicates that they were also
endothermic (354). Attacking Bakker's argument,
John Wilford quotes from Ostrom's work stating
that "'Haversian canals are present in some
ectotherms, and absent in some endotherms'"
(177). Another indicator of a creature's
physiology is the fibro-lamellar bone.
Christopher McGowan cites from Armand de
Ricqles, currently the world's most experienced
dinosaur bone histologist, who in 1976 found the
fibro-lamellar bone, a characteristic of
endothermic dinosaurs, in some dinosaur bones.
This discovery led Ricqles to conclude that some
dinosaurs may have been warm-blooded (153).
However, McGowan reminds us that in 1981
Ricqles, while studying a bone sample from a
Sauropod, a gigantic herbivore (Brachiosaurus

Kingsley 4

was a Sauropod), found both a fibro-lamellar
bone and a cyclic bone, an ectothermic
characteristic, in the same bone sample, casting
doubt on the value of fibro-lamellar bones as
indicators of either warm- or cold-bloodedness
(154). McGowan draws his argument together by
citing Ricqles's conclusion that Sauropods were
neither cold- nor warm-blooded; rather, they
were homiothermic, animals that maintain a
constant body temperature by sheer body weight
alone (154). Dr. David Norman further clarifies
how homiothermy operates by asserting that any
dinosaur whose volume (body mass) is
significantly greater than its surface area
(skin) will only gradually gain and lose body
temperature, enabling dinosaurs to warm
themselves during the day and then remain warm
throughout the night (80).

Dinosaur Heart Strength

The heart is responsible for pumping blood
throughout the body, especially to the brain.
Because, as Steve Parker notes, several of the
dinosaurs' heads were raised high above the rest
of their bodies, they would have required a
"fully divided heart like birds and mammals
(both of which are endotherms)" to pump blood to

Kingsley 5

their head and other extremities (107). However,
Michael Benton questions this assertion that
dinosaurs were endotherms since crocodilians
also have a primitive version of a four-
chambered heart and yet are ectotherms (172).

Dinosaur Leg Position

For some researchers, further evidence of
endothermy in dinosaurs is found in the position
of their legs. Bakker concludes that the
Diplodocus, a large herbivore, had a rib cage
that was so large that if its legs has been
splayed to the sides, as is characteristic of
most reptiles, its legs would not have been able
to touch the ground (204-05). Bakker further
argues that Diplodocus's ball-and-socket hip
joint would only have allowed the legs to be
directly under the dinosaur, and the knees would
have faced forward, allowing for walking similar
to the way humans walk (205).

Respiratory Turbinates for Endothermy?

The latest search for evidence in this debate is
found in the dinosaur's nose. Respiratory
turbinates, small scrolls of cartilage in the
nasal passage, help endotherms control water
loss and are found in almost all living
endotherms but not in any ectotherms

(Monastersky 330). The researchers into turbinates, John A. Ruben and William J. Hillenius, used CAT scans to examine the nasal passages of two major groups of dinosaurs, including Nanotyrannus and Velociraptor (Mestel 6). They did not find any respiratory turbinates. They also measured the nasal passages of many dinosaurs to see if a turbinate would even fit and decided that there was no room in the skinny nasal passages of dinosaurs (Mestel 6).

John R. Horner, a paleontologist at Montana State University, disagrees. He has a CAT scan of a Hadrosaur that has a turbinate ridge attachment in the nasal passage (Fischman 736). The ridge meets all of Ruben's criteria for being a respiratory turbinate. Fischman quotes Horner as saying that "maybe different dinosaurs had different strategies" for breathing (736).

Conclusion

Although years of research and debate have been recorded since 1964, when Ostrom found that obviously highly active dinosaur Deinonchyus, no one has been able to prove definitively that all dinosaurs were either endothermic or ectothermic. After examining dinosaur body size, bone structure, heart strength, leg position, and possible respiratory turbinates, there seems to be enough circumstantial evidence to conclude that some dinosaurs were endothermic. However, does that mean that no dinosaurs were ectothermic or homiothermic? The question is still open to debate. Paleontologists, like historians, are often plagued by a lack of evidence and a multitude of possibilities. But the missing evidence and many possibilities keep us in search of the answer to the question: Did dinosaurs have a warm or a cold furnace?

Kingsley 8

Works Cited

Bakker, Robert. <u>The Dinosaur Heresies</u>. New
    York: Morrow, 1986.

Benton, Michael J. <u>Vertebrate Paleontology:
    Biology and Evolution</u>. London: Unwin,
    1990.

Fischman, Joshua. "Were Dinosaurs Cold-Blooded
    after All? The Nose Knows." <u>Science</u> 270
    (1995): 735-36.

Lampton, Christopher. <u>New Theories on the
    Dinosaurs</u>. New York: Watts, 1989.

Lessem, Don. <u>Dinosaurs Rediscovered: New
    Findings Which Are Revolutionizing
    Dinosaur Science</u>. New York: Simon, 1992.

McGowan, Christopher. <u>Dinosaurs, Spitfires,
    and Sea Dragons</u>. Cambridge; Harvard UP,
    1991.

Mestel, Rosie. "Cold-Blooded Dinosaurs Ahead
    by a Nose." <u>New Scientist</u> 18 Mar. 1995:
    6.

Monastersky, Richard. "What Lurks Inside a
    Dinosaur's Nose?" <u>Science News</u> 148
    (1995): 330.

Norman, David B. <u>Dinosaur!</u> New York: Prentice,
    1991.

Kingsley 9

Parker, Steve. <u>The Practical Paleontologist</u>.

    Ed. Raymond L. Bernor. New York: Simon,

    1990.

Wilford, John Noble. <u>The Riddle of the</u>

    <u>Dinosaur</u>. New York: Knopf, 1986.

5

PRESENTING
AND
DOCUMENTING
RESEARCH

T his "nuts and bolts" chapter presents many specific guidelines for the proper formatting of research essays. The chapter also explains and illustrates correct in-text documentation of sources according to MLA guidelines. Although you cannot expect to learn every detail given here prior to drafting your paper, still you can benefit from studying this chapter carefully enough to become familiar with its contents and to know what you must pay attention to when drafting and documenting your essay. Later, when revising and editing, you will want to check your draft against the required forms for quotations, for handling numbers, for documentation, and so on, presented here. You can eliminate much revision and avoid undetected errors if you study the details of this chapter *before* you begin to write. For example, to avoid errors in documentation that can lead to plagiarism, you should place parenthetical documentation in your draft as you write. So, study the guidelines here and look closely at the many examples to become familiar with the rules and to develop your visual sense of what "looks right."

REFERRING TO PEOPLE AND WORKS

Research papers usually contain frequent references to authors and to published works. Learn the conventions for referring to people and to works and reinforce these conventions of style by making it a habit to use correct form when taking notes. Then check your draft against these guidelines for accuracy. Show your instructors that you can meet the expectations of readers in the academic community.

References to People

- In a first reference, give the person's full name (both the given name and the surname): Arthur Miller, Margaret Mead, Thomas Paine. In second and subsequent references, use only the last name (surname): Miller, Mead, Paine.

- Do *not* use Mr., Mrs., or Ms. Special titles (President, Chief Justice, Dr.) may be used in the first reference with the person's full name.

- *Never* refer to an author by her or his first name. Write Dickinson, not Emily; Whitman, not Walt.

References to Titles of Works

Titles of works must *always* be written as titles. Titles are indicated by capitalization and by either quotation marks or underlining. (Underlining in handwritten or typed papers represents italic type in printed works. MLA style calls for underlining rather than italics in research papers.)

Capitalizing Titles

- The first and last words are capitalized.
- The first word of a subtitle is capitalized.
- All other words in titles are capitalized except
  - Articles (*a, an, the*).
  - Coordinating conjunctions (*and, or, but, for, nor, yet, so*).
  - Prepositions of five or fewer letters (*in, with, about*); prepositions of more than five letters are capitalized (*Between, Through, Before*).

Titles Requiring Quotation Marks

Titles of works published *within* other works—within a book, magazine, or newspaper— are indicated by quotation marks.

essays	"Once More to the Lake"
short stories	"Young Goodman Brown"
poems	"The Road Not Taken"
articles	"Playing Dumb"
chapters	"Locating Sources"
lectures	"Henry VIII"
TV Episode	"Resolved: Drug Prohibition Has Failed" (one debate on the TV show *Firing Line*)

Titles Requiring Underlining (Italics in Print)

Titles of works that are separate publications and, by extension, titles of items such as works of art and films are underlined.

plays	<u>A Raisin in the Sun</u>
novels	<u>War and Peace</u>
nonfiction books	<u>A Brief History of Time</u>
textbooks	<u>Doing Research</u>
book-length poems	<u>The Odyssey</u>
magazines	<u>Scientific American</u>
newspapers	<u>Wall Street Journal</u>
pamphlets	<u>So You'd Like to Do Something about Water Pollution</u>
ballets	<u>Swan Lake</u>
films	<u>The Wizard of Oz</u>
operas	<u>Madame Butterfly</u>
paintings	<u>The Birth of Venus</u>
sculpture	<u>The Dying Slave</u>
ships	<u>Titanic</u>
recordings	<u>Eine Kleine Nachtmusik</u>
TV programs	<u>Nightline</u>

DOCUMENTING SOURCES

Depending on your course of study and specific research assignment, you may need the guidance of some but not all sections of this chapter. You may, for example, be quoting sources but not using charts in your research project. Everyone, though, needs to study the first part of this section on documentation. *All researchers must understand how to avoid misrepresenting material taken from sources.*

All research essays must contain correct documentation, but not all researchers will use the MLA documentation patterns presented in the second part of this section. Those using APA style, footnote/endnote style, or a number style will find guidelines for documentation in Chapter 7. Whatever pattern you use, if you have prepared an accurate working bibliography (see Chapter 3) and your notes contain all necessary information (see Chapter 4), then the required formal documentation will not be that difficult to prepare. Your goal is to make all references to sources accurate, consistent with required style, and concise. Follow the guidelines exactly as they are presented in this chapter for MLA style or in Chapter 7 for other styles. Handling documentation correctly takes, more than other skills, discipline and patience. However, there are challenges in working borrowed material into your paper without misrepresenting either the sources or your indebtedness to each source.

Avoiding Misleading Acknowledgment of Sources Within a Paper

Instructors assume that students are sincere and conscientious—until students give cause for instructors to think differently. If you are an honest student, you do not want to submit a paper that is plagiarized—even though the plagiarism is unintentional, resulting from careless note taking or careless writing.

Plagiarism usually occurs in one of two ways:

1. a researcher takes notes carelessly, neglecting to indicate precise page references, but uses the information anyway, without proper documentation

2. a researcher presents borrowed material in such a way that even though the paper contains documentation, the researcher has misrepresented the degree of indebtedness to the source.

Good note-taking strategies, explained in Chapter 4, will keep you from the first pitfall. The challenge of smoothly weaving borrowed material into your essay is met in Chapter 6. The part of the task dealing with appropriate documentation is examined here. This discussion will help you avoid the second cause of plagiarism.

The best way to identify quoted or paraphrased material in your essay is by identifying the author. You may even include the author's credentials (`"Ac-cording to Dr. Hays, a geologist with the Department of the Interior,. . ."`) or the location of the material (`"The presi-dent, as quoted by `Time` magazine, feels. . ."`). These *intro-ductory tags* give your reader a context for reading the borrowed material and also serve as part of the documentation in the paper. An introductory tag should help readers distinguish between your words and ideas and the mate-rial that you have borrowed. *Make certain that each tag clarifies rather than distorts an author's relationship to his or her ideas and your relationship to the source.* Here are three guidelines to follow to avoid misrepresenting bor-rowed material:

1. *Verbs in introductory tags:* Be careful when you vary such standard in-troductory tags as "Smith says" or "Jones states" that you do not select alter-native words that are misleading. Writing "Smith implies" rather than "Smith says" misrepresents Smith's attitude toward his work. (See pp. 211–22 for a discussion of varying word choice in introductory tags.)

2. *Location of introductory tags:* If you vary the pattern of tags by men-tioning Jones after you have mentioned her ideas in your paragraph, be sure that your reader can tell precisely which ideas in the passage belong to Jones. If your entire paragraph is a paraphrase of Jones's views, you are plagiarizing to conclude with "This idea is presented by Jones." Which of the several ideas in your paragraph is Jones's? Your reader will infer, incorrectly, that only the last idea has been taken from the source by Jones.

3. *Proper paraphrasing:* Be sure that paraphrases are *in your own words* so that you do not bring Smith's ideas into your paper in his style of writing. To use Smith's words and/or sentence structure, even in a condensed version, is to plagiarize from Smith.

> Note: putting a parenthetical reference at the end of a paragraph to document your source is not sufficient if you have used the source throughout the paragraph. Use introductory tags and parenthetical documentation throughout each paragraph to guide the reader through the material. Clearly distinguish among sources and between information from a source and your own ideas.

The paragraph on the following page (from Franklin E. Zimring's "Firearms, Violence and Public Policy" [Scientific American, November 1991]) provides material for the examples that follow of adequate and inadequate ac-knowledgment of sources. After reading Zimring's paragraph, study the three examples of student writing with these questions in mind: (1) Which example represents adequate acknowledgment? (2) Which examples do not represent adequate acknowledgment? (3) In exactly what ways is each plagiarized paragraph flawed?

> Although most citizens support such measures as owner screening, public opinion is sharply divided on laws that would restrict the ownership of handguns to persons with special needs. If the U.S. does not reduce handguns and current trends continue, it faces the prospect that the number of handguns in circulation will grow from 35 million to more than 50 million within 50 years. A national program limiting the availability of handguns would cost many billions of dollars and meet much resistance from citizens. These costs would likely be greatest in the early years of the program. The benefits of supply reduction would emerge slowly because efforts to diminish the availability of handguns would probably have a cumulative impact over time. (page 54)

Student Paragraph 1

One approach to the problem of handgun violence in America is to severely limit handgun ownership. If we don't restrict ownership and start the costly task of removing handguns from our society, we may end up with around 50 million handguns in the country by 2040. The benefits will not be apparent right away but will eventually appear. This idea is emphasized by Franklin Zimring (54).

Student Paragraph 2

One approach to the problem of handgun violence in America is to restrict the ownership of handguns except in special circumstances. If we do not begin to reduce the number of handguns in this country, the number will grow from 35 million to more than 50 million within 50 years. We can agree with Franklin Zimring that a program limiting handguns will cost billions and meet resistance from citizens (54).

MLA In-Text
Documentation

✓ You need a 100-percent correspondence between the sources listed on your Works Cited page(s) and the sources you cite (refer to) in your paper. Do not omit from your Works Cited any sources you refer to in your paper. Do not include in your Works Cited any sources not referred to in your paper.

✓ If it's in the text, it's on the Works Cited page:

As David Raup explains, tracking climate changes is difficult because climate itself is complicated, including wind patterns and seasonal changes as well as temperature (144).

Works Cited

Raup, David M. <u>Extinction: Bad Genes or</u>

   <u>Bad Luck?</u> New York: Norton, 1991.

✓ If it's on the Works Cited page, it's in the text:

Works Cited

Schneider, David. "The Rising Seas."

   <u>Scientific American</u> March 1997:

   112-17.

Scientists explain that tracking climate changes is difficult because climate itself is so complex (Raup 144; Schneider 117).

Student Paragraph 3

According to law professor Franklin Zimring, the
United States needs to severely limit handgun
ownership or face the possibility of seeing handgun
ownership increase "from 35 million to more than 50
million within 50 years" (54). Zimring points out that
Americans are "sharply divided" on restricting
handguns and that enforcing such laws would "cost many
billions of dollars." He concludes that the benefits
would not be seen immediately but that the
restrictions "would probably have a cumulative impact
over time" (54). Although Zimring paints a gloomy
picture of high costs and little immediate relief from
gun violence, he also presents the shocking
possibility of 50 million guns by the year 2040. Can
our society survive so much fire power?

Clearly, only the third student paragraph demonstrates adequate acknowledgment of the writer's indebtedness to Zimring. You may wonder about the
amount of direct quoting used by the third student, but he wants the power of
Zimring's words and statistics to build on. Notice that the placement of the
parenthetical page reference acts as a visual closure to the student's borrowing; then he turns to his response to Zimring and his own views on the problem of handguns.

MLA In-Text (Parenthetical) Citations

The student paragraphs above illustrate the most common form of parenthetical documentation in MLA style, that is, parenthetical references to author
and page number, or just to page number if the author has been mentioned in
an introductory tag. Because a reference only to author and page number is
an incomplete citation (readers could not find the source with such limited information), whatever is cited this way in the essay must refer to a specific
source presented fully in a Works Cited list that follows the text of the paper.
General guidelines for citing are given on the next page, followed by examples and explanations of the required patterns of documentation.

> ☑ You need a 100-percent correspondence between the sources listed on
> your Works Cited page(s) and the sources you cite (refer to) in your
> paper. Do not omit from your Works Cited any sources you refer to in your paper.
> Do not include in your Works Cited any sources not referred to in your paper.

Guidelines for Using Parenthetical Documentation

- The purpose of documentation is to make clear exactly what material in a passage has been borrowed and from what source the borrowed material has come.
- Parenthetical documentation requires specific page references for borrowed material.
- Parenthetical documentation is required for both quoted and paraphrased material.
- Parenthetical documentation provides as brief a citation as possible consistent with accuracy and clarity.

The Simplest Patterns of Parenthetical Documentation

The simplest parenthetical reference can be prepared in one of three ways:

1. Give the author's last name (full name in a first reference to an author) in the text of your paper and place the relevant page number(s) in parentheses following the borrowed material.

Frederick Lewis Allen observes that, during the 1920s,

urban tastes spread to the country (146).

2. Place the author's last name and the relevant page number(s) in parentheses immediately following the borrowed material.

During the 1920s, "not only the drinks were mixed, but

the company as well" (Allen 82).

3. On the rare occasion that you cite an entire work rather than borrowing from a specific passage, give the author's name in the text and omit any page numbers.

Tuchman argues that there are significant parallels

between the fourteenth century and our time.

Each one of these in-text references is complete only when the full citation is found in the Works Cited, thus:

Allen, Frederick Lewis. <u>Only Yesterday: An Informal
History of the Nineteen-Twenties</u>. New York:
Harper, 1931.

Tuchman, Barbara W. <u>A Distant Mirror: The Calamitous
14th Century</u>. New York: Knopf, 1978.

The three patterns just illustrated should be used in each of the following situations:

1. The work is not anonymous—the author is known.
2. The work is by one author.
3. The work cited is the only work used by that author.
4. No other author in your bibliography has the same last name.
5. The borrowed material is either quoted or paraphrased.

Placement of Parenthetical Documentation

The simplest placing of a parenthetical reference is at the end of the appropriate sentence *before* the period, but, when you are quoting, *after* the quotation mark.

During the 1920s, "not only the drinks were mixed, but
the company as well" (Allen 82).

Do not put any punctuation between the author's name and the page number.

If the borrowed material ends before the end of your sentence, place the parenthetical reference *after* the borrowed material and before any subsequent punctuation. This placement more accurately shows what is borrowed and what is your own work.

Sport, Allen observes about the 1920s, had developed
into an obsession (66), another similarity between the
1920s and the 1980s.

If a quoted passage is long enough to require setting off in display form (block quotation), then place the parenthetical reference at the end of the passage, *after* the last period. (Remember that long quotations in display form do not have quotation marks.)

It is hard to believe that when he writes about the
influence of science, Allen is describing the 1920s,
not the 1980s:

> The prestige of science was colossal. The
> man in the street and the woman in the
> kitchen, confronted on every hand with new
> machines and devices which they owed to the
> laboratory, were ready to believe that
> science could accomplish almost anything.
> (164)

And to complete the documentation for all three examples:

Works Cited

Allen, Frederick Lewis. Only Yesterday: An Informal
    History of the Nineteen-Twenties. New York:
    Harper, 1931.

Parenthetical Documentation for Complex Sources

Not all sources can be cited in one of the three simplest forms described above, for not all meet the five criteria listed on page 161. Works by two or more authors, for example, will need somewhat fuller references. Each sample form of parenthetical documentation illustrated below is completed with a full Works Cited reference.

Two Authors, Mentioned in the Text

Richard Herrnstein and Charles Murray contend that it
is "consistently. . . advantageous to be smart" (25).

Two Authors, Not Mentioned in the Text

The advantaged smart group form a "cognitive elite" in
our society (Herrnstein and Murray 26-27).

Works Cited

Herrnstein, Richard J., and Charles Murray. The Bell
    Curve: Intelligence and Class Structure in
    American Life. New York: Free, 1994.

A Book in Two or More Volumes

Sewall analyzes the role of Judge Lord in Dickinson's life (2: 642-47).

OR

Judge Lord was also one of Dickinson's preceptors (Sewall 2: 642-47).

Note: The number before the colon always signifies the volume number; the number(s) after the colon represents the page number(s).

Works Cited

Sewall, Richard B. The Life of Emily Dickinson.
   2 vols. New York: Farrar, 1974.

A Book or Article Listed by Title (Author Unknown)

According to the Concise Dictionary of American Biography, William Jennings Bryan's 1896 campaign stressed social and sectional conflicts (117).

The Times's editors are not pleased with some of the changes in welfare programs ("Where Welfare Stands" 4:16).

Always cite the title of the article, not the title of the journal, if the author is unknown.

Works Cited

Concise Dictionary of American Biography. New York:
   Scribner's, 1964.
"Where Welfare Stands." Editorial. New York Times
   18 May 1997, sec. 4: 16.

A Work by a Corporate Author

According to the report of the Institute of Ecology's Global Ecological Problems Workshop, the civilization

of the city can lull us into forgetting our
relationship to the total ecological system on which
we depend (13).

Although corporate authors may be cited with the page number within the parentheses, your presentation will be more graceful if corporate authors are introduced in the text. Then only page numbers go in parentheses.

Works Cited

Institute of Ecology. Man in the Living Environment.
    Madison: U of Wisconsin P, 1972.

Two or More Works by the Same Author

During the 1920s, "not only the drinks were mixed,
but the company as well" (Allen, Only Yesterday 82).

According to Frederick Lewis Allen, the early 1900s
were a period of complacency in America (The Big
Change 4-5).

In The Big Change, Allen asserts that the early
1900s were a period of complacency (4-5).

If your Works Cited list contains two or more works by the same author, the fullest parenthetical citation will include the author's last name, followed by a comma; the work's title, shortened if possible; and the page number(s). If the author's name appears in the text—or the author and title both, as in the third example above—omit these items from the parenthetical citation. When you have to include the title, it is best to simplify the citation by including the author's last name in the text.

Works Cited

Allen, Frederick Lewis. The Big Change. New York:
    Harper, 1952.

---. Only Yesterday: An Informal History of the
    Nineteen-Twenties. New York: Harper, 1931.

Two or More Works in One Parenthetical Reference

```
Several writers about the future agree that big

changes will take place in work patterns (Toffler

384-87; Naisbitt 35-36).
```

Separate each author cited with a semicolon. But if the parenthetical citation would be disruptively long, cite the works in a "See also" note rather than in the text.

```
                       Works Cited

Naisbitt, John. Megatrends: Ten New Directions

     Transforming Our Lives. New York: Warner, 1982.

Toffler, Alvin. The Third Wave. New York: Bantam,

     1981.
```

Complete Publication Information in Parenthetical Reference

Occasionally you may want to give complete information about a source within parentheses in the text of your paper. Then a Works Cited list is not used. Square brackets are used for parenthetical information within parentheses. This approach may be appropriate when you have used only one or two sources, even if many references are made to the few sources. Literary analyses are one type of paper for which this approach to citation may be a good choice. For example:

```
Edith Wharton establishes the bleakness of her

setting, Starkfield, not just through description of

place but also through her main character, Ethan, who

is described as "bleak and unapproachable" (Ethan

Frome [New York: Scribner's, 1911] 3. All subsequent

references are to this edition.). Later Wharton

describes winter as "shut[ting] down on Starkfield"

and negating life there (7).
```

Additional-Information Footnotes or Endnotes

At times you may need to provide additional useful information, explanation, or commentary that is not central to the development of your paper. These additions belong in content footnotes or endnotes. However, use these sparingly and never as a way of advancing your thesis. Many instructors object to content footnotes or endnotes and prefer only parenthetical citations in student papers.

"See Also" Footnotes or Endnotes

More acceptable to most readers is the footnote (or endnote) that refers to other sources of evidence for or against the point being established in the paper. Such footnotes or endnotes can be combined with parenthetical documentation. They are usually introduced with "See also" or "Compare," followed by the citation. For example:

```
Chekhov's debt to Ibsen should be recognized, as

should his debt to Maeterlinck and other playwrights

of the 1890s who were concerned with the inner lives

of their characters.²
```

```
    ² See also Eric Bentley, In Search of Theatre

(New York: Vintage, 1959) 330; Walter Bruford, Anton

Chekhov (New Haven: Yale UP, 1957) 45; and Raymond

Williams, Drama from Ibsen to Eliot (New York: Oxford

UP, 1953) 126-29.
```

PRESENTING DIRECT QUOTATIONS

As discussed in Chapter 4, most notes should be paraphrases so that most of your paper is in your own words and style. Still, there are times that quoting directly from sources is appropriate, even essential (e.g., in literary studies). When you need to quote from sources, follow these guidelines and conventions.

General Guidelines

1. **Quote accurately.** Take time to compare what you have written with the original. Pay attention to spelling and punctuation.
2. **Enclose all quoted material in quotation marks** and do not change words or punctuation within the quoted material.
3. **Keep quoted passages brief,** avoiding quoted passages of more than a few key lines. Long quoted passages throughout a paper are a quick visual signal to instructors that students have not learned much about their topics and are just trying to fill pages.

4. Introduce quoted passages with the author's name and other appropriate information to provide a context for readers. Consider the following examples.

Ineffective Long Quotation "Dumped" on Reader

"What a piece of work is man! He flushes fields, levels forests, covers waterways, creates swamps, drains swamps, changes the course of rivers. But at times his surgery on the land seems the work of a brilliant surgeon operating with a hatchet and buck knife, his mistakes and excuses sutured with leftover string" (Grove 159).

It is true that we have destroyed a majority of this country's wetlands, but just maybe with our intelligence, we can find a way to restore some of the loss and repair some of the damage with more than leftover string.

(Never let a long quotation rest by itself as a complete paragraph. Providing documentation at the end of the quotation is insufficient context for readers. These last two paragraphs of a paper on preserving wetlands should have been revised into one with a clear context for the quotation that includes identifying the author *before* quoting.)

Effective Context for Quotation

In developing this country, we have demonstrated great intelligence and skills. As Noel Grove puts it, man "flushes fields, levels forests, . . . changes the course of rivers" (159). Unfortunately, we have also destroyed most of the country's wetlands; our "surgery on the land," to use Grove's metaphor, "seems the work of a brilliant surgeon operating with a hatchet and buck knife" (159). We need to employ our surgical

skills and knowledge of the patient to repair the

damage to wetlands and restore some of the duck's lost

habitats.

5. **Combine quoting and paraphrasing when possible,** working key passages into sentences of your own. Consider the following examples.

Ineffective Long Quotation

Eliot shows Prufrock's anxiety in these lines:

And I have known the eyes already, known

them all—

The eyes that fix you in a formulated phrase,

And when I am formulated, sprawling on a pin,

When I am pinned and wriggling on the wall,

Then how should I begin

To spit out all the butt-ends of my days

and ways?

(Simply quoting lines of the poem without discussion does not do the job of analysis. The reader is left to figure out how the lines reveal anxiety. Instead, the writer should provide that explanation, as in the revision below.)

Effective Blend of Quoting and Analysis

Eliot has Prufrock reveal his anxiety and self-

consciousness when he worries about "the eyes that fix

you in a formulated phrase," eyes that will dissect

him as if he were an insect "sprawling on a pin," a

specimen "pinned and wriggling on the wall."

Form for Quotations

Words Added to Quoted Passages

Quoted passages must be reproduced exactly. Any words added to a quoted passage to make the meaning clear must be placed in *square brackets*, not parentheses. Add *[sic]* immediately after the necessary word or phrase to alert readers to an error in the original. When necessary, add words in square brackets to clarify a quoted passage.

> *Original:* "The most important common feature of American fiction today is that it has all been produced in the interval between two world wars." **From Joseph Warren Beach, *American Fiction 1920–1940* (New York: Macmillan, 1941), 11.**

> *Incorrect:* Joseph Warren Beach says that "the most important common feature of American fiction between 1920 and 1940 is that it has all been produced in the interval between two world wars" (11).

> *Correct:* Joseph Warren Beach says that "the most important common feature of American fiction today [between 1920 and 1940] is that it has all been produced in the interval between two world wars" (11).

Lowercase for Capitals: Your Only Change in Direct Quotations

When quoted material forms only part of a sentence, the first quoted word is not capitalized, even if it was capitalized in the original source. This is the only silent change you may make within quotations. *Exception:* The quoted passage follows an introduction that ends in a colon.

> *Incorrect:* In his book <u>Taking a Stand Against Environmental Pollution</u>, David Newton asserts that "Every living organism, from the simplest to the most complex, affects the environment and is in turn affected by it" (13).

> *Correct:* In his book <u>Taking a Stand Against Environmental Pollution</u>, David Newton asserts that "every living organism, from the simplest to the most complex, affects the environment and is in turn affected by it" (13).

> *Also correct:* David Newton explains our relationship to the environment in this way: "Every living organism, from the simplest to the most complex, affects the environment and is in turn affected by it" (13).

Punctuation with Quoted Material

1. Do not quote unnecessary punctuation. When quoted material comes at the end of a sentence, use only the punctuation needed to complete your sentence.

Original: "Trust thyself: every heart vibrates to that iron string." **From Ralph Waldo Emerson, "Self-Reliance."**

Incorrect: Emerson's faith in self-reliance is summed up in two words: "Trust thyself:."

Correct: Emerson's faith in self-reliance is summed up in two words: "Trust thyself."

2. Place commas and periods *inside* the closing quotation mark. Adhering to his own words "trust thyself," Emerson was an optimist, believing that the "filths of nature the sun shall dry up."

3. Place colons and semicolons *outside* the closing quotation mark. Rousseau believed that "the words 'slavery' and 'right' are contradictory"; his thinking was in advance of his time.

4. Depending on the structure of your sentence, use a colon, a comma, or no punctuation before a quoted passage. A colon provides a formal introduction; use it sparingly for emphasis and to introduce a long quotation. Use a comma only when sentence structure requires it. A quotation presented in a "that" clause is not preceded by a comma.

Original: "Hence a wise leader cannot and should not keep his word when keeping it is not to his advantage or when the reasons that made him give it are no longer valid." **From Machiavelli's *The Prince***

a: Machiavelli argues for pragmatism thus: "a wise leader cannot and should not keep his word when keeping it is not to his advantage" (51).

b: "Hence a wise leader cannot and should not keep his word," Machiavelli asserts, "when keeping it is not to his advantage" (51).

c: Machiavelli insists that "a wise leader cannot and should not keep his word when keeping it is not to his advantage" (51).

Ellipsis Points

To reduce the length of direct quotations, omit irrelevant portions. Indicate omitted words by using ellipsis points (three *spaced* dots:. . .). If the omitted material comes at the end of a sentence, a fourth dot is needed to serve as the period that completes the sentence. If a parenthetical reference is given, the period follows the parenthetical reference, as the third example illustrates.

```
1. Robert T. Bakker believes this is so because "the
   solution [to dinosaur extinction] is . . . obvious, so
   nonfantastic, that its very mundaneness comes as a
   jolt" (427).
```

Observe the use of explanatory words in square brackets to clarify the quoted material.

```
2. As Colbert explains, "the dinosaurs were not
   failures; they dominated the earth for more than one
   hundred million years . . . ." They could not have
   become extinct, Colbert concludes, merely because
   they were too big (201).
3. Colbert argues that "the dinosaurs were not failures;
   they dominated the earth for more than one hundred
   million years . . ." (201).
```

The use of ellipsis points between sentences that are continuously quoted indicates that one or more complete sentences have been omitted.

```
4. "It is unlikely," Colbert asserts, "that dinosaurs
   became extinct because a comet collided with the
   earth . . . . While this theory explains the demise of
   the dinosaurs and the marine plankton, it fails to
   explain how . . . so many animals managed to survive"
   (205).
```

Indicate that one or more lines of poetry have been omitted by using a line of spaced dots about the length of the omitted line(s).

```
5. Prufrock reveals the inaction of the anti-hero in his
   contrast to Hamlet:

                No! I am not Prince Hamlet, nor was meant

                    to be;

                Am an attendant lord, one that will do

                To swell a progress, start a scene or two,

                . . . . . . . . . . . . . . . . . . . . . . . . . . . .

                Almost, at times, the Fool.

                                        (11.111-119)
```

Single Quotation Marks

Use single quotation marks (the apostrophe key on your keyboard) to identify quoted material within quoted material.

1. In `The Social Contract`, Rousseau argues that "the words `'slavery'` and `'right'` are contradictory; they cancel each other out."

Periods are placed inside both the single and the double closing quotation marks, unless the sentence concludes with a parenthetical reference, as the following examples illustrate.

2. Lester Thurow complains that "when it comes to empirical analysis of consumer choice, economists retreat to the doctrine of 'revealed preferences.'"

3. Lester Thurow complains that "when it comes to empirical analysis of consumer choice, economists retreat to the doctrine of 'revealed preferences'" (449).

Display Form for Long Quotations

If quoted material runs to more than four typed lines, present it in *display form*. Indent the quoted material 10 spaces from the left margin and, when typing, continue to double space. Quotation marks are not used (the indenting signals a direct quotation). If the quotation includes more than one paragraph, indicate the beginning of a new paragraph by indenting an additional three spaces. Place a parenthetical reference two spaces *after* the final period. Long quotations need an introduction that identifies the author and (usually) concludes with a colon.

Daniel Boorstin conveys his dismay over the effects of television through the following effective metaphor:

> A new miasma—which no machine before could emit—enshrouds the world of TV. We begin to be so accustomed to this foggy world, so at home and solaced and comforted within and by its blurry edges, that reality itself becomes slightly irritating. (374)

Form for Quoting Poetry

1. When quoting two lines of poetry, or a portion of two lines, separate the lines with a slash (/) and retain the capital letter that (usually) begins the second line. Note that there is a space on either side of the slash. In the following example the first quoted word is not capitalized because it is not the first word in the poetic line.

```
Browning's Duke reveals his arrogance when he says:

"and I choose / Never to stoop."
```

2. More than two lines of poetry should be presented in display form and reproduced in the *exact* form of the original lines. As with most long quotations, introduce the quoted material and conclude the introduction with a colon. Line numbers are usually given for passages from long poems.

```
The "tight" lines near the end of "Patterns" reinforce

the image of Lowell's tightly controlled speaker who

seems to be willing herself to repress her feelings,

to meet the expected patterns of her life:

               I shall go

               Up and down

               In my gown.

               Gorgeously arrayed,

               Boned and stayed. (97-101)
```

Form for Quoting Drama

If you are quoting from a prose play, follow the guidelines for quoting prose passages. If you are quoting from a poetic drama, follow the guidelines for quoting poetry. Whether in prose or poetry, short passages from one character can be worked into the text, but long passages, or passages involving two speakers, should be reproduced in display form using the conventional pattern for indicating the speakers. For prose dramas, provide act and scene number (or indicate the appropriate section of the play and conclude with a parenthetical reference, as in the first example). For poetic dramas, give act, scene, and line numbers. Use arabic numerals separated by periods, as shown in the examples.

```
1. In Charley's speech to Biff and Happy during the

   Requiem, he eulogizes Willy:
```

> Willy was a salesman. And for a salesman
> there is no rock bottom to the life. He
> don't put a bolt to a nut, he don't tell
> you the law or give you medicine. He's a
> man way out there in the blue, riding on a
> smile and a shoeshine.

2. Creon shows his paranoia early in the play when he accuses the Sentry of taking bribes from those Creon believes to be plotting against him: "from the very beginning / There have been those who have whispered together / Stiff-necked anarchists" (1.110–112).

3. In the following exchange Iago subtly plants suspicion of Cassio in the mind of Othello:

> Oth.   Was not that Cassio parted from my wife?
>
> Iago. Cassio, my lord! No, sure, I cannot think it
>   That he would steal away so guilty-like
>   Seeing you coming.
>
> Oth.   I do believe 'twas he.
>
>   (3.3.37–40)

(Note that Othello's last remark is a continuation of line 40. His words are placed on a new line but moved to the right of "coming.")

Style for Quotations

Handling quotations effectively is an important part of many research tasks. You have just reviewed guidelines for presenting direct quotations in proper form. In addition to getting the form right, you need to pay attention to the style of sentences containing quoted material. Review the following four general guidelines and study the examples to avoid confusion or grammatical errors when quoting.

1. Do not distort the meaning or tone of the original material by quoting too little.

Original: Strauss tells his friends his wounds may be "incurable."

> *Misleading:* Strauss is said to have "incurable"
>   "wounds."
> *Better:* Strauss said that his wounds "may be
>   'incurable.'"

The use of the passive "is said" in the misleading version leaves the speaker's identity unknown. In addition, the misleading version does not make clear that "incurable" is Strauss's term and that it is qualified with "may be."

2. Do not distort or confuse meaning by quoting out of context or giving so little information that readers cannot evaluate the significance of quoted material.

> *Misleading:* Some words and phrases Evans and Novak use
>   to attack the liberals are "left-wing,"
>   "seized on the incident," "first opening to
>   attack," and "assault."

The writer is trying to present evidence that the language used by columnists Evans and Novak is slanted. But only the first word, "left-wing," which is a label, can be understood out of context. The other three phrases all point to some aggressive action, but there is too little context for readers to tell that the writers are indeed describing the action in a pejorative way.

3. Do not distort the meaning of a quoted passage by writing a misleading introduction to the quotation.

> *Original:* Indeed, it is the very high rate of violence in the U.S. that
>   makes the costs of gun use so large. The U.S. has both a
>   "crime problem" and a "gun problem," and each exacerbates
>   the other. No Western nation has ever instituted strict
>   controls under conditions similar to those in the U.S. (**From
>   Franklin E. Zimring, "Firearms, Violence and
>   Public Policy,"** *Scientific American* **54.**)
> *Misleading:* Zimring asserts that because the U.S. "has
>   both a 'crime problem' and a 'gun problem,'"
>   unlike any other Western country, strict
>   controls over guns will serve no purpose
>   (54).

This is misleading because Zimring is just describing certain realities: the U. S. is unique among Western countries in the amount of violence it has, both with guns involved and without guns. Zimring is not arguing that because these are the realities, we should not have strict gun controls.

4. Weave quoted passages smoothly into sentences and without grammatical error. Quotations must not distort the grammar, syntax, or logic of your complete sentence. Words, phrases, or clauses quoted in a series must maintain parallel structure, and quoting must be accomplished without leading to incomplete or illogical statements. Here are several examples of problems and their solutions.

Sentence fragment: Just below the picture a title to the article, "Watergate Notoriety Pays Off for Some."

Revised: Just below the picture is the title of the article: "Watergate Notoriety Pays Off for Some."

Not parallel: Time states that legalized abortion may help to solve such problems as "overpopulation," "the number of unwanted babies," and "probably lower the suicide rate of pregnant women."

Revised: Time states that legalized abortion may help to solve such problems as "overpopulation," "the number of unwanted babies," and the high "suicide rate of pregnant women."

Tense shift: As Mrs. Mallard looks out of the window she feels that there was "something coming to her."

Revised: As Mrs. Mallard looks out of the window she feels that there is "something coming to her."

Illogical structure: Time's description is ". . . prose style is a cross between 'Dear Abby' and early Chinese fortune cookie."

Revised: Time describes the style as "a cross between 'Dear Abby' and early Chinese fortune cookie."

Illogical word choice: Other unrealistic [?] words used by U. S. News and World Report are "topple," "jockeying for power," and "unofficial kingmaker."
(Revision is not possible. Only the writer knows what this sentence was supposed to mean.)

Many of the problems illustrated here can be solved by quoting less of a passage and using more of your own words. The revisions illustrate this principle.

USING PUNCTUATION CORRECTLY

This brief guide to punctuation emphasizes the required uses. Remember that while some uses are a matter of personal style, others are necessary, and consistency is essential.

Commas

1. Use commas between items in a series.

Professors Alleyne, Cromwell, and Johnson appeared on the panel.

2. Use commas with coordinating conjunctions (*and, or, but, for, nor, yet, so*) that join independent clauses.

Biff's initiation is sudden and devastating, but Chick develops more slowly.

3. Use commas between adjectives that, individually, modify the same noun.

Tabloids contain unreliable, titillating stories.

4. Use commas around parenthetical elements, or interrupters.

Huck, an outsider in his society, does not grow up. Scholarly journals, on the other hand, require the volume number and the year in parentheses.

5. Use commas after long introductory phrases or clauses.

Although this survey does not cover a large number of participants, some conclusions can be drawn.

6. Use commas around nonrestrictive phrases or clauses.

The painting, admired by the judges, received first prize. Walker's painting, hanging on the far wall, received first prize.

But: Do not use commas around restrictive elements.

The painting that won first prize has been sold.

Shaw's <u>Pygmalion</u> is the source for the musical <u>My Fair Lady</u>.

Other uses of commas—in dates, for example—and the placing of commas with quoted material and in bibliographic citations are explained in Chapter 3 or earlier in this chapter.

Colons and Semicolons

Colons and semicolons have different uses. Do not confuse them.

1. Use colons to introduce examples or explanations of what has been said.

The rules are simple: take drugs or break curfew and you are off the team.

2. Use colons to introduce quoted passages in display form or to introduce a list of items when preceded by such formal expressions as *the following* or *as follows*.

The steps in the experiment are as follows:

1. . . . . . (etc.)

3. Use semicolons to separate two independent clauses, two complete thoughts that could be separated by a period.

There is much compromise in growing up; Chick learns to compromise on some but not all.

4. Use semicolons in compound sentences if the clauses are long and contain commas within them.

Managing to "have its cake and eat it too," Time, on one level, is delivering news to the masses; but, on another level, it is serving up its own opinion for readers to digest.

Periods

1. Use periods to end complete sentences, endnotes, footnotes, bibliographic citations, and captions of figures (charts, maps, photographs, etc.).

2. Use periods between related numbers—for example, to separate act, scene, and line numbers for plays (3.2.6–8). Place periods outside the closing parenthesis, unless the statement within the parentheses is a complete sentence. Place periods within the closing quotation mark.

Exclamation Points

Rarely if ever use exclamation points in research essays. A clear, forceful statement is sufficient.

Hyphens

1. Use hyphens to form compound adjectives (*twentieth-century music*) and compound nouns (*anti-intellectual, know-how*). *Note:* Check a recent dictionary for the correct form of a compound noun: open (*fruit tree*), hyphenated (*ill-favored*), or closed (*notebook*).

2. Do not hyphenate words at the end of a line. Neither APA nor MLA approves of dividing words. Either leave the line short or use right justification so that words on the line are automatically spaced to create an even right margin. If you must divide a word between two lines, divide it between syllables and never leave only two letters on either one of the lines.

Dashes

A dash is formed by typing two hyphens without spacing. Use dashes—as illustrated here—to separate a shift in thought or parenthetical material. (Alternatives for parenthetical material include commas and parentheses.) Dashes are the most informal of the three possibilities.

Brackets

1. Use brackets around interpolations within quoted material.

"Ever since the 1830s, these diaries [fossil bones] have been telling the scientific community about dinosaurs' growth."

2. Use brackets around a phonetic transcript of a word.

Weltanschauung [velt´ än shou´ oong]

3. Use brackets as a sign of aggregation in mathematical equations:

$[(a + b - c) / (x - y)]$.

Do not confuse square brackets with parentheses.

Parentheses

1. Use parentheses to enclose added elements in a sentence.

```
Turning to the remaining types of social interaction
(with friends, strangers, children). . . .
```

2. Use parentheses to enclose series headings.

```
After controls, the following variables remain
significant: (1) age, (2) education. . . .
```

3. Use parentheses when first giving an abbreviation.

```
Studies of rapid eye movement (REM). . . .
```

4. Use parentheses with in-text citations.

```
During the 1920s, "not only the drinks were mixed, but
the company as well" (Allen 82).
```

PRESENTING NUMBERS

There are a few basic rules for presenting numbers in written works—and many exceptions and variations. To grasp the basic rules, keep in mind that the goals are clarity and consistency. Thus, when you are presenting many kinds of numbers, you may have to ignore one rule to maintain consistency throughout your paper. Also keep in mind that works written in the humanities will treat some numbers differently than texts in scientific and technological fields. You may find that you can solve a specific writing problem best by studying the examples given here for a model that corresponds to your particular use of numbers.

Words and Numerals

When deciding to write numbers as words or as numerals, you are choosing between *words* and *arabic numerals*. MLA style now requires the use of arabic numerals for chapter, section, and volume numbers of works; for act, scene, and line numbers in plays; for canto, stanza, and line numbers of poems. (The acceptable uses of Roman numerals are explained below.)

1. Use words for whole numbers under 10.

```
She began writing five years ago.
```

2. Write as figures (arabic numerals) numbers from 10 up. This rule applies to cardinal, ordinal, and percentage numbers.

There were `18` in the first and `26` in the second group.

He graduated `126th` (or `123rd`) in his class of `450`.

Tuition costs have increased `11` percent.

Variations: In discussions using numbers infrequently, the numbers may be expressed in words if they can be written in no more than two or three words. You can write:

```
fifteen hundred, eleven percent.
```

3. Use arabic numerals for partial numbers below 10.

```
8¹/₄    8.66    3.14
```

4. Regardless of its size, write out any number that begins a sentence.

```
Thirty-six percent of those interviewed responded with

a "yes" to question 1. (Note: Never use a symbol such

as "%" with a number written out.)
```

5. Express very large numbers by combining numerals and words.

```
4.5 billion years ago
```

6. Spell out round numbers (e.g., approximations) and numbers that are even hundred thousands.

```
Dinosaurs became extinct some sixty-five million years

ago.
```

```
The rally was attended by two hundred thousand fans.
```

7. Write as numerals numbers below 10 that appear in the same context as numbers from 10 up.

```
In 3 out of 15 case studies. . .
```

```
Compare lines 8, 25, and 56.
```

8. Use numerals with abbreviations and symbols.

```
65 mph      125 km     200 lb     5%
3" × 5"     70-80      6 P.M.     $2.50
```

9. *Scientific and technical usage.* Express physical quantities in numerals, regardless of size.

```
4 cubic feet      8 cubic centimeters
120 volts         60 miles
```

10.   Use the numeral "1" on your keyboard, not the lowercase "l" or the uppercase "L."

11.   Place commas between the third and fourth digits from the right, the sixth and seventh, and so on.

```
2,000   20,000   2,200,200
```

Exceptions: Commas are not used with page numbers, addresses, and years of four digits.

```
On page 3210. . .
```

```
8333 Little River Turnpike
```

```
The Norman Conquest of 1066. . . (But: 14,000BC)
```

Percentages, Mixed Numbers, and Money

1. Write percentages, mixed numbers, and decimal numbers as numerals.

```
20%   2¹/₂   3.14
```

2. Use an initial zero for decimal numbers less than 1.00.

```
0.6   0.617
```

Variations: (*a*) If the decimal fraction can never be 1.00 or greater, no zero is used:

$n = .32$ or $p < .08$.

(*b*) In some common decimal usage, such as batting averages, no zero is used.

```
He batted only .233 last year.
```

```
The murder weapon was a .38-caliber gun.
```

3. To write amounts of money, follow the rules for words and numerals.

```
Tickets cost five dollars each.
```

```
The fund-raiser netted $675.
```

```
The painting sold for $3.5 million.
```

(Combine figures and words for large numbers.)

4. Be consistent when writing amounts of money. If you use words for the amount, write out the unit of currency (five dollars). If you use a numeral, then use the appropriate symbol for the unit of currency ($675; 6¢). Do not use both symbol and word ($675 dollars). If some amounts are in dollars and cents, then use the decimal point and zeros for whole dollar amounts in the same context.

```
She sold the necklace for $49.50, the earrings for
$15.00.
```

Dates

1. Be consistent when writing dates. Use either the day-month-year pattern or the month-day-year pattern throughout. (*Note:* MLA style requires the day-month-year pattern with months abbreviated in the Works Cited.) Punctuate dates correctly, according to the following examples:

```
She was born on 5 May 1938. (No punctuation.)
```

```
She was born on May 5, 1938, and graduated in 1959.
```

(Commas before and after the year.)

```
Iraq invaded Kuwait in August 1990. (No punctuation.)
```

2. Write the year alone in figures: 1945.

3. Place BC **after the date,** AD **before the date.**

```
Octavian became the Emperor Augustus in 27 BC and ruled
until his death in AD 14.
```

4. Use words, without capitalization, for decades and centuries:

```
during the sixties, the twentieth century.
```

Variation: It is now acceptable to identify a decade in figures: the 1960s, the '60s.

5. Hyphenate centuries when they are used as adjectives.

```
sixteenth-century thought
```

```
twentieth-century music
```

Inclusive Numbers

1. Follow these rules for figures used to indicate a continuous sequence of numbers. Separate numbers by a hyphen.

From 1 through 99, write all digits: 4–16, 67–95

From 100 up, write only the last two digits of the second number, unless more are needed: 226–42, 695–720, 2003–07, 1863–912

2. Express inclusive numbers according to the following models:

the winter of 1990–91   BUT: from 1990 to 1992
the years 1914–1918   BUT: between 1914 and 1918
AD 312–37   BUT: AD 200–235
119–14 BC
43 BC – AD 17

Roman Numerals

1. **Use lowercase (i, iv) Roman numerals** to number the pages of a preface or introductory material or to cite pages that are so numbered.

2. **Use capital Roman numerals** for major divisions of an outline and for titles of persons (Henry VIII, Elizabeth I).

Equations

Write equations as simply as possible, preferably on one line rather than two whenever possible:

$$(x + y) \ / \ (3x - y) \qquad \text{NOT: } \frac{x + y}{3x - y}$$

Word processing software allows you to reproduce many mathematical symbols (such as Σ and ∞). If you cannot reproduce needed symbols on your keyboard, type as much of the equation as possible and fill in the rest in ink.

PRESENTING GRAPHICS

Although graphics (charts, graphs, maps, diagrams, photographs) are never a substitute for clear discussions, they are effective and efficient means for presenting statistical material or showing relationships and processes. When you plan to use one or more graphics in a paper, follow both the general guidelines and the specific instructions for the type of figure you use.

General Guidelines

1. Select the type of graphic best suited to illustrating the material you want to present.

2. Make a table or chart simple and clear. Use several, if necessary, rather than one that seeks to show too much information.

3. Prepare tables with the characters on any keyboard. Prepare other types of graphics either by using computer software or by working neatly by hand, in ink, using a ruler, compass or templates, as appropriate.

4. Place each graphic in your text as near as possible to your discussion of the material. *Exception:* If your project contains complex or numerous tables or other graphics, you may want to group them in an appendix. (When following MLA style, place an appendix between the end of the text and the Works Cited. See Chapter 7 for variations in other documentation styles.)

5. Number tables and other figures consecutively throughout the paper and label them appropriately: Table 1, Table 2, etc., or Figure 1, Figure 2, etc. Do not abbreviate Table. Figure may be abbreviated Fig.

6. Every table or figure needs (*a*) a number, (*b*) a caption that simply and clearly explains what the graphic shows, and (*c*) a reference to it in the text. *Always refer to the graphic before it appears in the paper and always refer to it by its label—either "Table" or "Figure" and its number, thus: "See Figure 3."* Do not write "the following Table" or "the Table below."

7. A graphic with its caption should be clear without textual discussion. Additionally, the textual discussion of the material should be clear without the table or figure. Do not repeat all of the information in a graphic, but explain the general points that the graphic illustrates. The following textual discussion and Figure 47, both from "Demographics Are Us, Revisited," by Jerry B. Reid (*Radiologic Technology* Mar./Apr. 1991), illustrate these guidelines.

> Of those employed full or part time, most are in hospital settings. (See Table 1.) The percentage employed by hospitals has decreased somewhat since 1972 for all three disciplines [radiography, nuclear medicine, and radiation therapy]. In 1972 it was 72 percent for radiography vs. 65 percent in 1990, 92 percent for nuclear medicine technology as opposed to 85 percent in 1990 and 89 percent for radiation therapy technology, which was 75 percent in 1990.

8. Place any explanatory notes below tables or figures. Introduce an explanation that refers to the entire table or figure with the word "Note" followed by a colon. Introduce an explanation of some specific element within the table or figure by using a superscript *letter* (not number) both after the specific element and before the note.

9. Tables and figures taken from sources must be documented. Introduce documentation with the label "Source" and a colon. Give author and page number, as for any in-text citation, and provide complete documentation in the Works Cited. When a table or figure is followed by both source information and explanatory notes, give the source information first.

Tables

Tables gather a series of related numbers together. They are the easiest figures to prepare because they can be typed as part of the text. Still, take time to align columns and space the material attractively. Prepare tables according to the following guidelines. Use Figures 47 and 48 as models.

Table 1
Employment Setting
(Active Part or Full-Time)

		RAD			NMT			RTT		
		Male	Female	Total	Male	Female	Total	Male	Female	Total
Hospital	1972	—	—	72%	—	—	92%	—	—	89%
	1990	80%	60%	65%	85%	86%	85%	76%	75%	75%
Clinic	1972	—	—	9%	—	—	4%	—	—	4%
	1990	7%	15%	13%	3%	4%	4%	9%	10%	10%
Private Office	1972	—	—	15%	—	—	1%	—	—	3%
	1990	6%	21%	17%	5%	7%	6%	8%	11%	11%
Educator	1972	—	—	—	—	—	—	—	—	—
	1990	2%	1%	1%	1%	1%	1%	2%	2%	2%
Other	1972	—	—	4%	—	—	3%	—	—	4%
	1990	5%	3%	3%	5%	2%	3%	4%	2%	2%

Note: Dash indicates data not available.

Figure 47 Illustration of Table That Is Discussed in Text.

Table 1
Incidences of Bias by Category

Bias Category	Positive Connotation	Negative Connotation
Contextual	9	3
Adjective	1	4
Attribution	4	3
Photographic	8	3
Opinion	21	9
Total	43	22

Note: Adverbial bias omitted for lack of occurrences.

Figure 48 Illustration of a Table with an Explanatory Note.

1. Place the label and caption *above* the table. The label comes first, typed flush with the left margin. Double space and then type the caption, again flush with the left margin. Capitalize the words of the caption according to the rules for titles (see page 155).

2. Use a line to separate the table caption and column headings. Use either a caption or a number for each column heading. Keep column headings brief; use two lines if necessary, as shown in Figure 48.

3. For tables with several parts, experiment with a combination of broken lines, solid lines, and double solid lines to aid visual presentation.

Bar Charts

Bar charts are relatively easy to prepare and to read by those not expert in statistics. They show quantitative relationships and highlight comparisons between two or more factors. Figure 49 gives an example. Follow these guidelines to prepare a bar chart.

1. Decide on the width of each bar on the basis of the number needed and whether the bars will be spaced or connected. (Note that in Figure 49 a combination of spacing and connection has been used. Spacing aids readability when a number of points of difference are shown.) Take time to create a balanced, neat visual.

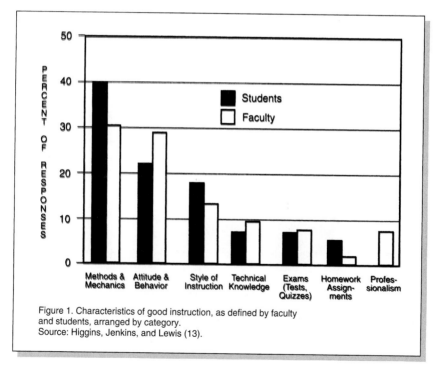

Figure 1. Characteristics of good instruction, as defined by faculty and students, arranged by category.
Source: Higgins, Jenkins, and Lewis (13).

Figure 49 Example of a Bar Chart.

2. Label each axis with numbers or captions. Keep captions (bar headings) brief; use two lines if necessary.

3. Place the label (e.g., Figure 1) and the caption *below* the bar chart. Place the label flush with the left margin. Put the caption either on the same line (as in Figure 49) or on a separate line and double space below the label. Captions for figures usually end in a period.

4. Bars can be shaded or patterned differently to highlight differences.

5. If shading or patterns are used, a legend will be needed. The legend can be placed within the lines framing the chart, as in Figure 49, or below the caption.

6. Frame your chart. The simplest method is to use the border icon on your PC's toolbar.

Pie Charts

A pie chart is a circle divided into segments. Each segment represents a portion of a whole. So, the segments must add up to a total of something—a group of people, an amount of money, and so on. A pie chart is a good visual for emphasizing differences in relationship to a whole. Prepare a pie chart according to these guidelines and use Figure 50 as your model.

1. Limit segments to no more than six. To accomplish this, combine small amounts into an "other" segment.

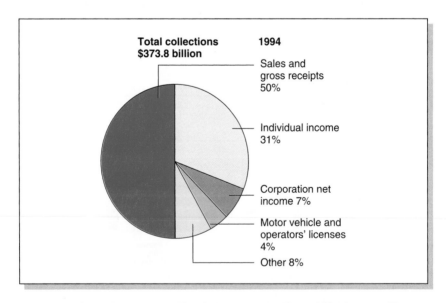

Figure 50 State Government Tax Collections, by Type: 1994 Source. Chart prepared by U.S. Bureau of the Census, Data from *Statistical Abstracts* 1997 (292).

2. Draw segments proportionally. If one segment represents 32 percent of the total "pie," then the segment at its widest part should be 32 percent of the circumference of the circle you have drawn.

3. Place the pie chart's label and caption *below* the chart.

4. Give each segment a label, written horizontally, not on an angle. Labels may be placed within segments if there is room. They may also be placed outside. Alternatively, the percentage numerals may be placed within the segments and the captions outside.

5. Segments may be shaded to emphasize differences. Computer software is available for producing smart-looking pie charts. If you are working by hand, keep your chart to black and white; do not use colored pencils.

Line Charts (Graphs)

Line charts, or graphs, are ideal for showing trends or changes over time or for showing a frequency distribution—a relationship of two variables, such as the number of participants per age group. Follow these guidelines when preparing a graph. (See Figure 51.)

1. Place the figure number and caption *below* the graph.

2. Label each axis.

3. If you are showing changes over time, put time periods on the horizontal axis. Then put the subject of the graph—such as numbers of people or dollar amounts—on the vertical axis.

4. If you are showing a frequency distribution, place the method of classification on the horizontal axis and the frequency on the vertical axis. Thus, if you wanted to show the distribution by age of the residents of a particular area, you would place age labels (0, 10, 20, etc.) on the horizontal axis and numbers of residents (0, 5,000, 10,000, etc.) on the vertical axis.

Flowcharts

Flowcharts show qualitative rather than quantitative relationships. They are good for showing a series of steps in a process or procedure, for indicating a sequence of events or ideas, for revealing causal relationships, and for instructing. Prepare flowcharts according to the following guidelines, using Figure 52 as a model.

1. Place the figure label and caption *below* the chart.

2. Select the shape—or shapes—to be used from a template. Prepare the chart with even spaces between shapes as much as possible. Connect all shapes with lines and arrows to show the pattern of movement through the steps or stages. Experiment with different shapes and flow patterns to find the most effective version.

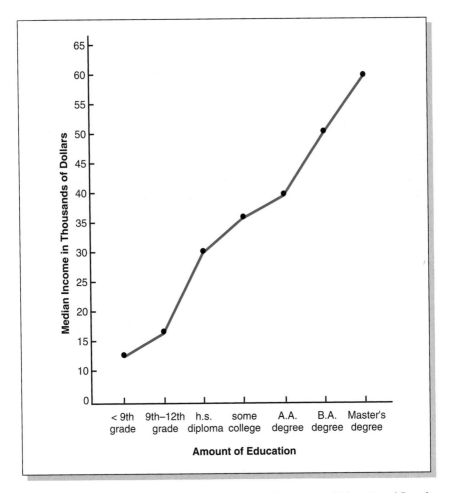

Figure 51 Median Income of Householders in Relation to Educational Level.
Source: *Statistical Abstracts*, Table 711 (462).
Note: Depicts households 25 years or older for 1994.

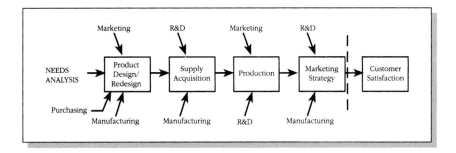

Figure 52 Customer Satisfaction Chain.
Source: Craven and Shipp. "Market Driven Strategies for Competitive
Advantage." *Business Horizons* Jan./Feb. 1991: 58.

3. Give each shape a label. The label is usually placed *within* the shape.

4. For simple flowcharts, arrange the shapes in a single horizontal or vertical line.

5. For complex patterns that involve "either/or" decision points or looping, use a combination of horizontal and vertical patterns of movement. Add "yes" and "no" terms above horizontal flow lines and beside vertical flow lines at the decision points.

6

WRITING
THE PAPER

As you near the end of your reading and note taking, and as you study Chapter 5 to become familiar with forms for presenting and documenting research, you may begin to worry about putting all your work together into a unified paper. You can ease your mind by remembering that the research process is not significantly different from the process of writing other essays. When selecting and focusing other writing topics, you search through the ideas, examples, and opinions you have on your topic. Then, as a due date approaches, you structure your ideas and material into a plan and write a first draft. This is the process you have been following with your research project, only you have searched through sources for material. If, throughout your study, you have continued to think about what your topic needs and how you can approach it, you have been developing and refining a plan all along. Now you need to settle on a final thesis and organization to guide your writing, and draft the paper.

ORGANIZING THE PAPER

To make decisions about your paper's organization, a good place to begin is with the identifying phrases at the top of your notes. They represent subsections of your topic that emerged as you studied sources and took notes. They will now help you organize your paper. Here are some guidelines for getting organized to write:

1. **Arrange notes by identifying phrases and read them through**. Read personal notes as well. Work all notes into one possible order as suggested by the identifying phrases and your preliminary outline. In reading through notes, you may discover that some now seem irrelevant. Set them aside, but do not throw them away yet. Some additional note taking may be necessary to fill in gaps that have become apparent. You know your sources well enough by now to be able to find the additional material you need.

2. **Reexamine your tentative thesis or research proposal and the preliminary outline that guided your research**. Consider: As a result of reading and reflection, do you need to alter or modify your thesis in any way? Or, if you began with a research question, what is the answer to the question? What, for example, was the impact of Prohibition on the 1920s? And, is Catherine Barkley a Hemingway hero? You need to decide.

3. **Decide on a final thesis**. To produce a unified and coherent essay with a clear central idea and a "reason for being," you need a thesis that meets the following criteria:

- *It is a complete sentence, not a topic or statement of purpose.*
  Topic: General Lee's strategy for the Battle of Chancellorsville.
  Thesis: General Lee's success at the Battle of Chancellorsville was the result of his skill as a military leader.
- *It is limited and focused.*

Unfocused: Prohibition affected the 1920s in many ways.

Focused: Prohibition was more acceptable to rural than urban areas because of differences in religious values, in patterns of socializing, in cultural backgrounds, and in the economic impact of prohibiting liquor sales.

- *It can be supported by your research.*

Unsupportable: Time magazine does not like George Bush.

Supportable: A study of *Time*'s coverage of President Bush during the 1990–91 winter months reveals a favorable bias during the Persian Gulf War but a negative bias after the war.

- *It establishes a new or interesting approach to the topic that makes your research worthwhile.*

Not inventive: A regional shopping mall should not be built adjacent to the Manassas Battlefield.

Inventive: Putting aside an appeal to our national heritage, one can say, simply, that the building of a regional shopping mall adjacent to the Manassas Battlefield has no economic justification.

4. **Write down the organization revealed by the way you have grouped notes and compare this organization with your preliminary plan**. If your newest outline adds, deletes, or reorders sections, justify those changes in your own mind. Consider: Does the new plan now provide a complete and logical development of your thesis? If, for example, your thesis asserts that there were *four* areas of Prohibition's effects on urban and rural America, then your organization must show that all *four* areas of impact will be examined for both urban and rural America. In short, you need eight sections for your plan in addition to an introduction and conclusion.

WRITING FORMAL OUTLINES

For many researchers, a clear thesis and a revised and expanded version of their preliminary outline are all they need as a guide to drafting their paper. Others benefit from preparing a detailed formal outline because they write better if they see the paper's complete and logical structure before beginning to write. If you decide to use a formal outline—or if your research assignment requires one—remember that you can change the outline as you write. If you are submitting the outline with your paper, make certain to revise it to correspond to any changes made while drafting or revising.

Conventional Outline Patterns

If you are preparing a formal outline, select one of the standard patterns and follow the conventions of logic and form. The most common pattern combines roman numerals, letters, and arabic numerals to show major sections and subdivisions of the paper. The outline takes this form:

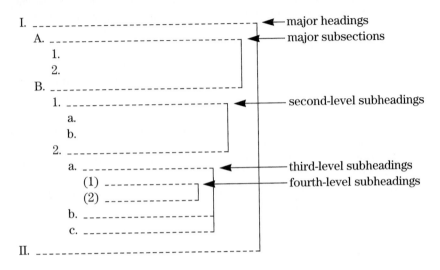

When typing the outline, align all headings and subheadings of equal weight by indenting those of the same weight the same number of spaces. (Begin major headings— the roman numerals—five spaces from the left margin.) Place a period after each letter or number, except for the fourth-level subheadings within parentheses. Allow two spaces after the period or parenthesis before typing words. Capitalize the first letter of the first word of each heading and subheading. Remember that each subdivision requires at least two parts: if there is a 1. under A., there must also be a 2. But any subsection may have more than two parts, and some subsections may not be divided at all.

An alternative pattern is the *decimal outline,* found with papers in business and the sciences. This pattern uses only numbers, with subsections indicated by adding onto the original section number:

1. _____
   1.1. _____
      1.1.1. _____
      1.1.2. _____
   1.2. _____
   1.3. _____
2. _____

Outline Styles

An outline's headings and subheadings can be written as *paragraphs*, *sentences*, or *topics*. You need to select one and then maintain that style throughout the outline. The paragraph outline is rarely used for relatively short papers. There is also a danger with the paragraph outline that you will write so much that the outline will begin to resemble the paper, yet, lacking specifics and documentation, it still isn't a real paper.

Some instructors encourage the use of the sentence outline as a strategy for eliminating headings that are too brief or vague to be helpful. If you are more used to writing topic outlines but are expected to produce a sentence outline, you can begin with topic headings and then expand them into complete sentences. This process, one that forces you to develop assertions about each section, can help clarify your thinking about the topic, not just about the ordering of its parts. One portion of the topic outline on pages 198–99 has been turned into sentences to illustrate the sentence outline:

Sentence Outline

II. Practical and economic issues demonstrate that building the shopping mall is a bad idea.
   A. An examination of existing shopping facilities shows that additional shopping facilities are not needed.
   B. The argument that the mall will bring new jobs to the area is unconvincing because the unemployment rate in the county is low and the income needed to live in the county is greater than could be obtained from clerking jobs.
   C. The increased county revenues from sales would be more than offset by the cost of providing and maintaining the new road system that would be needed to provide access to the proposed new mall.
   D. The increased traffic generated by another mall would create a level of congestion adversely affecting all retailers in the area.

The Topic Outline

The built-in advantages of the paragraph and sentence outlines—specific headings in parallel structure—must also be created in a topic outline for that outline to be helpful to you and to meet expected conventions of form. Here are guidelines for preparing useful and correct topic outlines.

Use Parallel Structure

When writing a topic outline, put headings of equal rank in parallel structure. That is, select a noun or noun phrase *(access to the media)*, a gerund phrase *(obtaining media access)*, or an infinitive phrase *(to obtain media access)*. Observe the lack of parallel structure in the following:

I. Steps in picking up a new sport
    A. Good equipment *(noun)*
    B. To take lessons *(infinitive)*
    C. Practicing *(gerund)*

Use Specific Headings

Vague headings put off the task of deciding what you want to say in each section of the paper, so make each heading concrete and content-filled to guide you through the paper. Avoid using "Introduction" and "Conclusion." They are useless labels, since every paper has to begin and end. In the sample topic outline below, one student, Tom Finley, uses "Background to the controversy" instead of "Introduction" and "Solutions to the controversy" instead of "Conclusion." Observe as well that Tom does not settle for "Background" only but develops the first section with several specific subheadings. Similarly, Tom lists specific solutions in the outline's final section.

Follow Conventions of Form

Since a topic outline does not contain complete sentences, do not place a period after each heading. Additionally, capitalize only the first word of each heading. Title the page "Outline"; place your thesis statement, labeled "Thesis," after the title; and double space throughout.

Sample Topic Outline

Outline

Thesis: The building of the William Center, a regional
        shopping mall adjacent to the Manassas
        Battlefield, cannot be justified on practical
        and economic grounds.

  I. Background of the controversy

      A. History of the shopping mall plan

      B. Explanation of the controversy

          1. Those favoring the mall

          2. Those opposing the mall

II. Practical and economic arguments against the mall

   A. Analysis of existing shopping facilities

   B. Analysis of "new jobs for the area" argument

   C. Cost of services in relation to new revenues

   D. Problems of traffic congestion

   E. County tax problems

III.Solutions to the controversy

   A. National park site

   B. Roads completed before mall

   C. Original office park plan

DRAFTING THE PAPER

Embrace your opportunity to draft your paper. You have been reading and writing and thinking about your topic for some time. Look forward, now, to putting all your new knowledge and ideas together in a format that can be shared with others.

Guidelines for the Drafting Process

Here are some strategies for getting started—and for getting through the drafting process successfully.

Give Yourself Enough Time

Good writing takes time and commitment to revision. Consider how much time you will need to complete an entire first draft. Working with notes and being careful about documentation make research paper writing more time-consuming than writing undocumented essays. A 10- or 12-page paper may take two or three afternoons or evenings to draft; a 20-page paper will obviously take longer. You should start writing, then, at least five days before your paper is due to allow time away from the draft before revising. You also need to calculate the time required to type and proofread the final version. If you have drafted on a word processor, preparing the final version will not be a lengthy process, because you will not retype the entire paper after revising and editing. If you are typing from a handwritten draft and are not a strong typist, allow 20 or 30 minutes a page. If you are paying someone to type your paper, you must schedule this service *in advance* and allow the typist from two days to a week to complete your paper. Do not sell short many weeks of research by trying to draft, revise, and complete a paper all in one day.

Prepare to Document as You Draft

Although you may believe that stopping to include parenthetical documentation as you write will cramp your writing, you really cannot wait until completing the draft to add the documentation. The risk of failing to document accurately is too great. Remember that parenthetical documentation is brief; take time to place in parentheses the author's name and relevant page number (or just the page number as appropriate) as you compose. Then, when your paper is finished and you are preparing your list of Works Cited, go through the paper carefully to make certain that there is a work listed for *every* parenthetical reference. Including documentation as you compose applies equally to writers using other forms of documentation. A parenthetical number is just as quickly placed in a draft as a parenthetical author and page reference. If you are using footnotes or endnotes, write out citations on a separate sheet of paper for each number you place in your draft. (Or, if composing on a word processor, follow directions for preparing footnotes. Once you master the procedure, footnote preparation at the keyboard is simple.)

Have All Material Within Reach

Whether working in your room or in a computer lab, you need to have all relevant materials at hand. Make sure that you have all notes and bibliography cards and your outline with you, as well as books and photocopied articles for checking the accuracy of direct quotations. If writing in longhand, you will also need paper, pencils, and a dictionary. If using one of the school's word processors, you will probably need to take your own formatted disk, and you may need to supply your own paper for a printer that processes single sheets. A few minutes spent collecting materials can save much time and considerable frustration.

Take Care of the Writer

Try, as much as possible, to provide the writer—you—with an environment conducive to the task of writing. Some writers can concentrate with background music; few can make much progress with a blaring stereo or television. An even greater challenge to concentration is conversation that you can hear but are not a part of. So, turn down the music and work when roommates are not around. Or plan to use the computer lab at times when it is not crowded (usually morning hours).

Remember that no paper needs to be written from top to bottom. If you have trouble getting started with the opening paragraph, move to the body of the essay. After you write several pages, a clever opening may occur to you. If you get stuck, take a short break: stretch, look out the window, get something to eat. Ten minutes of relaxation may be just what you need to get back in gear. After composing a few pages, and certainly after breaks, read over what you have written. This strategy will help you maintain a coherent style and inspire you to keep pressing forward.

Writing Style

Specific suggestions for composing the parts of your paper follow, but first here are some general guidelines for research paper style.

Use the Proper Person

Research papers are written primarily in the third person (*she, he, it, they*) to create objectivity and to direct attention to the content of the paper. You are not likely to use the second person (*you*) at all, for the second person occurs in instructions, in works such as texts that focus on what readers should understand or do. The usual question is over the appropriateness of the first person (*I, we*) in research essays. Do not try to skirt around the use of *I* if you need to distinguish your position from others you have presented. It is better to write "I" than "it is the opinion of this writer" or "the researcher learned" or "this project analyzed." On the other hand, avoid the qualifiers "I believe," "I feel," "I think." Just state your ideas.

Use the Proper Tense

When you are writing about people, ideas, or events of the past, the appropriate tense to use is the past tense. When writing about current times, the appropriate tense is the present. Both may occur in the same paragraph, as the following passage, from a student essay on computers, illustrates:

```
    Fifteen years ago "personal" computers were all

but unheard of. Computers were regarded as unknowable,

building-sized mechanized monsters that required a

precise 68-degree air-conditioned environment and

egghead technicians with thick glasses and white lab

coats scurrying about to keep the temperamental and

fragile egos of the electronic brains mollified.

Today's generation of computers is accessible,

affordable, commonplace, and much less mysterious. A

computer that used to require two rooms to house is

now smaller than a briefcase. A computer that cost
```

hundreds of thousands of dollars 15 years ago now has
a price tag in the hundreds. The astonishing progress
made in computer technology in the last few years has
made computers practical, attainable, and
indispensable. Personal computers are here to stay.

In the above example, when the student moves from computers in the past to computers in the present, he shifts tenses accurately.

When we write about sources, however, MLA convention requires the use of the present tense even for works or authors from the past. The idea is that the source, or the author, *continues* to make the point or use the technique into the present—every time there is a reader. Use of the *historical present tense* requires that you write "Lincoln selects the biblical expression 'Fourscore and seven years ago'" and "King echoes Lincoln when he writes 'five score years ago.'" Observe, in the following student paragraph, the use of the present tense, except in the first sentence, which refers to a past event.

Two weeks after the opening of <u>Death of a
Salesman</u>, Arthur Miller's essay "Tragedy and the
Common Man" was published in the <u>New York Times</u>. In
that reprinted piece, Miller stands in direct
contradiction to at least one premise of Aristotle's.
Miller writes that "the common man is as apt a subject
for tragedy in its highest sense as kings were" (143).
Miller reinterprets and updates the traditional
definition of tragedy when he describes "the tragic
right" as a "condition in which the human personality
is able to flower and realize itself" (145). Miller
concludes by challenging his contemporaries to
recognize that modern tragedy indeed exists in "the
heart and spirit of the average man" (147).

Use Vocabulary Appropriately

Although a research paper is more formal than a personal essay, it is still *your* writing, so it should sound like your writing. Avoid current slang expressions (*hang-up, okay, gross*) unless they are a part of your study, but do not seek unfamiliar, unnecessary five-dollar words or stilted sentence patterns on the mistaken notion that research papers are supposed to sound pompous.

On the other hand, as you explore a topic in a particular field, you need to learn the special terms of that field. As you read and took notes, you should have studied definitions of terms to make certain that you would be able to use them correctly in your paper. In a literary analysis, for example, you may need to discriminate among such terms as *image, metaphor,* and *symbol.* In his review of the literature on dinosaur warm-bloodedness, Aaron Kingsley must understand the difference between endothermic and ectothermic and write about respiratory turbinates. In many research projects, part of your task is to clarify, refine, or illustrate the meaning of a specialized concept such as *identity formation* in psychology or *surrealism* in art. The surest way to convince an instructor that you are only copying from sources but have not really learned about your topic is to string together key terms incorrectly.

Writing Good Beginnings

General guidelines for effective introductions apply to research papers as well. The best introduction is one that presents your subject in an interesting way to gain the reader's attention, states your thesis, and gives the reader an indication of the scope and limits of your paper. In a short research essay, you may be able to combine an attention-getter, a statement of subject, and a thesis in one paragraph. In longer papers, the introduction may expand to two or three paragraphs. In the physical and social sciences, the thesis may be withheld until the conclusion, but the opening introduces the subject and presents the researcher's hypothesis, often posed as a question. Since students sometimes have trouble with research-paper introductions in spite of knowing these general guidelines, several specific approaches are explained and illustrated in the following pages.

Present an Example or Anecdote

Begin with a brief example or anecdote to dramatize your topic. One student introduced her study of the nightly news with this attention-getter:

> When I watched television in the first weeks
>
> after moving to the United States, I was delighted by
>
> the relaxing display of the news programs. It was
>
> different from what I was used to on German
>
> television, where one finds a stern-looking man
>
> reading the news without any emotion. Here the

commentators laugh or show distress; their tone with each other is amiable. Watching the news in this country was a new and entertaining experience for me initially, but as my reading skills improved, I found that I preferred reading newspapers to watching television news. Then, reading Neil Postman's attack on television news shows in "Television News Narcosis" reminded me of my early experience with American TV and led me to investigate the major networks' presentation of the news.

In her second paragraph, the student completed her introduction by explaining the procedures she used for analyzing network news programs.

Relate to the Known

In the opening of her study of car advertisements, a student reminds readers of the culture's concern with image:

Many Americans are highly image conscious. Because the "right" look is essential to a prosperous life, no detail is too small to overlook. Clichés about first impressions remind us that "you never get a second chance to make a first impression," so we obsessively watch our weight, firm our muscles, sculpt our hair, find the perfect house, and buy our automobiles. Realizing the importance of image, companies compete to make the "right" products that will help us complete the "right" image. Then advertisers direct specific products to targeted groups of consumers. Although targeting may be labeled as stereotyping, it has been an effective strategy in advertising.

Challenge a Popular Attitude

Challenging a popular attitude or assumption is an effective attention-getting opening. For a paper on the advantages of solar energy, a student began:

> America's energy problems are serious, despite the popular belief that difficulties vanished with the end of the Arab oil embargo in 1974. Our problems remain because the world's supply of fossil fuels is not limitless.

Define Key Terms

Terms and concepts central to your project need defining early in your paper, especially if they are challenged or qualified in some way by your study. The following opening paragraph shows an effective use of definition:

> William Faulkner braids a universal theme, the theme of initiation, into the fiber of his novel Intruder in the Dust. From ancient times to the present, a prominent focus of literature has been a rite of passage, particularly that of childhood to adulthood. Joseph Campbell defines rites of passage as "distinguished by formal, and usually very severe, exercises of severance." A "candidate" for initiation into adult society, Campbell explains, experiences a shearing away of the "attitudes, attachments and life patterns" of childhood (9). This severe, painful stripping away of the child and emergence of the adult is central to Intruder in the Dust.

Provide Background

You can effectively begin by giving readers background information needed to clarify your later discussion of the topic. A student arguing against building a shopping mall next to the Manassas Battlefield began with the following brief history of the controversy:

The developer, Hazel-Peterson, said he wanted to
build a low-rise, campus-styled office park in rapidly
growing Prince William County. So the County Board of
Supervisors approved the rezoning of a 542-acre site
located adjacent to Manassas Battlefield Park to a
Planned Mixed-Use Development designation (PMD). Under
PMD zoning, the developer is not limited to the
original plan but can build just about anything. More
than a year after the zoning change, Hazel-Peterson
had a change of heart—or financial advice—and decided
that it really wanted to build a 1.2 million square
foot regional mall at the site. Not surprisingly, a
controversy has erupted over the use of these 542
acres next to the Manassas Battlefield.

Review the Literature

A review of relevant literature on a topic is essential to the report of research
in the sciences and social sciences. This review, part of the paper's introduction, does not usually appear in the opening paragraph. In shorter papers, and
in research essays in other fields, a brief review of the literature can be an
opening-paragraph strategy, as illustrated in the following:

Since opening on Broadway on February 10, 1949,
Arthur Miller's <u>Death of a Salesman</u> has been one of
the world's most discussed plays. Every fact of each
production, every nuance of dialogue, every opinion of
the author has been put under the critic's microscope.
In this immense body of words, the dominating question
emerges: Is <u>Death of a Salesman</u> a tragedy?
Commentators have drawn parallels between this play
and some of the classical tragedies of ancient Greece
and Elizabethan England (Fuller 243; Bierman et al.
265). Arthur Miller himself has written in defense of

his play as a tragedy (143-47). Others have disputed

his claim, citing the work of Aristotle (Clark 222;

Hynes 284). To resolve the conflict, we need first to

examine both Aristotle's and Miller's definitions of

tragedy and then see how they allow us to understand

and define the play itself.

Present Facts

Beginning with important, perhaps startling, facts, evidence, or statistics is an effective way to introduce a topic, provided the details are relevant to the topic. Observe the following example:

Teenagers are working again, but not on their

homework. Over 40 percent of teenagers have jobs by

the time they are juniors (Samuelson A22). And their

jobs do not support academic learning since almost

two-thirds of teenagers are employed in sales and

service jobs that involve mostly carrying, cleaning,

and wrapping (Greenberger and Steinberg 62-67), not

reading, writing, and computing. Unfortunately, the

negative effect on learning is not offset by improved

opportunities for future careers.

State and Expand the Thesis

Some topics do not lend themselves to arresting beginnings, and some writers get blocked trying to devise clever openings. Remember that presenting a clear statement of the paper's thesis, developed in several sentences, is always one appropriate way to get started. In a research essay on campus rape, one student began this way:

Rape, a criminal offense bordering on the

obstruction of civil rights, can be found on many

college campuses across the country. However, many

students do not realize the extent to which rape

occurs, even on their own campus. It is important to

```
recognize that rape on the college campus is a serious
problem, but that steps can be taken to reduce, if not
entirely eliminate, this problem.
```

Avoiding Ineffective Openings

Follow these guidelines for avoiding openings that most readers find ineffective or annoying.

1. **Do not restate the title** or write as if the title were the first sentence in paragraph 1. First, the title of the paper appears at the top of the first page of text. Second, it is a convention of writing to have the first paragraph stand independent of the title.

2. **Do not begin with "clever" visuals** such as artwork or fancy lettering.

3. **Do not begin with humor** unless it is part of your topic.

4. **Do not begin with a question that is just a gimmick, or one that a reader may answer in a way you do not intend**. Asking "What are the advantages of solar energy?" may lead a reader to answer "None that I can think of." A straightforward question ("Is *Death of a Salesman* a tragedy?") is appropriate.

5. **Do not open with an unnecessary definition quoted from a dictionary**. "According to Webster, solar energy means. . ." is a tired, overworked beginning that does not engage readers.

6. **Do not start with a purpose statement**. "This paper will examine. . ." Although a statement of purpose is a necessary part of a report of empirical research, such a report should open not with an immediate purpose statement but rather with some interesting introduction to the research subject.

Composing Main Paragraphs

As you write the body paragraphs of your paper, keep in mind that you want to meet three goals:

- maintain unity and coherence
- guide readers clearly through source material
- synthesize source material and your own ideas.

These are three demanding writing goals that take planning and practice on your part. Do not settle for paragraphs in which facts from note cards are just loosely run together. Review the following discussion and study the examples to see how to present what you have learned and want others to understand.

Provide Unity and Coherence

Paragraph unity is achieved when every sentence in a paragraph relates to and develops the paragraph's main idea or topic sentence. If you have a logical organization, composing unified paragraphs is not a great problem. Unity, however, does not automatically produce coherence; that takes attention to wording. Coherence is achieved when readers can follow the connection between one sentence and another and between each sentence and the topic sentence. Strategies for achieving coherence include repetition of key words, the use of pronouns that clearly refer to those key words, and the use of transition and connecting words. Observe these strategies at work in the following paragraph.

Perhaps the most important differences between the initiations of Robin and Biff and that experienced by Chick are the facts that Chick's epiphany does not come all at once and it does not devastate him. Chick learns about adulthood—and enters adulthood—piecemeal and with support. His first eye-opening experience occurs as he tries to pay Lucas for dinner and is rebuffed (15–16). Chick learns, after trying again to buy a clear conscience, the impropriety and affront of his actions (24). Lucas teaches Chick how he should resolve his dilemma by setting him "free" (26–27). As in most lives, Chick's passage into adulthood is a gradual process; he learns a little bit at a time and has support in his growing. Gavin is there for him, to act as a sounding board. Chick's initiation is consistent with Joseph Campbell's explanation: "all rites of passage are intended to touch not only the candidate, but also every member of his circle" (9). Perhaps Gavin is affected the most, but Chick's mother and father, and Lucas as well, are influenced by the change in Chick.

Coherence is needed not only within paragraphs but between paragraphs. Submitting an outline does not eliminate your responsibility to guide readers through your paper, connecting paragraphs and showing relationships by the use of transitions. Sometimes writers purposely avoid transition words because the words seem awkward, as indeed they can be if writers choose "My first point is. . ." "My second point is. . . ," and so on. But transitions can be smooth and still signal shifts in the paper's subtopics from one paragraph to another. The following opening sentences of four paragraphs from a paper on solutions to rape on the college campus illustrate smooth transitions:

¶3   Specialists have provided a number of reasons why men rape.

¶4   Some of the causes of rape on the college campus originate with the colleges themselves and with how they handle the problem.

¶5   Just as there are a number of reasons for campus rapes, there are also a number of ways to help solve the problem of these rapes.

¶6   If these seem like common-sense solutions, why, then, is it so difficult to significantly reduce the number of college campus rapes?

Without awkwardly writing "Here are some of the causes" and "Here are some of the solutions," the student guides her readers through a discussion of causes for and solutions to the problem of campus rape.

Guide Readers Through Source Material

To understand the importance of guiding readers through source material, first consider the following paragraph from a paper on the British coal strike in the 1970s:

The social status of the coal miners was far from good. The country blamed them for the dimmed lights and the three-day work week. They had been placed in the position of social outcasts and were beginning to "consider themselves another country." Some businesses and shops had even gone so far as to refuse service to coal miners (Jones 32).

Who has learned that the coal miners felt ostracized or that the country blamed them? As readers we cannot begin to judge the validity of these assertions without some context provided by the writer. Most readers are put off by an unattached direct quotation or some startling observation that is given no context within the paper.

> ✓ Use introductory tags to identify author and, when useful, the author's credentials, as a way to guide readers through source material. Vary both the words and their place in your sentences when using introductory tags.

The following revision of the student paragraph above provides both context and sentence variety:

```
The social acceptance of coal miners, according
to Peter Jones, British correspondent for Newsweek,
was far from good. From interviews both in London
shops and in pubs near Birmingham, Jones concluded
that Britishers blamed the miners for the dimmed
lights and three-day workweek. Several striking
miners, in a pub on the outskirts of Birmingham,
asserted that some of their friends had been denied
service by shopkeepers and that they "consider[ed]
themselves another country" (32).
```

Look again at the first sentence in the above paragraph. The tag is placed in the middle of the sentence, set off by commas. The sentence could have been written two other ways:

```
The social acceptance of coal miners was far from
good, according to Peter Jones, British correspondent
for Newsweek.
```

OR

```
According to Peter Jones, British correspondent for
Newsweek, the social acceptance of coal miners was far
from good.
```

Whenever you use a tag, you have these three sentence patterns from which to choose. Make a point to use all three options in your paper. Word choice can be varied as well. Instead of writing "According to Peter Jones" throughout your paper, consider some of the many options you have:

Jones *asserts*	Jones *contends*	Jones *attests to*
Jones *states*	Jones *thinks*	Jones *points out*
Jones *concludes*	Jones *stresses*	Jones *believes*
Jones *presents*	Jones *emphasizes*	Jones *agrees with*
Jones *argues*	Jones *confirms*	Jones *speculates*

Note: Not all words in this list are synonyms; you cannot substitute any one word for another in the list. *Confirms* is not the same as *believes*. On the other hand, *stresses* can be used instead of *emphasizes*. First, select the term that accurately states the writer's relationship to his or her material. Then, when appropriate, vary word choice as well as sentence structure.

Readers need to be told how they are to respond to the sources you use in your paper. They need to know which you accept as reliable and which you disagree with, and they need you to distinguish between fact and opinion. Ideas and opinions from sources need introductory tags and then some discussion from you.

Synthesize Source Material and Your Own Ideas

A smooth synthesis of source material is aided by an introductory tag and parenthetical documentation because these mark the beginning and ending of material taken from a source. But, a complete synthesis requires something more: your ideas about the source and the topic. To illustrate, let's look at another problem paragraph from the British-coal-strike paper:

```
    Some critics believed that there was enough coal

in Britain to maintain enough power to keep industry

at a near-normal level for 35 weeks (Jones 30). Prime

Minister Heath, on the other hand, had placed the

country's usable coal supply at 15.5 million tons

(Jones 30). He stated that this would have fallen to a

critical 7 million tons within a month had he not

declared a three-day work week (Jones 31).
```

This paragraph is a good example of random details strung together for no apparent purpose. How much coal did exist? Whose figures were right? And what purpose do these figures serve in the paper's development? Note that the entire paragraph is developed from one source. Do sources other than Jones offer a different perspective? This paragraph is weak for several reasons:

- it lacks a controlling idea (topic sentence) to give it purpose and direction
- it relies for development entirely on one source
- it lacks any discussion or analysis by the writer.

By contrast, the following paragraph, taken from a review-of-the-literature paper on dinosaur extinction, demonstrates a successful synthesis:

> Of course, the iridium could have come from other extraterrestrial sources besides an asteroid. One theory, put forward by Dale Russell, is that the iridium was produced outside the solar system by an exploding star (500). The theory of a nearby star exploding in a supernova is by far the most fanciful extraterrestrial theory; however, it warrants examination because of its ability to explain the widespread extinctions of the late Cretaceous Period (Colbert 205). Such an explosion, Russell states, could have blown the iridium either off the surface of the moon or directly from the star itself (500-01), while also producing a deadly blast of heat and gamma rays (Krishtalka 19). Even though this theory seems to explain the traces of iridium in the mass extinction, it does not explain why smaller mammals, crocodiles, and birds survived (Wilford 220). As Edwin Colbert explains, the extinctions of the late Cretaceous, although massive, were selective (205). So the supernova theory took a backseat to other extraterrestrial theories.

This paragraph's synthesis is accomplished by several strategies:

- the paragraph has a controlling idea
- the paragraph combines information from several sources
- information from different sources is clearly indicated to readers
- the student explains and discusses the information.

To sum up, good body paragraphs need (1) a controlling idea, (2) in most cases information from more than one source, (3) analysis and discussion from the student writer.

Writing Good Conclusions

Sometimes ending a paper seems even more difficult than beginning one. You know you are not supposed to just stop, but every ending that comes to mind sounds more corny than clever. Perhaps you are trying too hard for a "catchy" ending that may not even be appropriate. If you have trouble, try one of the following types of endings.

Restate and Extend the Thesis

Do not repeat your thesis as it was stated in your introduction, but expand on the original wording and emphasize the thesis's significance. Here is the conclusion of the solar energy paper:

> The idea of using solar energy is not as far-fetched as it seemed years ago. With the continued support of government plus the enthusiasm of research groups, environmentalists, and private industry, solar energy may become a household word quite soon. With the increasing cost of fossil fuel, the time could not be better for exploring this use of the sun.

Close with a Quotation

End with a quotation that effectively summarizes and drives home the point of your paper. Researchers are not always lucky enough to find the ideal quotation for ending a paper. If you find a good one, use it. Better yet, present the quotation and then add your comment in a sentence or two. The conclusion to a paper on the dilemma of defective newborns is a good example:

> Dr. Joseph Fletcher is correct when he says that "every advance in medical capabilities is an increase in our moral responsibility" (48). In a world of many gray areas, one point is clear. From an ethical point of view, medicine is a victim of its own success.

Present Discussion or Suggestions for Further Study

Conclusions of empirical reports will contain a discussion of the new data or the results of the experiment. This discussion can go beyond an explanation of the result's significance to suggest further research. In a review of the literature on a given issue, the paper can also conclude with suggestions for further study. In a paper that examined the empirical work conducted in infants' preference for infant-directed speech, the student ended with guidelines for further research. (Note that documentation is not in MLA style but in APA style—appropriate for a paper in the social sciences.)

Possibly the most important area of study to focus on is how we can use infants' auditory preferences to understand later language learning. For example, do the specific features of motherese help infants gain knowledge of segmentation of speech? Studies should determine whether infants benefit from features such as exaggerated use of pitch contouring and differential stress. Although some research has sought to examine this issue, more work needs to be done. Also, future research may look at how auditory preferences change ontogenetically, and how they may relate to other aspects of development (Cooper & Aslin, 1989).

Present Solutions

If you have researched a current problem, you can present your solutions to the problem in a final paragraph. The student opposing a mall adjacent to the Manassas Battlefield concluded with several solutions:

Whether the proposed mall will be built is clearly in doubt at the moment. What are the solutions to this controversy? One approach is, of course, not to build the mall at all. To accomplish this solution, now, with the rezoning having been approved, probably requires an act of Congress to buy the land and make it part of the National Park. Another solution, one that would please the County and the developer and satisfy citizens objecting to traffic problems, is to build the needed roads before the mall is completed. A third approach is to allow the office park of the original plan to be built, but not the mall. The local preservationists had agreed to this original development proposal, but now that the issue has received national attention, they may no longer be willing to compromise. Whatever the future of the William Center, the present plan for a new regional mall is not acceptable.

Avoiding Ineffective Conclusions

Follow these guidelines to avoid conclusions that most readers consider ineffective and annoying.

1. **Do not introduce a new idea**. If the point belongs in your paper, you should have introduced it earlier.

2. **Do not just stop or trail off**, even if you feel as though you have run out of steam. A simple, clear restatement of the thesis is better than no conclusion.

3. **Do not tell your reader what you have accomplished**: "In this paper I have explained the advantages of solar energy by examining the costs. . . ." If you have written well, your reader knows what you have accomplished.

4. **Do not offer apologies or expressions of hope**. "Although I wasn't able to find as much on this topic as I wanted, I have tried to explain the advantages of solar energy, and I hope that you will now understand why we need to use it more" is a disastrous ending.

5. **Do not end with a vague or confusing one- or two-sentence summary of complex ideas**. The following sentences make little sense: "These authors have similar and different attitudes and ideals concerning American desires. Faulkner writes with the concerns of man towards man whereas most of the other writers are more concerned with man towards money."

Choosing a Title

You should give some thought to your paper's title. It is what your reader sees first and how your work will be known. A good title provides information and creates interest. Make your title informative by making it specific. If you can create interest through clever wording, so much the better. But do not confuse "cutesiness" with clever wording. Better to be just straightforward than to demean a serious effort with a "cutesy" title. Study the guidelines in Chapter 5 for presenting titles of works to make certain that capitalization is correct. Review the following examples of acceptable and unacceptable titles.

Vague: A Perennial Issue Unsolved (There are many. Which one is this paper about?)

Better: The Perennial Issue of Press Freedom versus Press Responsibility

Too Broad: Earthquakes (What about earthquakes? This title is not informative.)

Better: The Need for Earthquake Prediction

Too Broad: The Scarlet Letter (Never use just the title of the work under discussion. You can use the work's title as a part of a longer title of your own.)

Better: Color Symbolism in The Scarlet Letter

Cutesy: Babes in Trouble (The slang "Babes" makes this title seem insensitive rather than clever.)

Better: The Dilemma of Defective Newborns

REVISING THE PAPER

After completing a first draft, catch your breath, pat yourself on the back, and then gear up for the next—and equally important—step in the writing process: revision. Revision actually involves three activities that can best be approached as three separate steps. *Revising*, step 1, means *rewriting*: actually adding text, deleting text, or moving parts of the draft around. Next comes *editing*, a rereading to correct errors from misspellings to awkward sentences. Finally, you need to *proofread* the typed copy. Trying to combine the first two steps often leads to incomplete revision. Ignoring the third step can lead to a lower grade than the research and writing deserve because easily corrected mistakes are overlooked.

Rewriting

If you have composed your first draft at a word processor, print a hard copy that is double- or triple-spaced so that you have room for revision. When composing a handwritten draft, skip lines or leave wide margins so that there is room for revision. Read your draft through and make changes—adding, deleting, moving parts around—as a result of answering the following questions:

Purpose and Audience

1. Is my draft long enough to fulfill assignment requirements and my purpose?
2. Are terms defined and concepts explained appropriately for my audience?

Content

1. Do I have a clearly stated thesis?
2. Have I presented sufficient evidence to support my thesis?
3. Are there any irrelevant sections that should be deleted?

Structure

1. Are paragraphs ordered to develop the topic logically?
2. Does the content of each paragraph help develop the thesis?
3. Is everything in each paragraph on the same subtopic to create paragraph unity?
4. Do body paragraphs have a balance of information and analysis, of source material and my own ideas?
5. Are there any paragraphs that should be combined? Are there any very long paragraphs that should be divided? (Length alone is not a reason to divide; check long paragraphs for unity.)

These questions guide your revision of the large elements of the paper. Clearly, if your draft is too short to meet requirements, you have a problem to solve before turning to issues of style or grammar. If you are facing too short a paper, examine your outline and note cards again to see if you have overlooked material you had intended to include. Then, with the questions on structure as your guide, examine each body paragraph for incomplete development. Consider: Are you assuming that the reader has information or understanding that it is really your task to provide?

Make any large-scale revisions involving length, content, organization, and paragraphing first. If you composed at a computer, you know how to add, delete, and move parts around. If your draft is handwritten, add above the line and in the margin, marking each place to add material with a caret (^). You can circle an entire paragraph and draw an arrow to mark its new placement, or cut the paragraph out and tape it to a new sheet that you place in front of the page to which the paragraph will be added. With handwritten drafts, be especially careful to make changes that can be read.

After rewriting, read the entire draft through again to assess length, content, order, and paragraph unity. Complete this first step of revision by judging your draft according to the following questions:

Coherence

1. Have connecting words been used and key terms repeated to produce paragraph coherence?
2. Have transitions been used to show connections between paragraphs?

Sources

1. Have I paraphrased instead of quoted whenever possible?
2. Have I avoided long quotations?
3. Have I used introductory tags to create a context for source material?
4. Have I used verbs in introductory tags that accurately represent the author's relationship to the material?
5. Have I documented *all* borrowed material, whether quoted or paraphrased?
6. Are parenthetical references properly placed after borrowed material? (See Chapter 5.)

After making the additional revisions generated by the above questions, you will be ready for the editing step. If you have been working with a handwritten draft, this is the time to type your paper into a word processor so that you can take advantage of its editing features. If you are going to turn over a handwritten paper to a typist, you may want to make a fresh copy at this point, especially if you have already made extensive changes. Remember that further changes are likely when you edit.

Editing

Although you may have corrected various errors and stylistic weaknesses as you made major revisions to the first draft, you are wise to examine the now completed second draft for specific "smaller" kinds of problems. Students often say that they would be happy to edit their papers if they only knew what to look for. Their point is well taken. What often passes for editing is a review of content primarily, what you have just done to revise your first draft. Here are five specific elements of writing that you should go over, one by one, to perform a thorough editing of your paper.

Tone

Read your second draft through to asses the paper's tone. Have you avoided humor or sarcasm, except as a part of your subject? Have you avoided condescending to or ridiculing readers? ("As everybody understands, surrealism refers to" is the kind of expression that needs deleting.) Do you maintain the appropriate level of seriousness throughout? (Do not be flip; do not complain about difficulties finding sources.)

Sentence Style

Examine your draft *sentence by sentence*, testing your sentences against the following questions:

1. Are the sentences grammatically complete, except for those fragments purposely used for emphasis? Look specifically for any beginnings with words such as *because* and *although*. These words introduce dependent clauses, which must be attached to an independent clause to make a complete sentence.

2. Are there instances of wordiness, clichés, trite expressions, or inflated phrases that can be eliminated? Go over your writing for phrases such as the following, and observe simpler alternatives that can be substituted.

Wordy, Trite, Inflated	*Revision*
very unique	unique
the study tends to suggest	the study suggests
in this day and age	today, now, currently
conduct an examination of	examine
at the present time	now
fewer in number	fewer
of great importance	important
in today's modern society	today

3. Do you need to increase sentence variety? Consider varying both length and structure. Begin some sentences with dependent clauses or phrases to avoid having most start with subject and verb.

4. Most important, do sentences present ideas clearly, and with precision? Look specially at uses of *this* and *which*. Do not use *this* to refer vaguely to a complex idea in the preceding sentence, and avoid attaching a *which* clause, as a vague comment, on the end of a complex statement. For example:

```
Huck never becomes an adult citizen of society despite

the broad experience he has in that society, which is

why he differs from Chick.
```

What does the *which* clause modify? You probably need two sentences:

```
Huck never becomes an adult citizen of society despite
the broad experience he has in that society. His lack
of growth sets him in contrast to Chick.
```

Discriminatory Language

Edit to eliminate all discriminatory language—language that stereotypes people by race, sex, nationality, religion, age, or handicap. Most people recognize ethnic or racial slurs and would not write such statements, but sometimes attitudes about young, old, or handicapped people can slip unnoticed into writing, and of course sexist writing is a particular problem because English lacks a neuter pronoun to refer to people. Remember that it is unacceptable to use *he* to refer to a noun that could be male or female. Here are some ways around the problem of sexist writing.

- Use "people," "humans," or "human beings" instead of "man."
- Use "spouse" or "family" instead of "wife," or use "families," as appropriate.

  Sexist: "The pioneer and his wife opened up the West."

  Nonsexist: "Pioneer families opened up the West."

- Use nonsexist terms for types of workers. Instead of "manpower" use "workers," "staff," or "personnel." Instead of "policeman" use "police officer"; instead of housewife" use "homemaker."
- Eliminate "he" or "his" to refer to a noun that could be either male or female by pluralizing the noun and then using the plural pronoun "they" or "their." Alternatively, recast the sentence to avoid the use of a pronoun. "He or she" can be used sparingly, but not more than once in a sentence.

  Sexist: "A good manager has learned how to motivate *his* employees."

  Nonsexist: "A good manager has learned how to motivate employees."

Word Choice

Examine your word choice and edit as necessary according to your answers to these questions:

1. Are specialized terms used correctly?
2. Have I avoided an excessive use of specialized terms and selected instead, where possible, simpler words?
3. Have I used, as much a possible, specific, concrete words instead of general, abstract words? Look for too much reliance on such words as *thing*, *factor*, or *aspect*.

4. Have I used correctly those troublesome words called homonyms: *there, their, they're; you're, your; where, wear; its, it's; affect, effect; aloud, allowed;* and so on?

5. Have I avoided contractions as too informal for research essays?

Punctuation

Finally, review the guidelines in Chapter 5 for punctuation usage and for all other technical issues such as presenting titles or quotations or numerals.

Proofreading

When your editing is completed, prepare a completed draft of your paper according to the format described and illustrated below. Try to print your final copy on a laser printer so that it looks good and is easily read. If you are preparing your paper on a typewriter, work with a new ribbon. Always use quality paper. Then proofread the final copy carefully, making necessary corrections neatly in ink. If a page has several errors, print a corrected page or retype the page. It is especially important that you carefully proof a paper typed by someone else. Remember: You are responsible for the work you hand in, and you will be receiving the grade, not the typist.

PREPARING THE COMPLETE PAPER (IN MLA STYLE)

Your paper may contain some or all of the following parts, in the order given, depending on requirements. All papers will contain parts 4 and 7. Adhere to the guidelines for each part included in your paper. (Double-space all parts of your paper.)

1. A title page, with your title, your name, the course name or number, your instructor's name, and the date—all centered. Place each item on a separate line and double space between lines. Do *not* underline your title or put it in quotation marks, but handle any title(s) within your title correctly (see Chapter 5). If your paper does not contain either an outline or an abstract, you may omit a separate title page. With this pattern, place your name, the name of the course, and the date on the first page of text, in the upper left corner, before the paper's title. Center the title on the page and double space all these elements. (See page 224 for an example.)

2. An outline if required. If the outline is more than one page, number the pages with small roman numerals (i. ii. iii).

3. An abstract, if required. The abstract, a summary of your paper in about 100 words, can be placed below the title on page 1 of your text, but more often it is placed on a separate page after the title page (and after the outline, if there is one) but before the first page of text. Title the page "Abstract." (See page 260 for a sample.)

4. The body, or text, of your paper. Begin the first page of text with the title of the paper centered 1 inch from the top. If you have not used a separate title page, center the title after the identifying information in the upper left corner of the page. Number all pages consecutively, placing the numeral "1" on the first page in the upper right corner of the page. A running head may be used with the page number. MLA style calls for the author's last name if a running head is used (see page 224). APA style calls for a short title (see page 259).

5. Content endnotes if used. Content notes can be presented as footnotes on appropriate pages of text, or they can be grouped as endnotes on one or more pages following the end of the text. Title the page "Notes," continue to number pages consecutively, and double-space throughout. Indent the first line of each note five spaces and begin each note with a raised (superscript) numeral that corresponds to the numeral placed within the text. (See page 159 for a discussion of content notes.)

6. An appendix if needed. Use an appendix for a number of visuals, lengthy tables of statistics or mathematical proofs, or detailed results of questionnaires that support a discussion within the text. Do not have a separate appendix for a few tables or charts that can easily be placed within the text of the paper. If you use an appendix, title a new page "Appendix" and continue to number pages consecutively and double-space throughout. If you have more than one appendix, title them "Appendix A," "Appendix B," and so on.

7. Your Works Cited list. Begin a new page titled "Works Cited" and continue to number consecutively and to double-space. See Chapter 3 (or Chapter 7) for citation formats and pages 231 and 245 for sample Works Cited pages.

SAMPLE RESEARCH PAPER 1: A SHORT LITERARY ANALYSIS

The following paper, in MLA style, illustrates the use of a few sources but many page references to one literary work. Alan's essay was written for a sophomore-level American literature course and was based in part on class discussion of *Intruder in the Dust* as an example of an initiation novel. Alan demonstrates considerable skill in literary analysis and shows, by his references to Nathaniel Hawthorne and Arthur Miller, that he remembers other studied works and sees parallels between them and *Intruder*. The ability to go beyond the current class discussion and to make connections with other works or concepts will be rewarded in any field of study.

Peterson 1

Alan Peterson

Professor Seyler

American Literature 242

May 5, 1998

Faulkner's Realistic Initiation Theme

William Faulkner braids a universal theme, the theme of initiation, into the fiber of his novel <u>Intruder in the Dust</u>. From ancient times to the present, a prominent focus of literature, of life, has been rites of passage, particularly those of childhood to adulthood. Joseph Campbell defines rites of passage as "distinguished by formal, and usually very severe, exercises of severance." A "candidate" for initiation into adult society, Campbell explains, experiences a shearing away of the "attitudes, attachments and life patterns" of childhood (9). This severe, painful stripping away of the child and installation of the adult is presented somewhat differently in several works by American writers.

One technique of handling this theme of initiation is used by Nathaniel Hawthorne in his story "My Kinsman, Major Molineaux." The story's main character Robin is suddenly awakened to the real world, the adult world, when he sees Major

---

Margin notes:

Appropriate heading when separate title page is not used. (See page 222.)

Center title. Double space throughout.

Opening ¶ introduces subject, presents thesis, and defines key term—initiation.

Student combines paraphrase and brief quotations in definition. (See page 162).

Summary and analysis combined to explain initiation in Hawthorne's story.

Peterson 2

Molineaux "in tar-and-feathery dignity"
(Hawthorne 528). A terrified and amazed Robin
gapes at his kinsman as the large and colorful
crowd laughs at and ridicules the Major; then an
acquiescent Robin joins with the crowd in the
mirthful shouting (Hawthorne 529). This moment
is Robin's epiphany, his sudden realization of
reality. Robin goes from unsophisticated rube to
resigned cynical adult in one quick scene.
Hawthorne does hold out hope that Robin will not
let this event ruin his life, indeed that he
will perhaps prosper from it.

A similar, but decidedly less optimistic,
example of an epiphanic initiation occurs in
Arthur Miller's play <u>Death of a Salesman</u>. Miller
develops an initiation theme within a flashback.
A teenaged Biff, shockingly confronted with
Willy's infidelity and weakness, has his boyhood
dreams, ambitions—his vision—shattered, leaving
his life in ruins, a truth borne out in scenes
in which Biff is an adult during the play
(1083-84, 1101). Biff's discovery of the vices
and shortcomings of his father overwhelm him.
His realization of adult life is a revelation
made more piercing when put into the context of
his naive and overly hopeful upbringing. A
ravaged and defeated Biff has adulthood wantonly

Transition to second example establishes contrast with Hawthorne.

¶ concludes with emphasis on contrast.

thrust upon him. Unlike Hawthorne's Robin, Biff never recovers.

William Faulkner does not follow these examples when dealing with the initiation of his character Chick in <u>Intruder in the Dust</u>. In Robin's and Biff's cases, each character's passage into adulthood was brought about by realization of and disillusionment with the failings and weaknesses of a male adult playing an important role in his life. By contrast, Chick's male role models are vital, moral men with integrity. Chick's awakening develops as he begins to comprehend the mechanisms of the adult society in which he would be a member.

Faulkner uses several techniques for illustrating Chick's growth into a man. Early in the novel, at the end of the scene in which Chick tries to pay for his dinner, Lucas warns Chick to "stay out of that creek" (Faulkner 16).[1] The creek is an effective symbol: it is both a physical creek and a metaphor for the boy's tendency to slide into gaffes that perhaps a man could avoid. The creek's symbolic meaning is more evident when, after receiving the

[1] Subsequent references to Faulkner's novel cite page numbers only.

Transition to Faulkner's story to contrast with Hawthorne and Miller.

Footnote first parenthetical reference to inform readers that subsequent citations will exclude the author's name and give only the page number. (See page 159).

Peterson 4

molasses, Chick encounters Lucas in town. Lucas again reminds Chick not to "fall in no more creeks this winter" (24). At the end of the novel, Lucas meets Chick in Gavin's office and states: "you ain't fell in no more creeks lately, have you?" (241). Although Lucas phrases this as a question, the answer is obvious to Lucas, as well as to the reader, that indeed Chick has not blundered into his naive boyhood quagmire lately. When Lucas asks his question, Chick's actual falling into a creek does not occur to the reader.

Another image Faulkner employs to show Chick growing into a man is the single file line. After Chick gets out of the creek, he follows Lucas into the house, the group walking in single file. In the face of Lucas's much stronger adult will, Chick is powerless to get out of the line, to go to Edmonds's house (7). Later in the novel, when Miss Habersham, Aleck Sander and Chick are walking back from digging up the grave, Chick again finds himself in a single file line with a strong-willed adult in front. Again he protests, then relents, but clearly he feels slighted and wonders to himself "what good that [walking single file] would do"

Note transition. (See pages 209–10 on transitions.)

Note interpolation in square brackets. (See page 169.)

(130). The contrast between these two scenes illustrates Chick's growth, although he is not yet a man.

Faulkner gives the reader other hints of Chick's passage into manhood. As the novel progresses, Chick is referred to (and refers to himself) as a "boy" (24), a "child" (25), a "young man" (46), "almost a man" (190), a "man" (194), and one of two "gentlemen" (241). Other clues crop up from time to time. Chick wrestles with himself about getting on his horse and riding away, far away, until Lucas's lynching is "all over finished done" (41). But his growing sense of responsibility and outrage quell his boyish desire to escape, to bury his head in the sand. Chick looks in the mirror at himself with amazement at his deeds (125). Chick's mother serves him coffee for the first time, despite the agreement she has with his father to withhold coffee until his eighteenth birthday (127). Chick's father looks at him with pride and envy (128-29).

Perhaps the most important differences between the epiphanic initiations of Robin and Biff and that experienced by Chick are the facts that Chick's epiphany does not come all at once and it does not devastate him. Chick learns

---

Good use of brief quotations combined with analysis. (See pages 162–63.)

Characteristics of Chick's gradual and positive initiation explained. Observe coherence techniques. (See pages 209–10.)

about adulthood—and enters adulthood—piecemeal
and with support. His first eye-opening
experience occurs as he tries to pay Lucas for
dinner and is rebuffed (15-16). Chick learns,
after trying again to buy a clear conscience,
the impropriety and affront of his actions (24).
Lucas teaches Chick how he should resolve *his*
dilemma by setting him "free" (26-27). Later,
Chick feels outrage at the adults crowding into
the town, presumably to see a lynching, then
disgrace and shame as they eventually flee (196-
97, 210). As in most lives, Chick's passage into
adulthood is a gradual process; he learns a
little bit at a time and has support in his
growing. Gavin is there for him, to act as a
sounding board, to lay a strong intellectual
foundation, to confirm his beliefs. Chick's
initiation is consistent with Joseph Campbell's
explanation: "all rites of passage are intended
to touch not only the candidate, but also every
member of his circle" (9). Perhaps Gavin is
affected the most, but Chick's mother and
father, and Lucas as well, are influenced by the
change in Chick.

In <u>Intruder in the Dust</u>, William Faulkner
has much to say about the role of and the
actions of adults in society. He depicts racism,

Peterson 7

Student
concludes
by
explaining
the values
Chick
develops in
growing up.

ignorance, resignation, violence, fratricide,
citizenship, hope, righteousness, lemming-like
aggregation, fear, and a host of other emotions
and actions. Chick learns not only right and
wrong, but that in order to be a part of
society, of his community, he cannot completely
forsake those with whom he disagrees or whose
ideas he challenges. There is much compromise in
growing up; Chick learns to compromise on some
issues, but not all. Gavin's appeal to Chick to
"just don't stop" (210) directs him to conform
enough to be a part of the adult world, but not
to lose sight of, indeed instead to embrace, his
own values and ideals.

Works Cited

Paging is continuous.

Place Works Cited on separate page.

Double-space throughout.

Use hanging indention.

Campbell, Joseph. <u>The Hero with a Thousand Faces</u>. Princeton: Princeton UP, 1949.

Faulkner, William. <u>Intruder in the Dust</u>. New York: Random, 1948.

Hawthorne, Nathaniel. "My Kinsman, Major Molineaux." 1832. Rpt. in <u>The Complete Short Stories of Nathaniel Hawthorne</u>. New York: Hanover-Doubleday, 1959. 517-30.

Miller, Arthur. <u>Death of a Salesman</u>. New York: Viking, 1949. Rpt. in <u>An Introduction to Literature</u>. 9th ed. Eds. Sylvan Barnet, Morton Berman, and William Burto. Boston: Little, 1985. 1025-111.

SAMPLE RESEARCH PAPER 2:
A POSITION PAPER ON A
CURRENT PUBLIC POLICY ISSUE

The following paper, in MLA style, illustrates a formal research essay format that includes a separate title page, an outline, and a Works Cited page. If an outline is required, use a separate title page instead of putting your name and course information in the upper left corner of page one. Notice, from the opening paragraph, that Connie has selected a current issue that is of personal interest to her. Note, as well, that she has researched the issue and provides relevant facts and figures as well as value statements to advance her argument. The Works Cited page shows a range of types of sources used.

Sample Student Paper

As you study the sample student paper, pay attention to these elements of formatting:

- Double spacing throughout the essay

- Using display form for long quotations—indent 10 spaces from the left margin, double space, do not use quotation marks, and place parenthetical citation after the last period

- Beginning the Works Cited on a new page

- Double spacing throughout the Works Cited

- Alphabetizing citations on the Works Cited page

Adoption: An Issue of Love, Not Race

Good example of a title page format in a three-part pattern of title, author, and course information.

Connie Childress

English 112. Section 27N.

Dr. Pamela Monaco

November 2, 1997

Childress 2

Outline

Thesis: It is not society's place to decide for
parents whether they are capable of
parenting a child of a different race or
ethnic background.

Begin with a
thesis
statement
and use one
standard
outline
pattern
consistently.
(See pp.
195–99.)

  I.   The Issue of Transracial Adoptions

       A. Discussion of Ashley's adoption

       B. Race or Ethnicity Not a Barrier to
          Adoption

  II. Transracial Adoption Problems

       A. What the Numbers Show

       B. Attitudes Toward Mixed-race Adoptions

       C. Arguments Against Transracial
          Adoptions

       D. Effects of Multiethnic Placement Act

  III. Some Consequences of Attitudes Against
       Transracial Adoptions

       A. Different-race Children Taken from
          Foster Parents

       B. U.S. Children Placed Overseas

  IV. What the Studies Show about Transracial
       Adoptions

  V.   Solutions to the Problem

Adoption: An Issue of Love, Not Race

Nine years ago when my daughter, Ashley, was placed in my arms, it marked the happy ending to a long, exhausting, and, at times, heartbreaking journey through endless fertility treatments and the red tape of adoption procedures. Ironically, she had not been in our home a day before we received a call from another adoption agency that specialized in foreign adoptions. The agency stated that it was ready to begin our home study. As I look at Ashley, with her brown hair, hazel eyes and fair complexion, I have trouble imagining not having her in my life. I know in my heart that I would have this feeling about my daughter whether she came to us from the domestic agency or the agency bringing us a child from a foreign country. To us the issue was only the child, not his or her race or ethnic background. The issue of race or ethnicity should be considered by adoptive parents along with all the other issues needing thought when they make the decision to adopt. But race or ethnicity alone should not be a roadblock to adoption. It is not society's place to decide for parents if they are capable

Last name and page number in upper right corner.

Repeat title on first page of text.

Double space throughout. (See page 222.)

The student introduces her topic by refering to her own adopted daughter. Paragraph 1 concludes with her thesis.

Childress 4

of parenting a child of a different race or
ethnic background.

Transracial adoptions are those adoptions
involving a family and a child of a different
race or ethnic background. Cultural differences
occur when the family is of one racial or ethnic
background and the adoptive child is of another.
In 1996, according to the U.S. Department of
Health and Human Services, "about 52 percent of
children awaiting adoption through state
placement services around the country are black"
(Kuebelbeck). On average, black children wait
longer to be adopted than white, Asian, or
Hispanic children. Why should it be more
difficult for a white family to adopt an African
American child than a child from China or
Russia? Or a Hispanic American or mixed-race
child? Any of these combinations still results
in a mixed-race adoption.

Although interracial adoptions are
"statistically rare in the United States,"
according to Robert S. Bausch and Richard T.
Serpe who cite a 1990 study by Bachrach et al.,
the issue continues to receive attention from
both social workers and the public (137). A New
Republic editorial lists several articles,
including a cover story in The Atlantic

in 1992, to illustrate the attention given to
transracial adoptions (6). All of the popular-
press articles as well as those in scholarly
journals describe the country's adoption and
foster-care problems. While the great majority
of families wanting to adopt are white, about
half of the children in foster care waiting to
be adopted are black ("All in the Family" 6).
Robert Jackson estimates, in 1995, that about
440,000 children are being cared for in foster
families (A26). The New Republic editorial
reports on a 1993 study revealing that "a black
child in California's foster care system is
three times less likely to be adopted than a
white child" (6). In some cases minority
children have been in a single foster home with
parents of a different race their entire life.
They have bonded as a family. Yet, often when
the foster parents apply to adopt these
children, their petitions are denied and the
children are removed from their care. For
example, Beverly and David Cox, a white couple
in Wisconsin, were asked to become foster
parents to two young sisters, both African
American. The Coxes provided love and nurturing
for five years, but when they petitioned to
adopt the two girls, not only was their request

denied, but the girls were removed from their home. Can removing the children from the only home they have ever known just because of their skin color really be in the best interest of the children? As Hillary Clinton has said, "Skin color [should] not outweigh the more important gift of love that adoptive parents want to offer" (Cole, Drummond, and Epperson 50).

The argument against transracial adoption has rested on the concern that children adopted by parents of a different race or ethnic background will lose their cultural heritage and racial identity, and that these losses may result in adjustment problems for the children (Bausch and Serpe 136). The loudest voice against mixed-race adoptions has been the National Association of Black Social Workers who passed a resolution in 1972 stating their "vehement opposition to the practice of placing Black children with white families" and reaffirmed their position in 1994 (Harnack 188). Audrey T. Russell, speaking at the 1972 conference, described white adoption of black children as "a practice of genocide" (189). Fortunately, for both children and families wanting to adopt, the NABSW has now reversed its position and concedes that placement in a home

Words added to a quotation for clarity are placed in square brackets.

Childress 7

of a different race is far more beneficial to the child than keeping the child in foster care (Jackson A26). The NABSW's new position may have come in response to the passage of the Multiethnic Placement Act of 1994, legislation designed to facilitate the placement of minority children into adoptive homes. As Randall Kennedy explains, while this legislation continues to allow agencies to consider "the child's cultural, ethnic and racial background and the capacity of prospective foster or adoptive parents to meet the needs of a child of this background," it prohibits the delaying of an adoption solely for the purpose of racial matching (44). Kennedy objects to the law's allowing for even some consideration of race matching because he believes that this results in some children never being adopted, as agencies search for a race match (44). Sandra Haun, a social worker from Fairfax County, Virginia, said in an interview that she does not oppose transracial adoptions but that the best choice for a child is with a family of the same race, if the choice exists. Providing that both adoptive homes could offer the child the same environment in every other aspect, then clearly the same-race home may be the best choice. More

Student uses a personal interview as one source.

Childress 8

often than not, however, placing a child in a home of the same race is not an option. How can we worry about a child's cultural identity when that child doesn't have a home to call his or her own? In the cases of minority children who have been with a foster family of a different race for most of their young lives, the benefits of remaining in a stable home far outweigh the benefits of moving to a family of the same race.

The emotional effects of removing a child from a home that he or she has lived in for an extended period of time is well illustrated in the movie <u>Losing Isaiah</u>. In the film, a black child is adopted by a white social worker and her husband after the child's birth mother has placed him in the garbage when he is three days' old so that she can be free to search for drugs. When Isaiah is three, the courts return him to his birth mother who is now off drugs. Is it fair to Isaiah for her reward to be at the expense of his emotional health? The attorney representing the adoptive parents sums up the plight of these children in one sentence: "The child is then wrenched from the only family they've ever known and turned over to strangers because of the color of their skin." In the end, Isaiah's birth mother realizes that this system is unfair to him. She

The student refers to a recent movie on adoption.

appeals to his adoptive parents to assist him in his adjustment to his new home.

　　To protect themselves from heartbreaking situations such as the one depicted in <u>Losing Isaiah</u>, potential adoptive couples in this country are seeking other alternatives. We know that many couples seeking to adopt often adopt children from foreign countries. One of the reasons for this is the assumed shortage of children in the United States available for adoption. What may be less widely known is that many American children of mixed-race or African American are placed with adoptive families overseas. One of the reasons for this situation is the continued unwillingness of social workers to place black or mixed-race children with white couples (Blackman et al. 65). The NABSW's years of resistance to placing black children with white parents has left its mark, although Edmund Blair Bolles speculates that the rare placing of black—or American Indian—children with white couples may reflect racial prejudices rather than a great concern to preserve black or Indian identities (72). Whatever the explanation, it is ironic that American babies are being "exported" to adoptive homes in other countries while babies from other countries are being "imported"

Childress 10

to American adoptive homes. The child social services system needs to be overhauled to remove the stigmas or concerns that keep American children from being adopted in the country of their birth. If one of the arguments against transracial adoptions is the possible loss of cultural identity, how can we tolerate a system which appears to prefer placing African American children outside their own country—their own cultural heritage?

The argument that adopted children may lose their cultural identity is no longer a justifiable objection to transracial adoptions. As Randall Kennedy asserts, "there exists no credible empirical support that substantiates" the idea that "adults of the same race as a child will be better able to raise that child than adults of a different race" (44). Bausch and Serpe cite four studies done between 1972 and 1992 that show that "most children of color adopted by white parents appear to be as well adjusted as children of color adopted by same-race parents" (137). Perhaps the most important study is one conducted over twenty years by Rita Simon, American University sociologist. She studied 204 interracial adoptees over the twenty-year period and found that many of the adoptees

supported transracial adoptions (Davis A3). Some
did report that they felt isolated from other
people of their own race, but we need to remember
that those who participated in this study were
adopted when adoptions were more secretive (and
when races were more separated). At that time,
most adoptees, regardless of race, may have felt
isolated because of this lack of openness. Simon,
in her book (with Howard Alstein and Marygold S.
Melli) draws these conclusions:

> The student shortens the block quotation by using ellipses. Note format of block quotation.

> Transracial adoptees do not lose their
> racial identities, they do not appear
> to be racially unaware of who they
> are, and they do not display negative
> or indifferent racial attitudes about
> themselves. On the contrary, . . .
> transracially placed children and
> their families have as high a success
> rate as all other adoptees and their
> families. (204)

With open adoptions becoming increasingly
popular, more adoptees today are aware of their
adopted state and often have knowledge of one or
both of their birth parents. It is not only
possible, but probably easier, to provide
opportunities for today's adoptee to learn about
his or her racial and cultural background. The

Childress 12

fact that the child is being raised by a family of a different race or ethnic background does not condemn that child to a life of ignorance concerning his or her own racial and cultural identity.

There can be only one logical solution to the issues surrounding mixed race adoptions. Children and their adoptive parents should be united as a family because they have passed the background investigations and screening interviews that show they are emotionally and financially able to provide loving and nurturing environments for the children. To keep children needing homes and loving parents apart because they are of different races or ethnic backgrounds is not fair to the children or the adoptive parents. Preventing or delaying such adoptions is detrimental to each child's development. Children require a consistent home environment to flourish, to grow to productive members of society. Legislation needs to support speedier adoptive placements for minority children to give them the same quality of life afforded other adoptees. Society needs to protect the rights of adoptive parents by not denying transracial adoptions as an option for couples seeking to adopt.

A strong conclusion stressing the student's position on transracial adoptions.

Childress 13

Works Cited

"All in the Family." Editorial. <u>New Republic</u>
24 Jan. 1994: 6-7.

Bausch, Robert S., and Richard T. Serpe.
"Negative Outcomes of Interethnic
Adoption of Mexican American Children."
<u>Social Work</u> 42.2 (1997): 136-43.

Blackman, Ann, et al. "Babies for Export."
<u>Time On-Disc</u>. CD-ROM. UMI-Proquest. Sept.
1997.

Bolles, Edmund Blair. <u>The Penguin Adoption
Handbook: A Guide to Creating Your New
Family</u>. New York: Viking, 1984.

Cole, Wendy, Tamerlin Drummond, and Sharon E.
Eppeson. "Adoption in Black and White."
<u>Time</u> 14 Aug. 1995: 50-51.

Davis, Robert. "Suits Back Interracial
Adoptions." <u>USA Today</u> 13 Apr. 1995: A3.

Harnack, Andrew. Ed. <u>Adoption: Opposing
Viewpoints</u>. San Diego: Greenhaven, 1995.
188.

Haun, Sandra. Personal Interview. 30 Sept.
1997.

Jackson, Robert L. "U.S. Stresses No Race Bias
in Adoptions." <u>Los Angeles Times</u>
25 Apr. 1995: A26.

Start a new page for the Works Cited. Include only works actually cited. Double-space throughout. Alphabetize and use hanging indention. (See page 223.)

Childress 14

Kennedy, Randall, and Carol Moseley-Braun. "At
Issue: Interracial Adoption—Is the
Multiethnic Placement Act Flawed?" <u>ABA
Journal</u> 81 (1995): 44-45. <u>ABA Journal On-
Disc</u>. CD-ROM. UMI-Proquest. Sept. 1997.

Kuebelbeck, Amy. "Interracial Adoption
Debated." AP US and World. 31 Dec. 1996.
26 pars. 8 Oct.1997 <http//www.donet.com/
~brandyjc/p6at111.htm>.

<u>Losing Isaiah</u>. Howard W. Koch, Jr., Dir. Perf.
Jessica Lange and Halle Berry. Paramount,
1995.

Russell, Audrey T. "Transracial Adoptions
Should Be Forbidden." From <u>Diversity</u>:
<u>Cohesion or Chaos—Mobilization for
Survival</u>; <u>Proceedings of the Fourth
Annual Conference of NABSW</u>, 1973. Harnack
189-96.

Simon, Rita J., Howard Altsteen, and Marygold
S. Melli. "Transracial Adoptions Should
Be Encouraged." From <u>The Case for
Transracial Adoption</u>, 1994. Harnack
198-204.

Cites a
CD-Rom
database.

Cites an
Internet
News
Source.

Cross
reference
citations

7

OBSERVING OTHER STYLES OF DOCUMENTATION

Although the research process is much the same regardless of the area of study, the presentation of research results varies from one discipline to another. Because of the similarity of process, we can examine, just once, topic selection, finding sources, studying sources, and writing the paper. But, we need a separate study of the various documentation styles to avoid confusion. You have found the guidelines for presenting papers in MLA style in Chapters 3 and 5. This style will be acceptable in many, but not all, undergraduate courses. Because MLA is not used in all disciplines, you need to be aware of three other styles of documentation, and of the fields of study that use them. With this knowledge, you will be able to document research papers for any of your courses, regardless of discipline.

The three most used styles, other than MLA, are

- author/year style (for the social sciences and some science fields)
- footnote or endnote style (for art and history fields primarily)
- number style (for some scientific and technical disciplines).

The *author/year style* identifies a source within the text by providing the author's name and the year of publication. This information is supported by a complete citation at the paper's end, similar to MLA style, except that specific details of format vary. The *footnote/endnote style* does not provide any parenthetical information in the text. Instead, citation is made by use of a raised (superscript) numeral after reference to a source that refers to the bibliographic information, attached to that same number, either at the "foot" of the page on which the reference occurs or at the "end" of the text in a listing of all notes in order by numeral. The format for presenting bibliographic information is similar to MLA style; the difference is location. Finally, the *number style* requires that each source be given a number as it is referred to and that only the number appear within the text whenever reference is made to that source. A list of references, usually following the order of references in the text, supports the textual numerals.

If explaining the details of each of these three styles were as simple as the previous paragraph suggests, the rest of this chapter would be simple and brief. Unfortunately, the facts are a bit more complicated. Within each of the three types of styles, variations in presentation are found. Some disciplines have their own style sheets. Other disciplines, such as those that seem to be partly in the humanities and partly in the social sciences (government, for example), will sometimes use footnotes/endnotes, sometimes the author/year style. In disciplines without a specific style sheet, many variations can be found in the scholarly journals serving those fields. As a reader of journal articles, you need to expect—and not be bothered by—variations in documentation patterns. Just remember that all patterns of documentation still provide the same information: author, title, and facts of publication for the source. Be prepared for some instructors to accept MLA style because they know you learned that pattern in your composition class; be prepared for other instructors to expect the style most commonly used in their disciplines.

Comparing Styles of Documentation

MLA

In-text: Michael Lesh explains that one of the difficulties facing the future of the digital library is the cost of reprinting works still under copyright (60).

Works Cited

Lesh, Michael. "Going Digital." <u>Scientific American</u> March 1997: 58-60.

APA

In-text: Michael Lesh (1997) explains that one of the difficulties facing the future digital library is the cost of reprinting works still under copyright.

References

Lesh, M. (1997). Going digital. <u>Scientific American, 276,</u> 58-60.

ACS (American Chemical Society)

In-text: Lesh (*3*) explains that one of the difficulties facing the future digital library is the cost of reprinting works still under copyright.

References

Lesh, M. <u>Sci Am.</u> **1997,** <u>276</u>, 58-60.

> ✓ **Remember:** If your instructor does not specify a pattern of documentation when assigning a research paper, it is your responsibility as a student to have a specific style approved and then to follow that style consistently in your paper.

In the following pages, the author/year, footnote/endnote, and number patterns of documentation will be explained and illustrated. Major disciplines are grouped below by type of documentation usually followed. For those disciplines with their own style manuals, the variations found in those manuals will be explained. APA style is also illustrated with a sample student paper.

GENERAL GUIDE TO DOCUMENTATION PATTERNS

Author/Year Style

APA style (250–83):	anthropology	economics	political science
	archeology	education	psychology
	astronomy	linguistics	sociology
	business	physical education	
CBE (Council			
of Biology Editors)	biology	physiology	
style (284–88):	botany	zoology	

USGS (U.S. Geological Survey) style (288–90): geology

Footnote/Endnote Style

art	history	philosophy
dance	music	religion

Number Style

computer science, health and medicine, engineering, related disciplines

ACS (American Chemical Society) style (300–03): chemistry

AIP (American Institute of Physics) style (303–05): physics

AMS (American Mathematical Society) style (305–07): mathematics

APA AUTHOR/YEAR STYLE

The APA *Publication Manual* (4th ed., 1994), designed primarily for scholars preparing papers for publication, distinguishes between the "draft copy" and the finished or "publication" form of a work. The key differences are as follows:

Draft Form	*Final or Publication Form*
First two–three words of title used to identify each page of MS.	Running head—short version of title—to be used in published form.
Double space throughout.	Printed format.
Ragged right margin.	Right-justified margin.
Titles underlined.	Titles in italics.
Citations with first lines indented.	Citations presented in hanging indentation (as in MLA style).

Editors of the *Manual* do suggest that students check with instructors regarding papers submitted for class. Since these papers are not designed for journal publication, instructors may regard them as finished and expect the publication format to be followed. Consult with your instructor before completing your paper. The examples of format for bibliographic citations are shown in "draft" form. In the sample student paper, the references are presented with hanging indention, and the paper uses a right-justified margin. However, titles have been underlined rather than put in italics.

Author/Year In-Text Citations

The simplest parenthetical reference can be presented in one of three ways:

1. Place the year of publication within parentheses immediately following the author's name in the text.

```
In a typical study of preference for motherese,

Fernald (1985) used an operant auditory preference

procedure.
```

Within the same paragraph, additional references to the author do not need to repeat the year if the researcher makes it clear that the same study is referred to.

Because the speakers were unfamiliar subjects,
Fernald's work eliminated the possibility that it is
the mother's voice per se that accounts for the
preference.

2. If the author is not mentioned in the text, place the author's last name, followed by a comma, and the year of publication within parentheses after the borrowed information.

One reason people become addicted to crack cocaine
so quickly is that its euphoric effects are felt
almost instantly (Medzerian, 1991).

3. Cite a specific passage by providing the page, chapter, or figure number following the borrowed material. Always give specific page references for quoted material.

- A brief quotation:

Deuzen-Smith (1988) argued that counselors must be
involved with clients and "deeply interested in
piecing the puzzle of life together" (p. 29).

- A quotation in display form:

Bartlett (1932) explained the cyclic process of
perception thus:

> Suppose I am making a stroke in a quick game,
> such as tennis or cricket. How I make the
> stroke depends on the relating of certain new
> experiences, most of them visual, to other
> immediately preceding visual experiences, and
> to my posture, or balance of posture, at the
> moment. (p. 201)

(Indent a block quotation five spaces from the left margin and double-space throughout. To show a new paragraph within the block quotation, indent the first line of the new paragraph an additional five spaces. Note the placing of the year *after* the author's name, and the page number *at the end* of the quotation.)

More complicated in-text citations should be handled as follows:

Two Authors, Mentioned in the Text

Kuhl and Meltzoff (1984) tested 4- to 5-month-olds in
an experiment. . .

Two Authors, Not Mentioned in the Text

. . . but are unable to show preferences in the
presence of two mismatched modalities (e.g., a face
and a voice; see Kuhl & Meltzoff, 1984).

Give both authors' last names each time you refer to the source. Connect their names with "and" in the text. Use an ampersand (&) in the parenthetical citation.

More Than Two Authors

For works coauthored by three, four, or five people, provide all last names in the first reference to the source. Thereafter, cite only the first author's name followed by et al.

As Price-Williams, Gordon, and Ramirez have shown
(1969), . . .

OR

Studies of these children have shown (Price-Williams,
Gordon, & Ramirez, 1969). . .

THEN

Price-Williams et al. (1969) also found that. . .

If a source has six or more authors, use only the first author's last name followed by et al. every time the source is cited.

Corporate Authors

In general, spell out the name of a corporate author each time it is used. If a corporate author has well-known initials, the name can be abbreviated after the first citation.

First in-text citation: (National Institutes of Health [NIH],
1996)

Subsequent citations: (NIH, 1996)

Two or More Works Within the Same Parentheses

When citing more than one work by the same author in a parenthetical reference, use the author's last name only once and arrange the years mentioned in order, thus:

```
The third and, according to Rescorla (1967, 1988). . .
```

When an author, or the same group of coauthors, has more than one work published in the same year, distinguish the works by adding the letters *a, b, c,* and so on, as needed, to the year. Give the last name only once, but repeat the year, each one with its identifying letter, thus:

```
Several studies (Smith, 1995a, 1995b, 1995c). . .
```

When citing several works by different authors within the same parentheses, list the authors alphabetically, alphabetize by the first author when citing coauthored works. Separate authors or groups of coauthors with semicolons, thus:

```
Although many researchers (Archer & Waterman, 1983;

Grotevant, 1983; Grotevant & Cooper, 1986; Sabatelli &

Mazor, 1985) have studied identity formation, . . .
```

> ✓ **Note:** APA style calls for the use of the past tense when referring to the work of scholars that took place in the definite past: "Fernald (1985) used"; "Fernald's work eliminated." (This is in contrast to the use of the present tense in MLA style: "Fitzgerald explores the nature and effects of the American Dream.") Use the present perfect tense to refer to an action begun in the past and continuing into the present: "Although many researchers. . . have studied identity formation." Use the present tense when discussing the results of your research: "The evidence suggests that . . ."

Preparing a List of References

Every source cited in the text of your paper needs a complete bibliographic citation. In APA style, these complete citations are placed on a separate page (or pages) after the text of the paper but before any appendices included in the paper. Sources are arranged alphabetically, and the first page is titled "References." For the "draft" format, indent the first line of each reference five spaces. Double space throughout the list. Follow these rules for alphabetizing:

1. Organize two or more works by the same author, or the same group of coauthors, chronologically.

```
Beck, A. T. (1991).

Beck, A. T. (1993).
```

2. Place single-author entries before multiple-author entries when the first of the multiple authors is the same as the single author.

> Grotevant, H. D. (1983).
>
> Grotevant, H. D., & Cooper, C. R. (1986).

3. Organize multiple-author entries that have the same first author but different second or third authors alphabetically by the name of the second author or third, as so on.

> Gerbner, G., & Gross, L.
>
> Gerbner, G., Gross, L., Jackson-Beeck, M., Jeffries-Fox, S., & Signorielli, N.
>
> Gerbner, G., Gross, L., Morgan, M., and Signorielli, N.

4. Organize two or more works by the same author(s) published in the same year alphabetically by title.

Form for Books

A book citation contains these elements in this form:

> Seligman, M. E. P. (1991). <u>Learned optimism</u>. New York: Knopf.
>
> Weiner, B. (Ed.) (1974). <u>Achievement motivation and attribution theory</u>. Norristown, NJ: General Learning Press.

<u>Authors:</u> Give all authors' names, last name first, and initials. Separate authors with commas, use the ampersand (&) before the last author's name, and end with a period. For edited books, place the abbreviation "Ed." or "Eds." in parentheses following the last editor's name.

<u>Date of Publication:</u> Place the year of publication in parentheses followed by a period.

<u>Title:</u> Capitalize only the first word of the title and of the subtitle, if there is one, and any proper nouns. Underline the title and end with a period. Place additional information such as number of volumes or an edition in parentheses after the title, before the period.

> Butler, R., & Lewis, M. (1982). <u>Aging and mental health</u> (3rd ed.).

<u>Publication Information:</u> Cite the city of publication; add the state (using the Postal Service abbreviation) or country if necessary to avoid confusion;

then give the publisher's name, after a colon, eliminating unnecessary terms such as Publishers, Co., and Inc. End the citation with a period.

Gardner, H. (1983). <u>Frames of mind: The theory of multiple intelligence</u>. New York: Basic Books.

Mitchell, J. V. (Ed.) (1985). <u>The ninth mental measurements yearbook</u>. Lincoln: University of Nebraska Press.

National Institute of Drug Abuse. (1993, April 13). <u>Annual national high school senior survey</u>. Rockville, MD: Author.

(Give a corporate author's name in full. When the organization is both author and publisher, place the word "Author" after the place of publication.)

Form for Articles

An article citation contains these elements in this form:

Changeux, J-P. (1993). Chemical signaling in the brain. <u>Scientific American, 269</u>, 58–62.

<u>Author</u>: Same rules as for author(s) of books.

<u>Date of Publication</u>: Place the year of publication for articles in scholarly journals in parentheses, followed by a period. For articles in newspapers and popular magazines, give the year followed by month and day (if appropriate).

(1997, March). (See also example below.)

<u>Title of Article</u>: Capitalize only the title's first word, the first word of any subtitle, and any proper nouns. Place any necessary descriptive information immediately after the title in square brackets.

Scott, S. S. (1984, December 12). Smokers get a raw deal [Letter to the editor].

<u>Publication Information</u>: Cite the title of the journal in full, capitalizing according to conventions for titles. Underline the title and follow it with a comma. Give the volume number, underlined, followed by a comma, and then inclusive page numbers followed by a period. If a journal begins each issue with a new page 1, then also cite the issue number in parentheses immediately following the volume number. Do not use "p." or "pp." before page numbers when citing articles from scholarly journals; do use "p." or "pp." in citations to newspaper and magazine articles.

Martin, C. L., Wood, C. H., & Little, J. K. (1990). The development of gender stereotype components. <u>Child Development, 61</u>, 1891–1904.

Werker, J. F., & McLeod, P. J. (1989). Infant preference for both male and female infant-directed talk: A developmental study of attentional and affective responsiveness. <u>Canadian Journal of Psychology, 43</u>(2), 230–246.

Hughes, M., & Gove, W. R. (1981, October). Playing dumb. <u>Psychology Today</u>, pp. 24–27.

Form for an Article or Chapter in an Edited Book

Gerbner, G., & Gross, L. (1980). The violent face of television and its lessons. In E. L. Palmer & A. Dorr (Eds.), <u>Children and the faces of television: Teaching, violence, selling</u> (pp. 149–62). New York: Academic Press.

Cite the author(s), date, and title of the article or chapter. Then cite the name(s) of the editor(s) in signature order after "In," followed by "Ed." or "Eds." in parentheses; the title of the book; the inclusive page numbers of the article or chapter, in parentheses, followed by a period. End with the place of publication and publisher of the book.

Forms for Dissertations

Bolt, J. A. (1986). A study of the effects of a bibliographic instruction course on achievement and retention of college students. <u>Dissertation Abstracts International, 47</u>, 4219A. (University Microfilms No. ASS87-08161.)

If the microfilm of the dissertation was used, give the microfilm number as well as the volume and page numbers of *DAI*. If the abstract only was used, follow this form:

Kuhlthau, C. C. (1983). The library research process: Case studies and interventions with high school seniors in advanced placement English classes using Kelly's theory of constructs (Doctoral dissertation, Rutgers University, 1983). <u>Dissertation Abstracts International, 44</u>, 1961A.

A Report

U.S. Merit Systems Protection Board. (1988). <u>Sexual harassment in the federal workplace: An update</u>. Washington, DC: U.S. Government Printing Office.

Electronic Sources

If a work exists in both print and electronic format, use the print format if at all possible. For other electronic sources, follow the basic pattern of:

Author, I. (date). Title of the article. <u>Periodical Title</u> [Online], <u>volume number</u>, Available: specify path

OR

Author, I. (date). <u>Title of work</u> [Online]. Available: specify path

(Note: Citations do not end with a period after the Internet address because the reader may think that the Internet address includes the period. The APA *Publication Manual* does not show electronic citations ending with the date you accessed the material. Your instructor may want you to include the access date.) Here is an example:

American Academy of Child and Adolescent Psychiatry (1992, October). Children's sleep problems. <u>Facts for Families Index</u> [Online], <u>34</u>, Available: http://www.psych.med.umich.edu/web/aacap/factsFam/sleep.htm

Electronic Bulletin Boards, Newsgroups, and E-mail

The APA *Publication Manual* discourages the use of these sources. Any that are used should be cited in the text of your paper but not included in the list of references. Treat as personal communications in the text only, supplying initials and last name and date:

```
P. Monaco (personal communication, June 15, 1997). . . .
```

Sample Paper in APA Style

As noted at the beginning of the discussion of APA style, the following student paper conforms to APA style and format for a finished or "publication" work, with the exception that titles of books are underlined, not placed in italics. Use one-inch margins and double space throughout, including any block quotations. Long block quotations should be indented *five* spaces from the left margin. (This varies from the 10 spaces required by MLA style.) Papers in the social sciences may contain these elements in the order indicated. Starred items must be in the paper.

*Title page, including running head (a separate page, numbered page 1)

*Abstract (a separate page, numbered page 2)

*Text of paper (begin on a new page, starting with page 3)

*References (begin on a separate page)

Appendixes (if there are any, begin each on a separate page)

Content footnotes (if there are any, list together, beginning on a separate page)

Tables (begin each on a separate page—for draft MS; for finished paper, place in the text)

Figures (begin each on a separate page—for draft MS; for finished paper, place in the text)

Mary Adams's paper, an exploration and evaluation of recent studies of two eating disorders, is a typical type of research assignment for undergraduates in the social sciences. As you read her paper on the epidemiology of anorexia and bulimia, observe Mary's use of headings and subheadings, the clear introduction of many sources, and the author/year style of in-text documentation.

Anorexia/Bulimia Epidemiology 1

Sample title
page for a
paper in
APA style.

The Epidemiology of Anorexia Nervosa

and Bulimia Nervosa

Mary M. Adams

Virginia Polytechnic Institute and State

University

Running Head: Anorexia/Bulimia Epidemiology

Observe placement of running head and page number.

A sample abstract, required in many kinds of research essays in social science and science fields.

Type abstract as one block paragraph.

Abstract

Both anorexia nervosa and bulimia nervosa occur most frequently in adolescence and overwhelmingly to females. Although sexual abuse may be a risk factor, evidence does not support the conclusion that sexual abuse causes eating disorders in either men or women. None of the theories used to explain why more women than men are prone to eating disorders seems adequate. Research that works with an integrated theory including genetics, cognitive patterns, family background, and sociocultural factors may help to explain why women are more susceptible than men to eating disorders.

Anorexia/Bulimia Epidemiology 3

The Epidemiology of Anorexia Nervosa
and Bulimia Nervosa

Student
begins with
a brief
statement of
the paper's
topic.

This paper defines and describes two eating

disorders, anorexia nervosa and bulimia nervosa,

examines the prevalence of the disorders, and

explores the relationship between these disor-

ders and two variables: gender and sexual abuse.

DEFINITION AND DESCRIPTION OF ANOREXIA NERVOSA

AND BULIMIA NERVOSA

Anorexia nervosa and bulimia nervosa are

two well-known types of eating disorders charac-

Observe
author/year
citation and
page
citation for
direct
quotations.

terized by a person's "excessive concern with

the control of body weight and shape" (Bryant-

Waugh & Lask, 1995, p. 13). The person attempts

to achieve the desired body shape and size by

drastically limiting the amount of food intake

and/or engaging in irregular or chaotic patterns

of food intake (Bryant-Waugh & Lask, 1995). The

disorder is diagnosed, using criteria provided

by the <u>Diagnostic and Statistical Manual</u>, 4th

ed. (DSM-IV) (1993), if the person meets the

following criteria: A body weight that is 15%

below the normal weight for age and height, an

intense fear of weight gain, becoming fat, dis-

tortion or inaccurate perception of body shape

and size, and endocrine disorder—shown in the

Anorexia/Bulimia Epidemiology 4

absence of at least three consecutive menstrual cycles (Bryant-Waugh & Lask, 1995). Physical signs and symptoms include emaciation, poor circulation demonstrated by low blood pressure, slow and weak pulse, cold hands and feet, discolored skin, and fine downy hair (Bryant-Waugh & Lask, 1995).

A person with bulimia nervosa is also greatly preoccupied with the control of weight, but the characteristic that distinguishes bulimia nervosa from anorexia nervosa is the occurrence and frequency of uncontrolled binge eating episodes followed by self-induced vomiting (Boumann & Yates, 1994). The bulimic will also engage in the use and abuse of diet pills and laxatives, excessive exercise, and periodic fasts (Boumann & Yates, 1994). As Bryant-Waugh and Lask (1995) state, using the DSM-IV, the disorder is diagnosed if the person meets the following criteria:

> (a) Recurrent episodes of binge eating (rapid consumption of a large amount of food in a discrete period of time),
>
> (b) A feeling of lack of control over eating behaviour,

Indent block quotation 5 spaces and add page number.

Anorexia/Bulimia Epidemiology 5

(c) Behaviour aimed at preventing weight gain such as self-induced vomiting, use of laxatives or diuretics, fasting,

(d) Persistent over-concern with body shape and weight. (p. 14)

Bulimia nervosa is characterized by several physical symptoms that include: menstrual irregularities, muscle weakness, fluid and electrolyte disturbance, gastro-intestinal bleeding, dental erosions, and enlarged salivary glands (Bryant-Waugh & Lask, 1995).

The ages of onset and duration of both disorders are similar: Both of the disorders tend to develop during adolescence and young adulthood and may persist for several years (Hsu, 1989). However, bulimia nervosa is about four times as common as anorexia nervosa (Pope & Hudson, 1984, p. 49). Two-thirds of the people who suffer from anorexia nervosa and bulimia nervosa will eventually recover and maintain a healthy diet and body weight, with about half of those who suffer from anorexia nervosa recovering within a five-year period even without treatment (Pope & Hudson, 1984, p. 116). For those who suffer from anorexia nervosa, there is a high mortality rate: as many as 19% of all diagnosed

Anorexia/Bulimia Epidemiology 6

cases die from the disorder (Brumberg, 1988, p. 13). Those suffering with bulimia nervosa, on the other hand, do not normally run the risk of death, although the disorder impacts negatively on the health of those who suffer from it (Pope & Hudson, 1984, pp. 25-29).

PREVALENCE OF ANOREXIA NERVOSA

AND BULIMIA NERVOSA

Walters and Kendler (1994) have estimated the overall prevalence of anorexia nervosa in the United States to be between 0.10 and 1.0%. Pope and Hudson (1984) have estimated the prevalence of bulimia nervosa in the general population to be 2.2% (pp. 33-34). In the United States, the prevalence of anorexia nervosa in males is estimated to be 0.05%; for bulimia nervosa the figure is 0.1-0.5% (Olivardia et al., 1995). It is further estimated that 5-10% of anorexics and 0.4-20% of bulimics are male (Olivardia et al., 1995).

In the United States, the prevalence of anorexia in adolescent females is estimated to be 0.5%, and the figure is the same for adult females (Shisslak, 1994). The prevalence of bulimia in adolescent females is estimated to be 0.0%-5.8%, and the prevalence of bulimia in adult females is probably 1-3% (Shisslak, 1994).

Section headings are frequently used in papers in the social sciences.

Observe Mary's presentation of figures.

Anorexia/Bulimia Epidemiology 7

The findings of Scott (1968) and Margo (1987) agree with Olivardia et al. (1995) that approximately 90-95% of anorexics are female.

Unlike anorexia nervosa, bulimia nervosa is a relatively new disorder first recognized as a clinical syndrome separate from anorexia nervosa in 1979 (Kendler et al., 1991). Therefore, it is difficult to estimate the true prevalence of the disorder.

The range in the estimated prevalence is the result of variation in the diagnostic criteria used (Walters & Kendler, 1994). The majority of the above estimates were derived using the DSM-III. Higher prevalence is found when the researcher also included individuals with a partial syndrome; that is, they met several but not all of the criteria (Drewnowski et al., 1994; Walters & Kendler, 1994).

The percentage of people who have either bulimia nervosa or anorexia nervosa and have been sexually abused varies somewhat based on the study cited; however, the percentage generally recognized is about 30% (Vize & Cooper, 1995). Unfortunately, because of the infrequency of eating disorders in males, most of the studies onanorexia nervosa and bulimia nervosa have focused on females instead of on males or

Anorexia/Bulimia Epidemiology 8

comparison groups (Olivardia, 1995). The result is a difficulty in determining an accurate percentage of males who have been sexually abused and have either anorexia nervosa or bulimia nervosa.

EVALUATION OF THE EVIDENCE

The evidence that gender is linked to anorexia nervosa and bulimia nervosa is overwhelming. Numerous articles report findings that the percentage of females with anorexia nervosa or bulimia nervosa is substantially greater than the percentage of males with these disorders (Bryant-Waugh & Yates, 1995; Drewnowski et al., 1988; Hsu, 1989; Kendler et al., 1991; Olivardia et al., 1995). Although it has been suggested that males suffering from anorexia nervosa or bulimia nervosa may be under-diagnosed, because men are less likely than women to seek treatment (Olivardia et al., 1994), one would be hard-pressed to find a study that reports findings where males account for more than 20% of the cases with anorexia nervosa or bulimia nervosa. It is widely recognized and accepted that males account for a very small number of the cases of eating disorders. However, Scott (1986) has pointed out in his article that diagnosis of anorexia in males has been neglected for a num-

After presenting some facts about eating disorders, Mary analyzes the facts.

Anorexia/Bulimia Epidemiology 9

ber of reasons ranging from the low overall prevalence of the disorder in both males and females to diagnostic criteria that required amenorrhea and fear of oral impregnation to be present in the patient with the disorder. While neither Scott (1986) nor Olivardia et al. (1994) dispute the rarity of the disorder in males, both have pointed out possible reasons for the *extremely* low prevalence of anorexia nervosa or bulimia nervosa in males as compared to females.

The vast majority of the articles do not dwell on the evidence that females are much more likely to have anorexia nervosa or bulimia nervosa than males, but instead focus on reasons why this is true or decline to conduct any studies that include males, because of the high prevalence of eating disorders in females. For example, prior to 1987, only three studies addressed the issue of bulimia nervosa in males (Schneider & Agras, 1987). The study of males with anorexia nervosa has also been limited due to the small numbers of males with the disorder (Herzog, 1984). However, more recently researchers are recognizing the need for comparison studies between males and females with eating disorders in order to identify the factors

Anorexia/Bulimia Epidemiology 10

that lead to or contribute to a person getting these disorders (Margo, 1987).

With regard to sexual abuse and eating disorders, the evidence that there is a correlation between these two variables is mixed. According to Fullerton et al. (1994), in a study of 712 females, using the DSM-III for the diagnostic criteria, 29% of the females who were diagnosed with anorexia or bulimia reported sexual abuse, 25% reported physical abuse, and 15% reported both physical and sexual abuse. In this study, sexual or physical abuse was more closely associated with bulimia nervosa than with anorexia nervosa, although it is evident from this study that abuse alone cannot explain why someone has an eating disorder. Fullerton et al. also addressed the issue of the severity of abuse and the severity of an eating disorder to see if there was a correlation, but failed to find a significant correlation between these two variables. The study did lead to the conclusion that childhood sexual abuse may be a risk factor in developing an eating disorder later in adolescence or young adulthood.

Vize and Cooper (1995) compared 28 cases of anorexia nervosa and 48 cases of bulimia nervosa with 35 cases of depression. The following cases

Anorexia/Bulimia Epidemiology 11

were all compared with 30 cases in a control group. They found that the rate of sexual abuse was significantly higher for the cases of eating disorders and depression than for the control group. Forty-three percent of subjects with anorexia nervosa and 27% of subjects with bulimia nervosa reported sexual abuse. Because of a greater percentage of subjects with anorexia nervosa reporting sexual abuse, this study is somewhat inconsistent with Fullerton's study. However, since 40% of the 35 cases of depression also reported sexual abuse, Vize and Cooper (1995) concluded that sexual abuse was a risk factor for any psychiatric disorder in general and not just a risk factor in the development of an eating disorder, a finding that is supported by others (Sullivan et al., 1995; Welch at al., 1994).

Sullivan et al. (1995) in a sample of 87 women with bulimia found that 44% of these women had a history of childhood sexual abuse. These findings support the findings of Fullerton et al. (1994) that women suffering with bulimia nervosa are more likely to have experienced childhood sexual abuse. Severity of the abuse and severity of the eating disorder were not significantly correlated, which supports the

Anorexia/Bulimia Epidemiology 12

findings of others (Fullerton et al., 1994; Pope et al., 1994). The prevalence of personality disorders was also studied, and the findings suggest that 49% of the subjects who reported sexual abuse also had an avoidant personality disorder, while only 24% of the subjects who did not report sexual abuse had an avoidant personality disorder. Although the DSM-III was used to determine that bulimia nervosa was present, this study was conducted using a clinical sample rather than a general population sample.

Pope et al. (1994), in a comparison study of American, Austrian, and Brazilian women, found that 15-32% of women reported childhood sexual abuse before the onset of the eating disorder. Unlike other studies that have focused on sexual abuse, Pope et al. differentiated between abuse that occurred before the onset of the eating disorder and abuse that occurred after the onset of the disorder. Severity of the abuse and severity of the disorder were not significantly correlated, which is in agreement with other researchers (Fullerton et al., 1994; Sullivan et al., 1995). However, contrary to the results of Fullerton et al. and Sullivan et al., Pope et al. did not find that women with bulimia nervosa

Anorexia/Bulimia Epidemiology 13

were more likely to have reported abuse than the general population.

While it can be said with a great deal of confidence that eating disorders are more prevalent in females than in males, it cannot be said with any confidence that sexual abuse causes eating disorders either in men or women. Although several studies have suggested that sexual abuse may be a risk factor in developing an eating disorder, Fullerton et al. (1994), Olivardia et al. (1995), Sullivan et al. (1995), and others have suggested that sexual abuse may be a risk factor in developing any psychiatric disorder (Vize & Cooper, 1995; Welch et al., 1994). Thus, the role that sexual abuse plays in the development of an eating disorder is unclear. More studies suggest a link between sexual abuse and bulimia nervosa, but sexual abuse is seen as a possible risk factor and not a cause of the eating disorder (Everill & Waller, 1994; Fullerton et al., 1994; Sullivan et al., 1995; Welch et al., 1994).

REVIEW OF THEORIES AND HYPOTHESES

There are several hypotheses as to why females are more prone to eating disorders than males. Scott (1986) suggested that there is a sociocultural explanation for the prevalence of

[Margin note:] Observe citing of multiple sources.

[Margin note:] Mary now turns to an explanation of possible causes for eating disorders.

Anorexia/Bulimia Epidemiology 14

eating disorders in females as opposed to males. Our society emphasizes thinness for women while no such emphasis exists for men. From early childhood girls are rewarded for dependence and, as a result, their self-esteem becomes tied to interpersonal approval. Boys, on the other hand, are rewarded for their ability to be assertive and aggressive, characteristics that promote self-reliance and autonomy. Scott (1986) has also suggested that young females face more role conflict than young males because of changes in the roles of women over the past thirty years. Some women cannot handle the new roles and responsibilities placed on them, and, as a result, they shift their focus to their bodies as a way of coping with the conflicting demands.

While Hsu (1989) agrees with Scott (1986) that there is a sociocultural explanation for the prevalence of eating disorders in females, he has argued that dieting alone is a powerful risk factor in the onset of an eating disorder. Since women are encouraged to diet from a young age to meet the thinness standard, this results in more women than men developing an eating disorder. Other risk factors for women include role conflict, poor self-esteem, and dysphoria. Sitnick and Katz (1984), focusing on sex role iden-

1. Socio-cultural explanation

2. Dieting factor.

Anorexia/Bulimia Epidemiology 15

tity, have hypothesized that females who are more prone to eating disorders have fewer masculine personality characteristics than females who do not suffer from eating disorders. Women who do not possess the necessary masculine traits to adapt to new societal roles are prone to developing an eating disorder.

3. Masculine traits as protection from eating disorders.

While these theories may explain the increasing numbers of females with eating disorders over the past thirty years, all fail to explain why young women throughout time have suffered with anorexia nervosa (Brumberg, 1988, p. 41-60). Women during the Middle Ages avoided food and wasted away for spiritual reasons, but the men did not engage in these practices to the same extent (Brumberg, p. 41). Taking this information into account, it becomes unclear why males have been protected from developing eating disorders.

Several studies have focused on males with eating disorders to find out why those of the less susceptible gender develop an eating disorder, because these clues may be valuable in understanding and explaining the higher prevalence of eating disorders in females (Fichter & Daser, 1987; Margo, 1987; Olivardia, 1995). Several studies have noted that sexual conflict may be a

Anorexia/Bulimia Epidemiology 16

risk factor for males developing an eating disorder (Fichter & Daser, 1987; Herzog et al.,
1984; Schneider & Steward, 1987; Scott, 1986).
While this does not explain the high prevalence
of eating disorders in females, it adds weight
to the argument that heterosexual males are protected against the development of an eating disorder (Fichter & Daser, 1987; Schneider & Steward, 1987). However, further research is needed
to establish what characteristics heterosexual
males possess that protect them from the development of eating disorders.

4. Sexual abuse

Everill and Waller (1994) sum up the theories on how sexual abuse may cause bulimia nervosa by using a functional model: Women use
bingeing and purging as a defense mechanism to
reduce awareness of emotional and cognitive
states that are linked to past abuse. They also
suggest that bingeing and purging may serve as a
way for the person to express anger, relieve
stress, gain some sense of control, and cleanse
himself or herself from the past abuse.

5. Cognitive styles

Everill and Waller (1994) also hypothesize
that a person's cognitive style is linked to the
development of an eating disorder. When a person
experiences the trauma of sexual abuse, he or
she develops a particular cognitive schemata as

Anorexia/Bulimia Epidemiology 17

a result of the abuse. This cognitive schemata heightens his or her sensitivity to abuse-related stimuli, to dissociation, to self-denigration, and to learned helplessness. The person uses bingeing and purging as a way to cope with his or her problems that are actually heightened by his or her cognitive style. While other studies fail to mention whether or not sexual abuse causes a particular cognitive style, these studies do conclude that individuals with eating disorders have different cognitive styles from those who do not suffer from an eating disorder (Bulik et al., 1994; Kaye et al., 1995; Yager et al., 1995).

EVALUATION OF THEORIES AND HYPOTHESES

Mary evaluates prevalent explanations for eating disorders.

None of the theories used to explain why more women are prone to eating disorders than men seem adequate. Although sociocultural explanations may give us some insight in uncovering the reasons why eating disorders are more prevalent in females than in males today, these explanations fail to address the reasons why people suffering with eating disorders can be found throughout history.

The theory of socioculture and dieting proposed by Hsu (1989) seems to be a more reasonable explanation than the sociocultural theory

Anorexia/Bulimia Epidemiology 18

alone for the higher prevalence of eating disorders among females. It seems possible that in
other times women may have been encouraged to
diet for different reasons (e.g., for religious
reasons instead of reasons relating to physical
appearance); however, a significant percentage
of people in the past did not develop an eating
disorder.

A woman's lack of masculine traits also
fails to address the long history of eating disorders. For most of the past, it was anything
but desirable or acceptable for a woman to possess masculine traits, but during those times,
women suffered eating disorders, and eating disorders were more prevalent among women than men.

To discover why eating disorders are more
prevalent among women there needs to be an integrated theory. So few people develop an eating
disorder to begin with that one factor, such as
socioculture, cannot begin to explain the higher
prevalence of eating disorders in females. Other
facts to explore may be genetics, temperament
and personality traits, and family background.
Comparison studies between males and females are
also needed to validate any claims. Since it is
difficult to separate genetics or temperament
from environmental factors such as culture and

Anorexia/Bulimia Epidemiology 19

Mary concludes with suggestions for further research into eating disorders.

family background, any integrated theory will have validity problems. However, the even greater challenge for researchers will be getting the necessary funding to conduct studies on both males and females who suffer from the same eating disorder. With such a small number of individuals, and a particularly small number of males, developing eating disorders compared to the general population, it seems reasonable that researchers will shift their attention from why one gender is more prone to eating disordersto other issues such as what are the possible causes and cures of eating disorders.

The theories on sexual abuse and the development of an eating disorder are also inadequate to explain why someone develops an eating disorder. Several studies have concluded that there is no clear evidence that sexual abuse causes eating disorders (Fullerton et al., 1994; Olivardia et al., 1995; Pope et al., 1994; Vize & Cooper, 1995; Welch et al., 1994). While the theories used to explain how sexual abuse causes eating disorders may be relevant to those who were sexually abused and have an eating disorder, a substantial number of people are sexually abused and do not develop an eating disorder (Pope et al., 1994) or develop some other psy-

Anorexia/Bulimia Epidemiology 20

chiatric disorder instead (Vize & Cooper, 1995; Welch et al., 1994). Furthermore, the majority of people suffering from an eating disorder do not report any sexual abuse (Vize & Cooper, 1995).

Even when applying the theories proposed by Everill and Waller (1994) only to those with an eating disorder who report sexual abuse, these theories still contain flaws. In these cases, sexual abuse may be complexly linked to eating disorders through the development of a particular cognitive style in individuals who suffered from abuse, but this is speculation at best. In the future, researchers may want to focus on an integrated theory that includes genetics, cognitive patterns, family background, and sociocultural factors.

Anorexia/Bulimia Epidemiology 21

References

Boumann, C. E., & Yates, W. R. (1994). Risk factors for bulimia nervosa: A controlled study of parental psychiatric illness and divorce. <u>Addictive Behaviors, 19</u>, 667-675.

Brumberg, J. J. (1988). <u>Fasting girls</u>. Cambridge: Harvard University Press.

Bryant-Waugh, R., & Lask, B. (1995). Eating disorders: An overview. <u>Journal of Family Therapy, 17</u>, 13-30.

Bulik, C. M., Sullivan, P. F., Weltzin, T. E., & Kaye, W. H. (1995). Temperament in eating disorders. <u>International Journal of Eating Disorders, 17</u>, 251-261.

Drewnowski, A., Hopkins, S. A., & Kessler, R. C. (1988). The prevalence of bulimia nervosa in the U.S. college student population. <u>The American Journal of Public Health, 78</u>, 1322-1325.

Drewnowski, A., Yee, D. K., Kurth, C. L., & Krahn, D. D. (1994). Eating pathology and DSM-III-R bulimia nervosa: A continuum of behavior. <u>The American Journal of Psychiatry, 151</u>, 1217-1219.

Title the page "References." Double-space throughout. Alphabetize by author last name (See pages 253–58.)

Anorexia/Bulimia Epidemiology 22

Everill, J. T., & Waller, G. (1995). Reported sexual abuse and eating psychopathology: A review of the evidence for a causal link. International Journal of Eating Disorders, 18, 1–11.

Fitcher, M. M., & Daser, C. (1987). Symptomology, psychosexual development, and gender identity in 42 anorexic males. Psychological Medicine, 17, 409–418.

Fullerton, D. T., Wonderlich, S. A., & Gosnell, B. A. (1994). Clinical characteristics of eating disorder patients who report sexual or physical abuse. International Journal of Eating Disorders, 17, 243–249.

Herzog, D. B., Norman, D. K., Gordon, C., & Pepose, M. (1984). Sexual conflict and eating disorders in 27 males. The American Journal of Psychiatry, 141, 989–990.

Hsu, L. K. G. (1989). The gender gap in eating disorders: Why are the eating disorders more common among women? Clinical Psychology Review, 9, 393–407.

Kaye, W. H., Bastiani, A. M., & Moss, H. (1995). Cognitive style of patients with anorexia nervosa and bulimia nervosa. International Journal of Eating Disorders, 18, 287–290.

Anorexia/Bulimia Epidemiology 23

Kendler, K. S., MacLean, C., Neale, M., Kessler, R., Heath, A., & Eaves, L. (1991). The genetic epidemiology of bulimia nervosa. The American Journal of Psychiatry, 148, 1627–1637.

Margo, J. L. (1987). Anorexia nervosa in males: A comparison with female patients. British Journal of Psychiatry, 151, 80–83.

Olivardia, R., Pope, H. G., Mangweth, B., & Hudson, J. (1995). Eating disorders in college men. The American Journal of Psychiatry, 152, 1279–1285.

Pope, H. G., & Hudson, J. I. (1984). New hope for binge eaters. New York: Harper & Row.

Pope, H. G., Mangweth, B., Negrao, A. B., Hudson, J. I., & Taki, A. C. (1994). Childhood sexual abuse and bulimia nervosa: A comparison of American, Austrian, and Brazilian women. The American Journal of Psychiatry, 151, 732–737.

Schneider, J. A., & Agras, S. W. (1987). Bulimia in males: A matched comparison with females. International Journal of Eating Disorders, 6, 235–242.

Scott, D. W. (1986). Anorexia nervosa in the male: A review of clinical, epidemiologi-

Anorexia/Bulimia Epidemiology 24

cal and biological findings. <u>International
Journal of Eating Disorders, 5</u>, 799-819.

Shisslak, C. M., Crago, M., & Estes, L. S.
(1995). The spectrum of eating distur-
bances. <u>International Journal of Eating
Disorders, 18</u>, 209-219.

Sitnick, T., & Katz, J. L. (1984). Sex role
identity and anorexia nervosa. <u>Interna-
tional Journal of Eating Disorders, 3</u>,
81-87.

Sullivan, P. F., Bulik, C. M., Carter, F. A.,
& Joyce, P. R. (1995). The significance
of a history of childhood sexual abuse in
bulimia nervosa. <u>British Journal of Psychiatry, 167</u>, 679-682.

Vize, C. M., & Cooper, P. J. (1995). Sexual
abuse in patients with eating disorder,
patients with depression, and natural
controls: A comparison study. <u>British
Journal of Psychiatry, 167</u>, 80-85.

Walters, E. E., & Kendler, K. S. (1995).
Anorexia nervosa and anorexic-like syn-
dromes in a population-based female twin
study. <u>The American Journal of Psychiatry, 152</u>, 64-71.

Anorexia/Bulimia Epidemiology 25

Welch, S. L., & Fairburn, C. G. (1994). Sexual abuse and bulimia nervosa: Three integrated case control comparisons. The American Journal of Psychiatry, 151, 402–407.

Yater, J., Rorty, M., & Rossotto, E. (1995). Coping styles differ between recovered and nonrecovered women with bulimia nervosa, but not between recovered women and non-eating-disordered control subjects. The Journal of Nervous and Mental Disease, 183, 86–94.

CBE (COUNCIL OF BIOLOGY EDITORS) NAME/YEAR STYLE

The latest edition (6th, 1994) of *Scientific Style and Format: The CBE Manual for Authors, Editors, and Publishers* is significantly different from previous editions. The title page underscores a key shift. The *Manual* asserts that it now covers "the physical sciences and mathematics as well as the life sciences." The *Manual* calls for a single, international style for all scientists. So instead of presenting an author/year—or name/year, to use their language—style that varies just a bit from APA style and has been used in the life sciences, the *Manual* now covers both name/year and a number system, used in the physical sciences and mathematics. (It also recognizes that there are traditions within disciplines that many want to retain. And, in fact, many fields in the life sciences continue to use the CBE name/year pattern.) A review of CBE name/year format follows. The number system will be illustrated for chemistry, physics, and mathematics.

In-Text Citations

Give name (author) and year (plus precise page numbers when quoting) within the text according to the guidelines presented under APA style on pages 250–53. Authors may be mentioned in a sentence with the year following in parentheses, or both author and year may be placed in parentheses. Here are two examples.

(1) One type of glial cells, the astrocytes (star cells), perform more than support and clean-up tasks in the central nervous system. Nedergaard (1994) has demonstrated the astrocytes have functional neurotransmitter receptors and can communicate directly with neurons. This research, states Nedergaard, "challenges the general assumption that neurons alone are responsible for information processing in the central nervous system" (p. 1770).

(2) In the case of apple leaf wax, it is known that the dihydrochalcone phloridzin is present. Although this is used by the apple aphid as a signal to feed,

```
it is known to be repellent to the pea aphid
Acyrthrosiphon pisi (Klingauf, 1971).
```

References

Start references on a new page, after the text but before any tables or figures, and title the page "Literature Cited" or "References Cited." (List only those works cited in the paper.) Arrange citations alphabetically by author's last name. Two styles are shown—and are found in journals in the field. (1) Begin each citation flush with the left margin and indent second and subsequent lines four spaces. (2) Begin each citation flush with the left margin and do not indent any lines. The first format will be illustrated in examples provided with explanation. The second pattern is illustrated in the sample "References Cited" page.

Form for Books

1. Give the author's name, last name first, *not followed by a comma*, followed by initials without spacing or periods until after the last initial. Give the year of publication. Follow with the title (and subtitle, if there is one), *not* underlined. Capitalize only the first word of the title (and of the subtitle) and any proper nouns. End with a period.

```
Desmond A. 1995. Kew: The history of the royal botanic
    gardens.
```

With two or more authors, use the same pattern of last name and initials without spacing. Place a comma between names of authors.

```
Henry JG, Heinke GW. 1996. Environmental science and
    engineering.
```

2. Give edition information, or name(s) of editor(s), as appropriate.

```
Henry JG, Heinke GW. 1996. Environmental science and
    engineering. 2nd ed.
```

3. Provide the facts of publication: place of publication, followed by a colon; publisher, followed by a period.

```
Desmond A. 1995. Kew: The history of the royal botanic
    gardens. London (UK): Harvill.
```

4. For parts of books, cite author, year, and title of the part used, followed by "In:" and the title of the book. Give place and publisher and then the inclusive pages of the part used. Use "p," *without a period after*, for page or pages.

```
Stevens PF. 1990. George Bentham and the Kew Rule. In:

    Hawksworth DL, ed. Improving the stability of

    names: Needs and options. Koningstein (Germany):

    Koeltz. p 157-68.
```

5. The CBE *Manual* calls for giving the total number of pages for a book, at the end of the citation. This practice is found in some journals related to the life sciences but is not a standard practice.

```
Kirk PM, Sutton BC, Pegler DN, editors. 1995.

    Ainsworth and Bisby's dictionary of the fungi. 8th

    ed. Wallingford: C.A.B. International. 616 p.
```

6. For works with no author identified, use [Anonymous] in square brackets.

Form for Journal, Magazine, and Newspaper Articles

1. Cite the author, last name first and initials, followed by the year for journal articles. For magazine and newspaper articles, give the full date in this order: year—month—day. Then give the article title, *not* in quotation marks, capitalizing only the first word and any proper nouns.

```
Lentz TL, Trinkaus JP. 1971. Differentiation of the

    junctional complex of surface cells in the

    developing Fundulus blastoderm.
```

2. Give the journal title, *not* underlined, using standard abbreviations as listed in the CBE *Manual*.

```
Lentz. . . blastoderm. J. Cell Biol.
```

3. Cite the volume number, followed by a colon and then the article's inclusive page numbers.

```
Lentz. . . J. Cell Biol. 48:455-472.
```

4. For journals that page each issue separately rather than paging consecutively throughout all the issues in one year, add the issue number in parentheses—without spacing—following the volume number.

```
Rice AL. 1970. Decapod crustacean larvae collected

    during the International Indian Ocean Expedition.

    Bull. Br. Mus. [Nat. Hist.] Zool. 21(1): 1-24.
```

5. For magazine and newspaper articles, cite the full date thus:

Karl TR, Nicholls N, Gregory J. 1977 May. The coming

climate. Sci. Am.: 78-83.

[Anonymous]. 1990 Aug 24. Gene data may help fight

colon cancer. Los Angeles Times; Sect A:4.

Form for Technical Bulletins, Reports, Conferences, or Symposiums

Treat as a book, but add information to identify the special type of publication. Bulletins and technical publications usually have a number (abbreviated "nr") that needs to be included.

Wells PG, Butler JN, Hughes JS, editors. 1995. *Exxon*

Valdez oil spill: Fate and effects in Alaskan

waters. Philadelphia: American Society for Testing

and Materials. ASTM Special Technical Publication

nr 1219.

Form for Electronic Sources

The CBE *Manual* suggests that most electronic sources used will be journal articles, electronic books or their parts, and computer software. In all cases, follow the appropriate forms given above—for an article or a book—but include the type of medium in square brackets after the journal or book title and end the reference with an availability statement and the date you accessed the material.

Briggs DJ, France J. 1982. Mapping noise pollution

from road traffic for regional environmental

planning. J. Envrion. Manage [online database];

14(2): 173-79. Available from Cambridge Scientific

Abstracts via the Internet. Accessed 1997 June 18.

Sample References

Use the following sample references as a guide to preparing a list of references according to CBE name/year style.

References Cited

Cole DW, Rapp M. 1981. Element cycling in forest

ecosystems. In Reichle DE, ed. Dynamic properties of

forest ecosystems. Cambridge (UK): Cambridge Univ
Pr. p 341-401.

Houghton RA. 1994. The worldwide extent of land-use
change. BioScience 44: 305-13.

Redfield AC. 1985. The biological control of
chemical factors in the environment. Am Scientist
46: 205-21.

Sibly RM, Smith RH, eds. 1985. Behavioural ecology:
Ecological consequences of adaptive behaviour. 25th
symposium of the British Ecological Society 1984.
Blackwell: Oxford.

Tyree MT, Ewers FW. 1991. The hydraulic architecture
of trees and other woody plants (Tansley Review nr
34). New Phytologist 119: 345-60.

Willis R, trans. 1965. The works of William Harvey.
[London 1847]. Sources of science nr 13. New York:
Johnson Reprint.

Wright HA, Bailey AW. 1982. Fire ecology. New York:
J Wiley.

USGS (U.S. GEOLOGICAL SURVEY) STYLE

In its *Suggestions to Authors of the Reports of the United States Geological Survey* (7th ed., Washington, DC: Department of the Interior, 1991), the USGS establishes guidelines for its geologists' papers. You should know, however, that the variations of APA style found in this manual are not used in many of the journals relevant to geologists, including the *Journal of the Geological Society*. The variations can perhaps be explained by the close connection between geology and many applied sciences that use other styles. When preparing papers in geology courses, learn each professor's preference for APA style, CBE style, USGS style, or the number style.

In-Text Citations

In-text citations should provide author, year, and page references (unless the work cited is a dictionary or glossary or the reference is to a body of work). "And others" is preferred to "et al." when a citation refers to three or more authors. Here are examples of in-text citations:

Some of the dated granitoids intrude parts of the

Warrawoona stratigraphic units (A. H. Hickman,

1981:59). . . .

More recent work by Copper, James, and Rutland

(1982). . .

A variation of this hypothesis, proposed by G. K.

Gilbert (1893:289-90). . .

References

Title the alphabetical list of sources "References Cited" or "References." The order of information is:

author, last name first followed by initials or by first name if only one name is used

year of publication, not in parentheses

title of work, not underlined, followed by a colon.

For Books: the city of publication, the name of the publisher, and the number of book pages

For Articles: the name of the periodical, capitalized but not underlined, volume and issue numbers, not underlined, and inclusive page numbers.

Use commas between elements of a citation except for the colon after the source title. End each citation with a period. Here are several examples in USGS style:

References Cited

Brindze, Ruth, 1972, Charting the Oceans: New York,

Vanguard Press, 108p.

Brush, S. G., 1982, Nickel for your thoughts: Urey

and the origin of the Moon: Science, v. 217,

p. 891-98.

Compston, W., Williams, I. S., and Meyer, C., 1984, U-Pb geochronology of zircons from lunar breccia 73217 using a sensitive high mass-resolution ion microprobe, Proceedings of the 14th Lunar and Planetary Science Conference: Journal of Geophysical Research, v. 89 supplement, p. B525-34.

Heymsfield, A. J., and Miloshevich, L. M., 1991, Limit to greenhouse warming?: Nature, v. 351, no. 6321, p. 14-15.

Stacey, F. D., 1977a, Physics of the Earth, 2nd ed.: New York, Wiley.

---, 1977b, A thermal model of the Earth: Physics of the Earth and Planetary Interiors, v. 15, p. 341-48.

Van der Veen, C. J., 1986, Ice sheets, atmosphere CO_2 and sea level: Thesis, Univ. Utrecht, 185p.

World Bank, 1988, The World Bank Atlas, 1988: Washington, DC.

FOOTNOTE/ENDNOTE STYLE

Instructors in history, philosophy, and the arts frequently prefer the footnote or endnote form of documentation to any form of parenthetical citation. There are two chief guides to footnote and endnote style:

MLA Handbook, 4th edition, 1995

Chicago Manual of Style, 14th edition, 1993

The required information and the order of that information in a footnote are the same in these two style manuals. But they do differ in minor ways in formatting.

Since the *MLA Handbook* recommends the author/page citation over footnotes or endnotes and the *Chicago Manual of Style* includes author/year, make certain that an instructor requiring that you follow either one of these manuals actually wants you to use footnotes or endnotes. Once footnotes or endnotes has been established as the pattern of documentation, find out if your instructor has a preference. The *MLA Handbook*, for example, advises writers to use endnotes unless specifically requested to use footnotes, and Chicago also prefers endnotes. However, some instructors now expect and prefer footnotes, probably because they assume that students will be using PCs, which make footnoting much easier than if they have to be prepared on a typewriter. Finally, ascertain if your instructor wants a bibliography in addition to footnotes or endnotes. Because the first footnote or endnote reference contains complete bibliographic information, a list of works cited or bibliography is not necessary. Still, some instructors want both documentation notes and a Works Cited page at the end of the paper.

The guidelines below follow the *Chicago Manual of Style* for preparing footnotes and endnotes. The few differences in presentation found in the *MLA Handbook* are explained where appropriate.

In-Text Citations

Use a raised (superscript, such as this[2]) arabic numeral immediately following all material from a source, whether quoted or paraphrased. The number follows all punctuation except the dash, and it always follows, never precedes, material needing documentation. Number footnotes or endnotes consecutively throughout the paper, beginning with the number 1. Study the following brief excerpt from Everard H. Smith's study of the Civil War as an example:

> A cautious scholar, Clausewitz was unwilling to predict whether the democratic nationalism unleashed by Napoleon would lead to even more violent future wars. Yet he was not hopeful, for he believed that the passions of the people, once engaged, could not easily be restrained.[61] Alexis de Tocqueville, who toured the United States during the same period, reached similar conclusions about the relationship of warfare to popular will. A democracy, he surmised, would fight with irresistible determination because of the totality of its involvement: "War. . . in the end becomes the one great industry, and every eager and ambitious desire sprung from equality is focused thereon."[62]

With footnoting, use the same care to present material from sources with introductory tags and with a placing of superscript numerals so that readers can tell where borrowed material begins and where it ends. Regularly placing citation numerals only at the ends of paragraphs will not result in accurate documentation.

Location and Presentation of Footnotes

1. Place footnotes on the same page as the borrowed material. If you are using a typewriter, calculate the number of lines needed at the bottom of the page to complete all the footnotes for that page. If you miscalculate, retype the page. A word processor will make the spacing calculations for you.

2. Begin the first footnote four lines (two double spaces) below the last line of text.

3. Indent the first line of each footnote five spaces. Type the superscript numeral that corresponds to the one in the text, leave one space, and then type the reference information. (This is the most common practice in research papers, but the *Chicago Manual* also shows online numerals followed by a period—for example: 1. This Chicago style can be found in books and some journals. It is most often used with endnotes.)

4. If a footnote runs to more than one line of text, single-space between lines and begin the second line flush with the left margin.

5. If more than one footnote appears on a page, double-space between notes.

Location and Presentation of Endnotes

1. List endnotes in consecutive order corresponding to the superscript numbers in the text.

2. Indent the first line of each endnote five spaces. Type the raised number, leave one space, and then type the reference. (Again, this is the traditional pattern in research papers, but Chicago style also shows an online numeral followed by a period. See the alternative example under Form for Books below.)

3. If the endnote runs to more than one line, double-space between lines and begin the second line flush with the left margin.

4. Double-space between endnotes.

5. Start endnotes on a new page titled "Notes." Endnotes follow the text and precede a list of works cited, if such a list is included.

Footnote/Endnote Form: First (Primary) Reference

Each first reference to a source contains all the necessary author, title, and publication information that would be found in a works cited or reference list. Subsequent references to the same source use a shortened form. Prepare all first-reference notes according to the following guidelines.

Form for Books

1. Cite the author's full name in signature order, followed by a comma.

2. Cite the title of the book, and underline it. Include the complete subtitle, if there is one, unless a list of works cited is also provided. No punctuation follows the title.

3. Give the facts of publication in parentheses: city of publication followed by a colon, publisher followed by a comma, and year of publication.

4. Give the precise page reference. Do not use "p." or "pp." *MLA Handbook* style: Use no punctuation between the closing parenthesis and the page refer-

ence. *Chicago Manual* style: Place a comma after the closing parenthesis, before the page number.

¹Daniel J. Boorstin, The Americans: The Colonial

Experience (New York: Vintage-Random, 1958), 46.

(The most common footnote/endnote pattern uses a superscript number and a comma after the closing parenthesis.)
Alternative

1. Daniel J. Boorstin, The Americans: The Colonial

Experience (New York: Vintage-Random, 1958), 46.

(If you use this less common style for student papers, do not indent the first line of the note. Format as this example illustrates.)

Form for Articles

1. Cite the author's full name in signature order, followed by a comma.
2. Cite the title of the article in quotation marks and place a comma *inside* the closing quotation mark.
3. Give the facts of publication:

the title of the journal, underlined

the volume in arabic numerals

the date followed by a colon.

4. For scholarly journals, give the volume number followed by the date in parentheses. For popular magazines and newspapers do not use the volume number. Instead give the date only, not in parentheses.
5. For scholarly articles, provide a precise page reference following the colon, without using "p." or "pp." For popular articles, place a comma after the magazine or newspaper title, give the date, followed by a comma and the page number. All notes end with a period.

²Everard H. Smith, "Chambersburg: Anatomy of a

Confederate Reprisal," American Historical Review 96

(April 1991): 434.

³Andrew Rosenthal, "White House Retreats on

Ruling That Curbs Minority Scholarships," New York

Times, 18 Dec. 1990, A1.

Sample Footnotes/Endnotes

Additional information must be added as necessary to the simplest examples given above. Some of the most common variations are illustrated here. Note that the examples are presented as endnotes: The lines of each note are double spaced. (Footnotes are single-spaced within each note but double-spaced between notes.) The examples illustrate the most common pattern of indenting the first line, using a raised numeral, and placing a comma after the facts of publication in a book citation.

A Work by Two or Three Authors

[4]Charles A. Beard and Mary R. Beard, The American Spirit (New York: Macmillan, 1942), 63.

A Work by More Than Three Authors

[5]Leonard W. Levy et al., eds., American Constitutional History (New York: Macmillan, 1989), 52.

An Edited Work

[6]The Autobiography of Benjamin Franklin, ed. Max Farrand (Berkeley: University of California Press, 1949), 6-8.

(Begin with the title—or the editor's name—if the author's name appears in the title.)

A Translation

[7]Max Weber, From Max Weber: Essays in Sociology, trans. and ed. H. H. Gerth and C. Wright Mills (London: Routledge & Kegan Paul, 1948), 142.

[8]Jean Jacques Rousseau, The Social Contract and Discourses, trans. with an introduction by G. D. H. Cole (New York: Dutton, 1950), 42-43.

A Preface, Introduction, or Afterword

[9]Ernest Barker, introduction, The Politics of Aristotle, trans. and ed. Ernest Barker (New York: Oxford University Press, 1962), xiii.

A Book in Two or More Volumes

[10]Paul Tillich, Systematic Theology, 3 vols. (Chicago: University of Chicago Press, 1951–63), 1:52.

(Make the page reference first to the volume, followed by a colon, and then the page number.)

A Work in Its Second or Subsequent Edition

[11]Frank J. Sorauf and Paul Allen Beck, Party Politics in America, 6th ed. (Glenview, IL: Scott, Foresman/Little, Brown, 1988), 326.

A Work in a Series

[12]Charles L. Sanford, ed., Benjamin Franklin and the American Character, Problems in American Civilization (Lexington, MA: D. C. Heath, 1955), 4.

A Work in a Collection

[13]George Washington, "Farewell Address, 1796," in A Documentary History of the United States, ed. Richard D. Heffner (New York: New American Library, 1965), 64–65.

An Encyclopedia Article

[14]The Concise Dictionary of American Biography, 1964 ed., s.v., "Anthony, Susan Brownell."

(Do not cite a page number for reference works arranged alphabetically. Instead, cite the entry in quotation marks after "s.v." [*sub verbo*—"under the word"]. The edition number or year is needed, but no other facts of publication are required for well-known reference works.)

An Article in a Scholarly Journal

[15]Ellen Fitzpatrick, "Rethinking the Intellectual Origins of American Labor History," American Historical Review 96 (April 1991): 426.

An Article in a Popular Magazine

[16]Robert B. Reich, "Dumpsters: The End of an Unfair Trade Practice," The New Republic, 10 June 1991, 9.

An Editorial

[17]"The Third World's Peace Dividend," editorial, Washington Post, 28 May 1991, A18.

A Review

[18]Gabriel P. Weisberg, "French Art Nouveau," rev. of Art Nouveau in Fin-de-Siecle France: Politics, Psychology, and Style by Deborah Silverman, Art Journal 49 (Winter 1990): 427.

A Speech

[19]Speech by William J. Brennan, Jr., at Georgetown University, Text and Teaching Symposium, October 10, 1985, Washington, DC.

A Dissertation

[20]Beth Reingold, "Representing Women: A Comparison of Female and Male Legislators in Arizona and California" (Ph.D. dissertation, University of California, Berkeley, 1992), 117.

An Online News Service

[21]Laurene McQuillan, "Bush Urges Senate to Avoid Abortion Litmus Test on Souter," <u>Reuters</u>, July 24, 1990, available from NEXIS.

Footnote/Endnote Form: Short Forms

After the first complete footnote or endnote, subsequent references to the same source should be shortened forms. The simplest short form for any source with an author or editor is the author's or editor's last name followed by a comma and a precise page reference: Fitzgerald, 425. If there is no author cited, use a short title and page number. If two sources are written by authors with the same last name, then add first names or initials to distinguish between them. For example, if you cited "The Tendency of History" by Henry Adams and *The Founding of New England* by James T. Adams, then the short forms would be:

[22]Henry Adams, 16.

[23]James T. Adams, 253.

More typically, you will use two or more sources by the same author. In that case, add a short title to the note; thus:

[24]Boorstin, <u>American Politics</u>, 154.

[25]Boorstin, <u>The Americans</u>, 44–47.

The Latin abbreviations *loc. cit.* and *op. cit.* are no longer recommended, and Ibid. is almost as obsolete. Ibid. is usually replaced by the simple short form of author's last name and page number. Remember that Ibid. can be used only to refer to the source cited in the immediately preceding note. The following footnotes, appearing at the bottom of a page from a history paper, illustrate the various short forms.

Sample Footnotes from a History Paper

While mid-twentieth century historians may be more accurate, they have lost the flavor of earlier American historians who had a clear ideology that shaped their writing.[20]

[11]William Bradford, <u>Of Plymouth Plantation</u>, <u>The American Puritans: Their Prose and Poetry</u>, ed. Perry Miller (New York: Anchor-Doubleday, 1956), 5.

[12]Daniel Boorstin, The Americans: The Colonial
Experience (New York: Vintage-Random, 1958), 16.

[13]Ibid., 155. [OR [13]Boorstin, The Americans, 155.]

[14]James T. Adams, 139.

[15]Henry Adams, The Education of Henry Adams, ed.
D. W. Brogan (Boston: Houghton Mifflin, 1961), 342.

[16]Boorstin, American Politics, 167.

[17]Henry Adams, "The Tendency of History," 16.

[18]Ibid, 71. [OR: [18]Henry Adams, "The Tendency of
History," 71.]

[19]Henry Adams, Education, 408.

[20]John Higham, "The Cult of the 'American
Consensus': Homogenizing Our History," Commentary 27
(Feb. 1959): 94-96.

NUMBER STYLE

As noted at the beginning of this chapter, the number style of documentation
requires that each source cited be given a number when it is first referred to
and that only the number— the same number—appear in parentheses within
the text, whenever reference is made to the source. The in-text citation by
number is supported by a complete list of references organized (usually) in
the order in which the sources are referred to in the paper. (A variation of this
pattern is to organize the reference list alphabetically.) The following paragraph from a paper on the global tectonics of Venus illustrates one version of
number-style in-text citation:

One of the principal hypotheses concerning the nature
of Venusian tectonics is that it is dominated by the
effects of convective plumes rising in the mantle,
impinging on the lithosphere, and producing hot spots-
areas of volcanism and uplift created by the magmatic,
thermal, and dynamic effects of the plumes (*3, 5, 6*).
Two major elements of this model are (i) that large-

scale horizontal motion of the lithosphere does not
take place or is, at most, a minor process (*6, 7*) and
(ii) that Venus loses most of its heat through
lithospheric conduction, which is enhanced at the thin
lithosphere associated with hot spots (*6, 8*).

The *Chicago Manual of Style* describes the number system as tedious for readers, particularly when several numbers are cited together but no authors' names are mentioned in the text. Not surprisingly, some journals relevant to the fields that have used the number style (chemistry, physics, mathematics, computer science, and the medical sciences) have now switched to, or allow as an alternative, the author/year style of documentation. The American Chemical Society, for example, now lists the author/year style as one option. To add to the confusion, experts in some special fields in the earth sciences must employ the number system in some of the interdisciplinary journals for which they write. The paper on Venus, for example, was written by two geologists and published in the journal *Science*.

> ✓ Do not assume! Ascertain each instructor's preference for documentation style and then follow that style as explained in this text. Some instructors ask only that you select an appropriate style and be consistent. Others care greatly about which style you use.

What follows is a general guide to in-text citations with numbers and then the styles for citing references according to the American Chemical Society (*ACS Style Guide*, 1986), the American Institute of Physics (*AIP Style Manual*, 4th ed., 1990), and the American Mathematical Society (*A Manual for Authors of Mathematical Papers*, rev. ed., 1990).

In-Text Citation: In General

1. Select the appropriate pattern of number citation, according to your field or your instructor's preference:

A superscript number[2]

An online number in parentheses (2)

An online number in parentheses either in italic type *(2)* or underlined in the paper (2)

An online number, usually in italic type, placed within square brackets [*2*]

2. Place the number immediately after the author's name

```
Head and Crumpler (3) have proposed. . .
```

OR

```
Head and Crumpler³ have proposed. . .
```

or after a sentence, clause, or phrase that contains the borrowed material:

```
Subthreshold field steering currents have been used to
improve selectivity of peripheral nerve stimulation
with nerve cuff electrodes [14],[29],[35].
```

3. When citing several sources at once, place numbers in ascending order:

```
in the literature (2,3,6)

in the literature ²,³,⁶
```

(Note that superscript numbers are separated by commas with no spaces between commas and numbers.)

ACS (American Chemical Society) Style

In-Text Citations

The *ACS Style Guide* lists 11 journals requiring superscript numbers for in-text citation, 5 journals (plus books published by ACS) requiring online italic numerals, and 3 requiring author/year citations. References should be listed in the order of in-text citations when the writer is using numerals, alphabetically when the writer is using the author/year style.

References

Most journals in the chemistry field follow a style of beginning each reference with its number and repeating the form of the numeral that was used in the text. Thus, if superscript numerals were used in the text, then each reference would begin with a superscript numeral. In the *ACS Style Guide*, however, no number is shown at the beginning of a reference, and there is no indenting of either the first line or of second and subsequent lines of each reference. Follow these guidelines for preparing references:

1. Begin your list of references on a new page after the text but before any tables or illustrations. Title the page "References."

2. Cite authors by last name and initials, last name first for all authors. Separate multiple authors' names with a semicolon:

```
Littman, M.; Yeomans, D. K.
```

Form for Books

1. Cite the book title, with normal capitalization, in italics (underlined), followed by a semicolon:

   `Comet Halley: Once in a Lifetime;`

2. Provide publication information in this order: publisher first, followed by a colon; place, followed by a comma; and date:

   `American Chemical Society: Washington, DC, 1985.`

3. Specific volume, chapter, and/or page numbers are often cited, if only one part of the book is used. If many pages throughout a book have been cited in the text, then exclude specific pages from the reference. When citing portions of a book, use the following abbreviations or spelled-out forms, noting capitalization when used:

   Abstract

   Chapter

   ed. (for *edition*, but Ed. or Eds. for *editor* or *editors*)

   No. (for *number*)

   p. (for *page*); pp (for *pages*—no period used)

   Part

   Vol. (for a specific volume; vols. for number of volumes)

   Example

   `Armstrong, G. W. et al. In Analytical Chemistry of`

   `the Elements; Kolthoff, I. M.; Elving, P. J., Eds.;`

   `Interscience-Wiley: New York, 1961; Part 2, Vol. 7.`

Form for Articles

1. Do not give the title of the article. Cite the journal title after the author's name, in abbreviated form and in italics (underlined):

   `Bercovici, D.; Schubert, G. Science`

2. Cite the year in bold type, indicated by a wavy line under the date. (If you are using a word processor, use the bold function key for the year.) There is no punctuation between the journal title and the year; a comma follows the year.

   `Bercovici, D.; Schubert, G. Science 1989,`

OR

`Bercovici, D.; Schubert, G. `<u>`Science`</u>` **1989**,`

3. Without spacing, cite the volume number, in italics (underlined), followed by a comma:

`Bercovici. . . `<u>`Science`</u>` **1989**,`<u>`244`</u>`,`

4. Without spacing, cite either the initial page of the article or, preferred by ACS, the inclusive page numbers for the article:

`Bercovici, D.; Schubert, G. `<u>`Science`</u>` **1989**,`<u>`244`</u>`,950.`

5. When citing references to articles in journals that are not paged continuously throughout the issues in a year, include the issue number in parentheses following the volume number. Note that there is no space between the volume number and the opening parenthesis or between the comma and the page numbers.

`Ewen, J. A. `<u>`Sci. Amer.`</u>` **1997**,`<u>`276`</u>`(5),86-91.`

6. Indicate when a reference is to an English translation of an article by adding "Engl. Transl." in parentheses after the journal title. Then, if possible, add a reference to the original article.

Sample References

Use the following sample references as models for preparing citations for papers in chemistry.

References

`Steudel, R. `<u>`Chemistry of Nonmetals`</u>`; deGruyter:`

`Berlin, 1977; p. 15.`

`Pojman, J. A.; Craven, R; Leard, D. `<u>`J. Chem. Educ.`</u>

`**1994**,`<u>`71`</u>`,84-90.`

`Bowen, C. W. `<u>`Abstracts of Papers`</u>`, 208th National`

`Meeting of the American Chemical Society,`

`Washington, DC, August 1994; Abstract 162.`

`Head, J. W.; Crumpler, L. S. `<u>`Nature`</u>` **1990**,`<u>`346`</u>`,525.`

`Wainscoat, R. J. In `<u>`The World of Galaxies`</u>`; Corwin,`

`H. G.; Bottinelli, L., Eds.; Proceedings of the`

Conference "Le Monde des Galaxies," Paris, France;

New York and Berlin: Springer-Verlag, 1989; pp

290-292.

Lubetkin, S. Chem Soc. Rev. **1995**,24,243-250.

Dorin, H.; Demmin, P. E.; Gabel, D. L. Chemistry,

The Study of Matter; Prentice Hall: Englewood

Cliffs, NJ, 1992; p. 341.

Wan, J. R. Ph.D. dissertation, Department of

Chemistry, University of Washington, 1993.

Grimm, R. E.; Phillips, R. J. J. Geophys. Res., in

press.

AIP (American Institute of Physics) Style

In-Text Citation

The preferred style of documenting sources is the use of superscript numerals in consecutive order throughout the text supported by a list of references organized in the order of citation in the text. The AIP also recognizes the alternative of author/year citation but advises writers to get approval for this pattern of citation before using it in a paper submitted for publication. So, the same advice applies to students: know what style your instructor wants you to use and then follow that style only.

References

The list of references should be placed after the text and any appendices but before tables and figures. Title the page "References." Double-space throughout the list. Start each reference on a new line, beginning with the superscript number flush with the left margin. Subsequent lines are also flush with the left margin.

1. Give authors' names in signature form as they appear on the title page of the work cited and follow with a comma:

[1]D. F. Shriver and M. A. Drezden,

Form for Books

2. Cite the title of the book in italics (underlined), with normal capitalization:

The Manipulation of Air-Sensitive Compounds

3. Add the number of volumes or edition number, as necessary:

<u>The Manipulation of Air-Sensitive Compounds</u>, 2nd ed.

4. Place publication information within parentheses—publisher first, then place, then date, each element separated by a comma:

[1]D. F. Shriver and M. A. Drezden, <u>The Manipulation of Air-Sensitive Compounds</u>, 2nd ed. (Wiley, New York, 1986).

5. For edited books, first give the author(s) of the particular part used. Cite the editor(s) after the title:

[2]J. M. Rehm, G. L. McLendon, P. M. Fauchet, in <u>Advanced Luminescent Materials</u>, edited by D. J. Lockwood, P. M. Fauchet, N. Koshida, S. R. J. Brueck (The Electrochemical Society, Pennington, NJ, 1996), p. 212.

Form for Articles

1. Article titles are not usually given. Cite the journal title, in abbreviated form, *not* underlined, after the name(s) of the author(s):

[3]T. A. Germer and W. Ho, J. Chem. Phys.

2. Give the volume number in bold type, indicated in the manuscript with a wavy line. (If you are using a word processor, use the bold function key for the volume number.)

T. A. Germer. . . Phys. 89 (OR:**89**)

3. Place a comma *after* the volume number, then the *first* page number, and then the year of publication in parentheses:

T. A. Germer and W. Ho, J. Chem. Phys. **89**, 652 (1988).

4. When citing references to articles in journals that are not paged continuously throughout the issues in a year, include the issue number in parentheses following the volume number:

[4]Barbara Goss Levi, Phys. Today **44** (2), 17 (1991).

Sample References

Use the following sample references as models for preparing papers in physics.

[1]M. S. Hybertsen, Phys. Rev. Lett. **10**, 1514 (1994).

[2]Lawrence Badash, ed., <u>Rutherford and Boltwood:</u> <u>Letters on Radioactivity</u> (Yale Univ. Press, New Haven, 1969), pp. 76-77.

[3]D. J. Adams and E. M. Adams, Mol. Phys. (1991), in press.

[4]<u>Albert Einstein: Philosopher-Scientist</u>, P. A. Schilpp, ed. (Open Court, La Salle, CA, 1970), p. 683.

[5]D. Hull and T. W. Clyne, <u>An Introduction to Composite Materials</u>, 2nd ed. (Cambridge Univ. Press, New York, 1996), p. 169.

[6]J. T. Spencer, P. A. Dowben, and V.-G. Kim, U.S. Patent No. 4,957,773 (18 Sept. 1990).

[7]Callery Chemical Company, Technical Bulletin No. CM-070, 1971.

[8]G. T. Horowitz, D. Marolf, preprint hep-th/9610171 (Los Alamos server, http://xxx.lanl.gov/).

AMS (American Mathematical Society) Style

In-Text Citations

In its revised second edition of *A Manual for Authors of Mathematical Papers*, the AMS encourages the use of specific references that include page numbers. The reference citation number, followed by precise pages, is placed in *square brackets*, and the numeral is in bold type.

As Jones [**3**, pp. 15-17] has demonstrated. . .

References

The AMS *Manual* shows the listing of references consecutively by number as cited in the text. However, the manual does include the possibility of listing references alphabetically. When numbering consecutively, use an online numeral, *not* in bold and *not* in brackets. Indent each number three spaces from the left margin. Subsequent lines in each reference are flush with the left margin.

1. Cite the author(s) by initial(s) and last name in signature order, followed by a comma:

        1. U. Grenander,

Form for Books

2. Give the title of the book in italics (underlined), capitalizing only the first word of the title (and subtitle, if there is one) and any proper nouns. Place a comma after the title:

        1. U. Grenander, <u>Lectures in pattern theory</u>,

3. Add number of volumes, edition number, or series name and number, as appropriate:

        1. U. Grenander, <u>Lectures in pattern theory</u>,

    Applied mathematical sciences no. 33,

4. Give the facts of publication in the order of publisher, city of publication, and year. Separate all elements by commas:

        1. U. Grenander, <u>Lectures in pattern theory</u>,

    Applied mathematical sciences, no. 33, Springer-

    Verlag, New York, 1981.

Form for Articles

5. Following the author's name, cite the article title, <u>underlined</u>, capitalizing only the first word and any proper nouns. Follow the title with a comma:

        2. C. Lance, <u>On nuclear C*-algebra</u>,

6. Give the journal title, abbreviated and *not* underlined:

        2. C. Lance, <u>On nuclear C*-algebra</u>, J. Funct. Anal.

7. Follow the journal title with the volume number in bold (indicated in manuscript with a wavy line), the year in parentheses, a comma, and inclusive page numbers:

        2. C. Lance, <u>On nuclear C*-algebra</u>, J. Funct. Anal

    12 (1973), 157–176.

Sample References

Use the following sample-references as models for preparing papers in mathematics.

References

1. S. M. Ross, <u>Introduction to probability models</u>, 4th ed., Academic Press, Boston, 1989.

2. D. Knuth, <u>Semi numerical algorithms</u>, Vol. 2, <u>The art of computer programming</u>, 2nd ed., Addison-Wesley, Reading, MA, 1981.

3. C. Keutenauer, <u>Series rationnelles et algebres syntactiques</u>, These, Univ. Paris, VI (1980).

4. H. Azad, M. Barry, and G. Seitz, <u>On the structure of parabolic subgroups</u>, Comm. In Alg. **18** (1990), 551-561.

5. G. M. Seitz, <u>Maximal subgroups of exceptional algebraic groups</u>, Amer. Math. Soc. Memoirs 441 (1991), 1-197.

6. S. Richman, <u>A defect relation for quasi-meromorphic mappings</u>, Annals of Math, in press.

7. R. Courant and D. Hilbert, <u>Methods of mathematical physics, Part I</u>. Interscience, New York, 1953.

8. S. Hammarling, <u>Parallel algorithms for singular value problems</u> in <u>Numerical linear algebra, digital signal processing and parallel algorithms</u>, G. H. Golub and P. Van Dooren, eds. Springer Verlag, Berlin, Germany, 1991, 173-187.

A List of
Abbreviations

You will see many of the abbreviations listed below in your college reading and research. Some of them are appropriate for your use in research papers. In general, you
are encouraged by MLA and most style sheets to use abbreviations or short titles of literary works and books of the Bible in both parenthetical citations and content notes.
Abbreviations are not always acceptable in the text of papers, but those well known to
readers in a given discipline should be used. Examples include MLA for Modern Language Association or APA for American Psychological Association, REM for rapid eye
movement, Btu for British thermal unit. Keep in mind, though, that many Latin abbreviations, once regularly used in footnote and endnote citations, are now discouraged.

SCHOLARLY ABBREVIATIONS

abbr.	abbreviated, abbreviation
abr.	abridged, abridgment
anon.	anonymous
art.	article
b.	born
bk., bks.	book(s)
ca. *or* c.	circa (about). Used with approximate dates: "ca. 1850."
cf.	confer (compare). Do not use "cf." when "see" is meant.
ch., chaps.	chapter (s)
chap., chaps.	chapter(s)
col., cols.	column(s)
comp.	compiled by, compiler
d.	died
diss.	dissertation
ed., eds.	edited by, edition(s), editor(s)
e.g.	*exempli gratia* (for example)
enl.	enlarged (e.g., "enl. ed.")

esp.	especially
et al.	*et alii* (and others)
et seq.	*et sequens* (and the following). Used with a page number, as in "p. 5 et seq.," to mean "page 5 and the following page."
f., ff.	And the following page(s). Exact references are better— e.g., "pp. 24–26" rather than "pp. 24 ff."
fig.	Figure
ibid.	*ibidem* (in the same place). Used to cite a different page in the immediately preceding cited work; not acceptable in MLA style; discouraged in most style manuals.
i.e.	*id est* (that is)
illus.	illustrated by, illustrations, illustrator
incl.	includes, including, inclusive
inf.	infra (below). The phrase "see below" is preferred.
introd.	Introduction
l., ll.	line(s). Do not use in text; no longer used in MLA parenthetical citations.
loc. cit.	*loco citato* (in the place cited). Not acceptable in MLA style
MS, MSS	manuscript(s).
n., nn.	note(s)
N.B.	*nota bene* (mark well, take careful note)
n.d.	no date (of publication) given
n.p.	no place (of publication) given
n.s. *or* ns	new series
obs.	obsolete
op. cit.	*opere citato* (in the work cited). Not acceptable in MLA style.
o.s. *or* os	old series
p., pp.	page(s). Do not use "ps." for "pages."
pass.	*passim* (here and there, throughout the work)
pseud.	pseudonym
pt., pts.	part(s)
rev.	review, revised, revision
rpt.	reprint, reprinted
sec.	section
ser.	series
st., sts.	stanza(s)
sup.	supra (above). The phrase "see above" is preferred.
trans.	translated by, translation, translator(s)
v.	*vide* (see)
v., vv.	verse(s)

viz.	*videlicet* (namely)
vol., vols.	volume(s)
vs. *or* v.	versus (against)

ABBREVIATIONS OF PUBLISHERS' NAMES

Abrams	Harry N. Abrams, Inc.
ALA	American Library Association
Allen	George Allen and Unwin Publishers, Inc.
Allyn	Allyn and Bacon, Inc.
Appleton	Appleton-Century-Crofts
Barnes	Barnes and Noble Books
Basic	Basic Books, Inc.
Beacon	Beacon Press, Inc.
Bobbs	The Bobbs-Merrill Co., Inc.
Bowker	R. R. Bowker Co.
Clarendon	Clarendon Press
Dell	Dell Publishing Co., Inc.
Dodd	Dodd, Mead, and Co.
Doubleday	Doubleday and Co., Inc.
Dutton	E. P. Dutton, Inc.
Farrar	Farrar, Straus, and Giroux, Inc.
Free	Free Press
Gale	Gale Research Co.
GPO	(U.S.) Government Printing Office
Harcourt	Harcourt Brace Jovanovich, Inc.
Harper	Harper & Row Publishers, Inc.
Heath	D.C. Heath and Co.
Holt	Holt, Rinehart, and Winston, Inc.
Houghton	Houghton Mifflin Co.
Knopf	Alfred A. Knopf, Inc.
Lippincott	J. B. Lippincott Co.
Little	Little, Brown, and Co.
Macmillan	Macmillan Publishing Co., Inc.
McGraw	McGraw-Hill, Inc.
Merrill	Merrill Publishing Co.
MLA	Modern Language Association
Norton	W. W. Norton and Co., Inc.
Prentice	Prentice-Hall, Inc.

Putnam's	G. P. Putnam's Sons
Random	Random House, Inc.
St. Martin's	St. Martin's Press, Inc.
Scott	Scott, Foresman and Co.
Scott/Little	Scott, Foresman/Little, Brown, Inc.
Scribner's	Charles Scribner's Sons
Simon	Simon and Schuster, Inc.

ABBREVIATIONS FOR MONTHS

Abbreviate the months as shown below. (*May, June,* and *July* are not shortened.) Use abbreviated forms in citations but not in the text of your papers.

Jan.	Apr.	July	Oct.
Feb.	May	Aug.	Nov.
Mar.	June	Sept.	Dec.

ABBREVIATIONS FOR STATES

Use the following postal abbreviations (without periods) when giving the state after a city in a citation. Do not abbreviate the names of states in the text of your papers.

Alabama	AL	Maine	ME
Alaska	AK	Maryland	MD
Arizona	AZ	Massachusetts	MA
Arkansas	AR	Michigan	MI
California	CA	Minnesota	MN
Colorado	CO	Mississippi	MS
Connecticut	CT	Missouri	MO
Delaware	DE	Montana	MT
District of Columbia	DC	Nebraska	NE
Florida	FL	Nevada	NV
Georgia	GA	New Hampshire	NH
Hawaii	HI	New Jersey	NJ
Idaho	ID	New Mexico	NM
Illinois	IL	New York	NY
Indiana	IN	North Carolina	NC
Iowa	IA	North Dakota	ND
Kansas	KS	Ohio	OH
Kentucky	KY	Oklahoma	OK
Louisiana	LA	Oregon	OR

Pennsylvania	PA	Utah	UT
Rhode Island	RI	Vermont	VT
South Carolina	SC	Virginia	VA
South Dakota	SD	Washington	WA
Tennessee	TN	West Virginia	WV
Texas	TX	Wisconsin	WI
		Wyoming	WY

ABBREVIATIONS FOR BOOKS OF THE BIBLE

Abbreviate books of the Bible in parenthetical references. Combine the abbreviations with chapter and verse citations as in this example: (Gen. 2.12). Do not underline titles or place them within quotation marks. All the books of the Bible are listed below; note that those of one syllable are not abbreviated.

Old Testament(OT)

Gen.	Genesis
Exod.	Exodus
Lev.	Leviticus
Num.	Numbers
Deut.	Deuteronomy
Josh.	Joshua
Judg.	Judges
Ruth	Ruth
1 Sam.	First Samuel
2 Sam.	Second Samuel
1 Kings	First Kings
2 Kings	Second Kings
1 Chron.	First Chronicles
2 Chron.	Second Chronicles
Ezra	Ezra
Neh.	Nehemiah
Esth.	Esther
Job	Job
Ps.	Psalms
Prov.	Proverbs
Eccles.	Ecclesiastes
Song. Sol.	Song of Solomon
Isa.	Isaiah

Jer.	Jeremiah
Lam.	Lamentations
Ezek.	Ezekiel
Dan.	Daniel
Hos.	Hosea
Joel	Joel
Amos	Amos
Obad.	Obadiah
Jon.	Jonah
Mic.	Micah
Nah.	Nahum
Hab.	Habakkuk
Zeph.	Zephaniah
Hag.	Haggai
Zech.	Zechariah
Mal.	Malachi

New Testament (NT)

Matt.	Matthew
Mark	Mark
Luke	Luke
John	John
Acts	Acts of the Apostles
Rom.	Romans
1 Cor.	First Corinthians
2 Cor.	Second Corinthians
Gal.	Galatians
Eph.	Ephesians
Phil.	Philippians
Col.	Colossians
1 Thess.	First Thessalonians
2 Thess.	Second Thessalonians
1 Tim.	First Timothy
2 Tim.	Second Timothy
Tit.	Titus
Philem.	Philemon
Heb.	Hebrews
Jas.	James

1 Pet.	First Peter
2 Pet.	Second Peter
1 John	First John
2 John	Second John
3 John	Third John
Jude	Jude
Rev.	Revelation

ABBREVIATIONS FOR LITERARY WORKS

When appropriate in parenthetical documentation, use abbreviations for the titles of literary works. In general, abbreviate by using the initial letters of the key words of a title (e.g., SL for The Scarlet Letter) or by using a short form of a one-word title (e.g., Can. for Candide). Note that these abbreviated titles are underlined, in contrast to the books of the Bible. Use the following abbreviations for Shakespeare's plays.

Ado	Much Ado about Nothing
Ant.	Antony and Cleopatra
AWW	All's Well That Ends Well
AYL	As You Like It
Cor.	Coriolanus
Err.	The Comedy of Errors
Ham.	Hamlet
1H4	Henry IV, Part I
2H4	Henry IV, Part II
H5	Henry V
1H6	Henry VI, Part I
2H6	Henry VI, Part II
3H6	Henry VI, Part III
H8	Henry VIII
JC	Julius Caesar
Jn.	King John
LLL	Love's Labour's Lost
Lr.	King Lear
Mac.	Macbeth
MM	Measure for Measure
MND	A Midsummer Night's Dream
MV	The Merchant of Venice

Oth.	Othello
Per.	Pericles, Prince of Tyre
R2	Richard II
R3	Richard III
Rom.	Romeo and Juliet
Shr.	The Taming of the Shrew
TGV	The Two Gentlemen of Verona
Tim.	Timon of Athens
Tit.	Titus Andronicus
Tmp.	The Tempest
TN	Twelfth Night
Tro.	Troilus and Cressida
Wiv.	The Merry Wives of Windsor
WT	The Winter's Tale

Key Reference Works by Discipline

The following list of reference works by discipline can aid your research in a specific field. Of course not all the works will be found in every library, and your library may have other, similar reference aids. In large college libraries many more works will be found than those listed here, arranged in the reference room by Library of Congress classification number, that is, grouped by subject field. This appendix begins with an index to the disciplines and then organizes works under the alphabetically arranged disciplines. For each discipline general works (including bibliographies, guides, encyclopedias, dictionaries, and histories) are listed first, followed by indexes in print form and electronic databases (either CD-ROM or online). Indexes in both paper and electronic formats will be so indicated. The electronic databases include both indexes to journals and indexes that contain full texts of articles.

INDEX TO LIST OF REFERENCE WORKS BY DISCIPLINE

LIST OF REFERENCE WORKS BY DISCIPLINE

ART AND ARCHITECTURE

GENERAL WORKS AND BIBLIOGRAPHIES

American Art Directory. New York: Bowker, 1952–present.

Annotated Bibliography of Fine Art. 1897. Rpt. Boston: Longwood, 1976.

Art Books. 1950–1979. New York: Bowker, 1981. Supplement 1985.

Bibliographic Guide to Art and Architecture. Boston: Hall, 1976–1985.

Britannica Encyclopaedia of American Art. Chicago: Encyclopaedia Britannica, 1973.

Contemporary Architects. 2nd ed. Chicago: St. James, 1987.

Contemporary Artists. 4th ed. New York: St. James's, 1995.

Dictionary of American Painters, Sculptors, and Engravers. New York: Reprint Service, 1993.

Encyclopedia of World Art. 16 vols. New York: McGraw, 1959–1983. Supplement 1987.

Fine and Applied Arts Terms Index. Detroit: Gale, 1983.

Fine Arts: A Bibliographic Guide. 3rd ed. Littleton, CO: Libraries Unlimited, 1990.

Guide to the Literature of Art History. Chicago: ALA, 1981.

A History of Architecture. New York: McGraw, 1985.

Larousse Dictionary of Painters. New York: Larousse, 1981, 1990.

Macmillan Encyclopedia of Architects. 4 vols. New York: Free, 1982.

Oxford Companion to Twentieth Century Art. Oxford: Oxford UP, 1988.

Pelican History of Art. 50 vols. in progress. Baltimore: Pelican, 1953–present.

Random House Library of Painting and Sculpture. 4 vols. New York: Beazley, 1981.

Research Guide to the History of Western Art. Chicago: ALA, 1982.

Web Museum. Internet. Available: http://sunsite.unc.edu/wm/

INDEXES AND ELECTRONIC DATABASES

ART ABSTRACTS (E)
ACADEMIC INDEX ASAP (E)
Art Index. New York: Bowker, 1929–present.
(P) (E—ART ABSTRACTS)
Bibliography of the History of Art (BHA).
1991-Quarterly. (Formerly RILA) (E)

Index to Art Periodicals. 11 vols. Boston:
Hall, 1962. Supplements.
ARTS AND HUMANITIES SEARCH (E)

BIOLOGICAL SCIENCES

GENERAL WORKS AND BIBLIOGRAPHIES

Biology Data Book. Madison: FASEB, 1983.
The Concise Oxford Dictionary of Zoology.
New York: Oxford UP, 1996.
Dictionary of Flowering Plants and Ferns.
New York: Cambridge UP, 1982.
Dictionary of Genetics and Cell Biology.
New York: New York UP, 1988.
*Dictionary of Theoretical Concepts in
Biology*. Metuchen: Scarecrow, 1981.
Encyclopedia of the Biological Sciences.
New York: Kreiger, 1981.
*Guide to Sources for Agricultural and
Biological Research*. Berkeley: U of
California P, 1981.

Henderson's Dictionary of Biological Terms.
New York: Wiley, 1995.
Information Sources in the Life Sciences.
4th ed. London: Bowter-Saur, 1996.
*Library Research Guide to Biology:
Illustrated Search Strategy and Sources*.
Ann Arbor: Pierian, 1978.
*Macmillan Illustrated Animal
Encyclopedia*. New York: Macmillan,
1984.
*Smith's Guide to the Literature of the Life
Sciences*. 9th ed. Minneapolis: Burgess,
1980.

INDEXES AND ELECTRONIC DATABASES

ACRICOLA (E)
Bibliography of Bioethics. Detroit: Gale,
1975–. Annual. (P) (E—BIOETHICSLINE
PLUS)
Biological Abstracts. 1926–present. (P) (E—
BIOSIS)
Biological and Agricultural Index. New
York: Wilson, 1947–present. (P) (E—
WILSONDISK)

General Science Index. New York: Wilson,
1978–present. (P)
LIFE SCIENCES COLLECTION (E)
SCISEARCH (E)
ZOOLOGICAL RECORD (E)

BUSINESS AND ECONOMICS

GENERAL WORKS AND BIBLIOGRAPHIES

AMA Management Handbook. New York:
American Management Assoc., 1994.
Basic Business Library: Core Resources.
2nd ed. Phoenix: Oryx, 1989.

*Bibliographic Guide to Business and
Economics*. Boston: Hall, 1975–present.
Annual.

Business and Economics Books,
1876–1983. 4 vols. New York: Bowker,
1983.
Business Information Sources. 3rd ed.
Berkeley: U of California P, 1993.
Business Rankings Annual. Detroit: Gale,
Annual.
Dictionary of Banking and Financial
Services. New York: Wiley, 1985.
MIT Dictionary of Modern Economics. 3rd
ed. Cambridge: MIT, 1992.
Economics Information Resources
Directory. Detroit: Gale, 1984–present.

Encyclopedia of American Economic
History: Studies of the Principal
Movements and Ideas. 3 vols. New York:
Scribner's, 1980.
Information Sources in Economics. 2nd ed.
London: Butterworth, 1984.
The New Palgrave: A Dictionary of
Economics. New York: Stockton, 1992.
The New Palgrave Dictionary of Money and
Finance. New York: Stockton, 1992.
Standard & Poor's Register of Corporations,
Directors, and Executives. New York:
Standard, 1928 –. Annual.

INDEXES AND ELECTRONIC DATABASES

ABI/INFORM (E)
ACADEMIC INDEX ASAP (E)
Accountants' Index. New York: AICPA,
1921–present.
Business Periodicals Index. New York:
Wilson, 1958–present. (P) (E)
D&B DUN's FINANCIAL RECORDS PLUS
(E)
D&B'S ELECTRONIC BUSINESS
DIRECTORY (E)

DISCLOSURE, 1977–. Weekly (E)
ECONOMIC LITERATURE INDEX (E)
MOODY'S CORPORATE NEWS US (also
INTERNATIONAL) (E)
STANDARD & POOR'S DAILY NEWS (E)
Wall Street Journal Index. New York: Dow
Jones, 1958–present. (P) (E)

CHEMISTRY

GENERAL WORKS AND BIBLIOGRAPHIES

Chemical Publications, Their Nature and
Use. New York: McGraw, 1982.
Encyclopedia of Chemical Technology. New
York: Wiley, 1991–present. Available
electronically also.
Hawley's Condensed Chemical Dictionary.
New York: Reinhold, 1992.

How to Find Chemical Information: A
Guide to Practicing Chemists, Teachers,
and Students. New York: Wiley, 1987.
Lange's Handbook of Chemistry. New York:
McGraw, 1992.
Riegel's Handbook of Industrial Chemistry.
New York: Reinhold, 1992.

INDEXES AND ELECTRONIC DATABASES

Chemical Abstracts. Easton: ACS,
1907–present. Weekly. (P) (E—as CA
SEARCH)
GENERAL SCIENCE ABSTRACTS (FULL
TEXT) (E)
General Science Index. New York: Wilson,
1978–present. (P) (E—WILSONDISK)

CHEMICAL INDUSTRY NOTES (E)
CHEMNAME (E)
COMPENDEX (E)
INSPEC (E)
SCISEARCH (E)

COMPUTER SCIENCE

GENERAL WORKS AND BIBLIOGRAPHIES

Annotated Bibliography on the History of Data Processing. Wesport: Greenwood, 1983.

Computer-Readable Databases. Detroit: Gale, 1991.

Dictionary of Computing. New York: Oxford UP, 1990.

Encyclopedia of Artificial Intelligence. New York: Wiley, 1992.

Encyclopedia of Computer Science and Engineering. New York: Van Nostrand Reinhold, 1993.

Historical Dictionary of Data Processing: Technology, Biographies, Organizations, 3 vols. Westport: Greenwood, 1987.

Scientific and Technical Information Sources. Cambridge: MIT, 1988.

Software Encyclopedia 1997. New Providence, NJ: Bowker, 1997.

INDEXES AND ELECTRONIC DATABASES

ACM Guide to Computing Literature. 1978–present. Annually.

Applied Science and Technology Index. New York: Wilson, 1958–present. (P) (E—WILSONDISK)

BUSINESS SOFTWARE DATABASE (E)

COMPUTER DATABASE (E)

INSPEC (E)

MICROCOMPUTER ABSTRACTS (E)

EDUCATION (INCLUDING PHYSICAL EDUCATION AND HEALTH)

GENERAL WORKS AND BIBLIOGRAPHIES

American Educator's Encyclopedia. Westport: Greenwood, 1991.

Bibliographic Guide to Education. Boston: Hall, 1978–present.

A Bibliographic Guide to Educational Research. 3rd ed. Metuchen: Scarecrow, 1990.

Digest of Education Statistics. Washington: GPO, 1962–present. Annually.

Education Journals and Serials. Metuchen: Scarecrow, 1988.

Encyclopedia of Educational Research. 6th ed. New York: Free, 1992.

Foundations of Physical Education and Sport. Mosby Year Book, 1994.

A Guide to Sources of Educational Information. 2nd ed. Arlington, VA: Information Resources, 1982.

Handbook of Research on Teaching. New York: Free, 1985.

International Encyclopedia of Education. Paris: UNESCO, 1948–. Annual.

Introduction to Reference Sources in Health Science. 2nd ed. Metuchen: Scarecrow, 1984.

The Philosophy of Education: A Guide to Information Sources. Detroit: Gale, 1980.

Research Processes in Physical Education, Recreation, and Health. 2nd ed. Englewood Cliffs: Prentice, 1984.

Educational Resources Information Center (ERIC). Phoenix: Oryx, 1956–present. (P) (E)

Sports an Physical Education: A Guide to the Reference Resources. Westport: Greenwood, 1983.

Subject Bibliography of the History of American Higher Education. Westport: Greenwood, 1984.

World Education Encyclopedia. 3 vols. New York: Facts on File, 1988.

INDEXES AND ELECTRONIC DATABASES

ACADEMIC INDEX ASAP (E)
Current Index to Journals in Education.
Phoenix: Oryx, 1969–present. (P) (E)
Education Index. New York: Wilson,
1929–present. (P) (E)
ERIC (EDUCATIONAL RESOURCES
INFORMATION CENTER) (E)
EXCEPTIONAL CHILD EDUCATION
RESOURCES (E)

MEDLINE (E)
Physical Education Index. Cape Girardeau,
MO: Ben Oak, 1978–present. (P)
Physical Fitness and Sports Medicine.
Washington: GPO, 1978–present. (P)
SPORT (E)

ENVIRONMENTAL STUDIES

GENERAL WORKS AND BIBLIOGRAPHIES

*Atlas of United States Environmental
Issues.* New York Macmillan, 1994.
*Beacham's Guide to Environmental Issues
and Sources.* 5 vols. Washington, DC:
Beacham, 1993.
*Encyclopedia of Community Planning and
Environmental Management.* New York:
Facts on File, 1984.
Energy Abstracts for Policy Analysis. Oak
Ridge, TN: TIC, 1989.
Energy Information Guide. 3 vols. San
Carlos, CA: Energy Information P, 1994.
Environment Abstracts. New York:
Environment Information Center,
1971–present.

*Environmental Impact Assessment: A
Bibliography with Abstracts.* New York:
Bowker, 1988.
Handbook of Air Pollution Technology. New
York: Wiley, 1984.
*The Information Please Environmental
Almanac.* Boston: Houghton, 1991–.
Annually.
Pollution Abstracts. Washington, DC:
Cambridge Scientific Abstracts,
1970–present. (E)
U.S. Geological Survey Home Page. Internet.
Available: http://www.usgs.gov.
World Resources. Oxford: Oxford UP,
1986–present. Annually.

INDEXES AND ELECTRONIC DATABASES

ACADEMIC INDEX ASAP (E)
Biological Abstracts. Philadelphia: Biological
Abstracts, 1926–present. (P)
BIOSIS PREVIEWS (E)

ENVIRONLINE (E)
ENVIRONMENTAL BIBLIOGRAPHY (E)
GEOBASE (E)
WATER RESOURCES ABSTRACTS (E)

ETHNIC STUDIES

GENERAL SOURCES

*Dictionary of American Immigration
History.* Metuchen: Scarecrow, 1990.
*Ethnic Periodicals in Contemporary
America: An Annotated Guide.* Westport:
Greenwood, 1990.

*Guide to Multicultural Resources,
1995–1996.* Atkinson, WI: Highsmith,
1995.
*Multiculturalism in the United States: A
Comparative Guide.* Westport:
Greenwood, 1992.

AFRICAN-AMERICAN STUDIES

African American Encyclopedia. 6 vols. North Bellmore, NY: Cavendish, 1993.
Afro-American Reference. Westport: Greenwood, 1985.
Bibliographic Guide to Black Studies. Boston: Hall, 1975–. Annually.
Black Index: Afro-Americans in Selected Periodicals 1907–1949. New York: Garland, 1981.
Dictionary of American Negro Biography. New York: Norton, 1983.

The Kaiser Index to Black Resources, 1948–1986. 5 vols. Brooklyn: Carlson, 1992.
The Negro Almanac: A Reference Work on the Afro-American. Detroit: Gale, 1990.
Who's Who among Black Americans. Northbrook, IL: WWABA, 1976–present.
Voices of the Spirit: Sources for Interpreting the African-American Experience. Chicago: ALA, 1994.

ASIAN-AMERICAN STUDIES

Asian American Studies: An Annotated Bibliography and Research Guide. Westport: Greenwood, 1989.
Asians in America: Filipinos, Koreans, and East Indians. New York: Hippocrene, 1981.
The Chinese in America. New York: Harper, 1982.

East to America: A History of the Japanese in the United States. New York: Quill, 1980.
Japanese-American History: An A to Z Reference from 1868 to the Present. New York: Facts on File, 1993.

HISPANIC-AMERICAN STUDIES

Chicano Literature: A Reference Guide. Westport: Greenwood, 1985.
Hispanic-American Almanac. Detroit: Gale, 1993.
The Hispanic Presence in North America. New York: Facts on File, 1991.

Literature Chicana. Encino: Floricanto, 1985.
Sourcebook of Hispanic Culture in the United States. Chicago: ALA, 1982.
Statistical Record of Hispanic Americans. Detroit: Gale, 1993.

NATIVE AMERICAN STUDIES

American Indian Novelists: An Annotated Critical Bibliography. New York: Garland, 1982.
Guide to Research on North American Indians. Chicago: ALA, 1983.
Indians in North America: Methods and Sources for Library Research. Hamden, CT: Library Professional Pubs., 1983.

Reference Encyclopedia of the American Indian. West Nyack, NY: Todd, 1993.
American Indian Literature: An Introduction, Bibliographic Review, and Selected Bibliography. New York: MLA, 1990.

INDEXES AND ELECTRONIC DATABASES

MLA International Bibliography. New York:
MLA, 1921–present. (P) (E)
Sage Race Relations Abstracts. London and
Beverly Hills, 1976–present.
SOCIAL SCISEARCH (E)

Social Sciences Index. New York: Wilson,
1974–present. (P) (E)
SOCIOABS. *Sociological Abstracts.* La Jolla,
CA: Sociological Abstracts, 1952–present.
(P) (E)

FILM

GENERAL WORKS AND BIBLIOGRAPHIES

Dictionay of Film Terms. New York:
McGraw, 1983.
Film: A Reference Guide. Westport:
Greenwood, 1980.
The Film Encyclopedia. New York:
HarperCollins, 1994.
Film Study: A Resource Guide. Rutherford:
Fairleigh Dickinson UP, 1973.
The Filmgoer's Companion. New York:
Scribner's, 1990.

International Motion Picture Almanac. New
York: Quigley, 1929–present. Annually.
Main Page: The Internet Movie Database.
Internet. Available: http://us.imdb.com
New York Times Film Reviews 1913–1968.
10 vols. New York: New York Times and
Arno, 1971–72. Biennial supplements.
The Oxford Companion to Film. New York:
Oxford UP, 1976.

INDEXES AND ELECTRONIC DATABASES

Film Literature Index. New York: Filmdex,
1973–present. Quarterly. (P)
Film Quarterly. Berkeley: U of California P,
1945–present. Bimonthly. (P)

International Index to Film Periodicals.
New York: Bowker, 1972–present. Annual.
(P)
MAGILL'S SURVEY OF CINEMA (E)

FOREIGN LANGUAGES

FRENCH

*Concise Oxford Dictionary of French
Literature.* Oxford: Clarendon, 1976.
Critical Bibliography of French Literature.
Syracuse: Syracuse UP, 1947–85. In
progress.
*Dictionnaire etymologique de la langue
francaise.* Paris: Presses Universitaires de
France, 1975.

*French Language and Literature: An
Annotated Bibliography.* New York:
Garland, 1989.
*French Literature: An Annotated Guide to
Selected Bibliographies.* New York: MLA,
1981.
New History of French Literature. 2 vols.
Cambridge: Harvard UP, 1989.

GERMAN

*A Critical Bibliography of German
Literature in English Translation:
1481–1927.* Metuchen: Scarecrow, 1965.
Supplements.

Der Grosse Duden. 10 vols. New York:
Adler's, 1971.
*Introduction to Library Research in
German Studies.* Boulder: Westview,
1984.

Oxford Companion to German Literature.
New York: Oxford, 1986.
Reallexikon der deutschen
Literaturgeschichte. 3 vols. New York:
DeGruyter, 1958–77.

Selected Bibliography of German Literature
in English Translation: 1956–1960.
Metuchen: Scarecrow, 1972.
Who's Who in Germany: A Biographical
Dictionary. 2 vols. New York: IPS, 1985.
Supplements.

LATIN

Ancient Writers: Greece and Rome. 2 vols.
New York: Scribner's, 1982.
Cambridge History of Classical Literature.
New York: Cambridge UP, 1982–present.
In progress.
The Classical World Bibliography of Roman
Drama and Poetry and Ancient Fiction.
New York: Garland, 1978.

Introduction to Medieval Latin Studies: A
Syllabus and Bibliographical Guide.
Washington: Catholic UP, 1977.
Oxford Companion to Classical Literature.
New York: Oxford UP, 1989.
Studies in Roman Literature, Culture and
Religion. New York: Garland, 1978.

RUSSIAN

Basic Russian Publications: A
Bibliographic Guide to Western-
Language Publications. Chicago: U of
Chicago P, 1965.
Bibliography of Russian Literature in
English Translation to 1945. 1963. Rpt.
Totowa, NJ: Rowman, 1972.
Dictionary of Russian Literature. 1956. Rpt.
Westport: Greenwood, 1971.
Guide to Bibliographies of Russian
Literature. Nashville: Vanderbilt UP, 1970.
Handbook of Russian Literature. New
Haven: Yale UP, 1990.

Introduction to Russian Language and
Literature. New York: Cambridge UP,
1977.
Modern Encyclopedia of Russian and Soviet
Literature. Gulf Breeze, FL: Academic
International, 1971–present. In progress.
Russia, the USSR, and Eastern Europe: A
Bibliographic Guide to English
Language Publications, 1975–1980.
Littleton, CO: Libraries Unlimited, 1982.
Supplements.

SPANISH

Bibliography of Old Spanish Texts. Madison:
Hispanic Seminary, 1984.
Bibliographic Dictionary of Hispanic
Literature in the United States.
Westport: Greenwood, 1989.
Handbook of Latin American Literature.
New York: Garland, 1992.
Handbook of Latin American Studies.
Gainesville: U Press of Florida,
1935–present.

Modern Spanish and Portuguese
Literatures. New York: Ungar, 1988.
Oxford Companion to Spanish Literature.
Oxford: Clarendon, 1978.
A Sourcebook for Hispanic Literature and
Language. Metuchen: Scarecrow, 1983.
Spanish and Spanish-American Literature:
An Annotated Guide to Selected
Bibliographies. New York: MLA, 1983.

INDEXES AND ELECTRONIC DATABASES

ARTS AND HUMANITIES SEARCH (E)
Humanities Index. New York: Wilson,
1974–present. (P) (E—HUMANITIES
ABSTRACTS FULL TEXT)

LLBA (Linguistics and Language Behavior
Abstracts) (E)
MLA International Bibliography. New York:
MLA, 1921–present. (P) (E)

GEOLOGY

GENERAL WORKS AND BIBLIOGRAPHIES

Bibliography of North American Geology. 49
vols. Washington: GPO, 1923–71.
*Catalog of the U.S. Geological Survey
Library.* Boston: Hall, 1964. Supplements.
Dictionary of Geology. New York: Oxford,
1986.
Encyclopedia of Field and General Geology.
New York: Chapman & Hall, 1988.
*Geological Reference Sources: A Subject and
Regional Bibliography.* Metuchen:
Scarecrow, 1981.

Glossary of Geology. Falls Church, VA: AGI,
1987.
*Magill's Survey of Science: Earth Science
Series.* 5 vols. Englewood Cliffs, NJ:
Salem, 1990.
*McGraw-Hill Encyclopedia of the Geological
Sciences.* New York: McGraw, 1988.

INDEXES AND ELECTRONIC DATABASES

Bibliography and Index of Geology. Boulder:
AGA, 1933–present. (P)
CAMBRIDGE SCIENTIFIC ABSTRACTS (E)
COMPENDEX (E)
GEOARCHIVE (E)

General Science Index. New York: Wilson,
1978–present. (P) (E—WILSONDISK)
GEOBASE (E)
GEOREF (E)

HISTORY

GENERAL WORKS AND BIBLIOGRAPHIES

*America: History and Life: A Guide to
Periodical Literature.* Santa Barbara:
ABC-Clio, 1964–present. (Also in
electronic format.)
Bibliography of British History. Oxford:
Clarendon, 1928–present.
Encyclopedia of American History. New
York: Harper, 1996.
Encyclopedia of American Social History. 3
vols. New York: Scribner's, 1993.
Encyclopedia of Asian History. 4 vols. New
York: Scribner's, 1988.
Encyclopedia of the Renaissance. New York:
Facts on File, 1987.

Explorers and Discovers of the World.
Detroit: Gale, 1993.
Guide to Historical Literature. New York:
Oxford UP, 1995.
*Handbook for Research in American
History: A Guide to Bibliographies and
other Reference Works.* Lincoln: U of
Nebraska P, 1994.
The Historian's Handbook. Norman: U of
Oklahoma P, 1986.
Library Research Guide to History. New
York: Pierian, 1980.
The Modern Researcher. New York:
Harcourt, 1992.

Times Atlas of World History. Maplewood, NJ: Hammond, 1993.

The Timetables of History: A Horizontal Linkage of People and Events. New York: Simon and Schuster, 1991.

INDEXES AND ELECTRONIC DATABASES

America: History and Life. Santa Barbara: ABC-Clio, 1964–present. (P) (E)
American Historical Association. Recently Published Articles. 1976–present.
The English Historical Review. Harlow, Essex, England: Longman, 1886–present.

Historical Abstracts. Santa Barbara: ABC-Clio, 1955–present. (P) (E)
Humanities Index. New York: Wilson, 1974–present. (P) (E—HUMANITIES ABSTRACTS FULL TEXT)

JOURNALISM AND MASS COMMUNICATIONS

GENERAL WORKS AND BIBLIOGRAPHIES

Annotated Media Bibliography. Washington: ACC, 1985.
The Associated Press Stylebook and Libel Manual. New York: AP, 1992.
Basic Books in the Mass Media. Champaign: U of Illinois P, 1990.
Broadcasting Cablecasting Yearbook. Washington: Broadcasting Publications, 1982–present. Annually.
Communications and the Mass Media, A Guide to the Reference Literature. Englewood, CO: Libraries Unlimited, 1991.
Communications Research. Belmont, CA: Wadsworth, 1993.
Encyclopedia of Twentieth-Century Journalists. New York: Garland, 1984.
Halliwell's Film Guide. New York: Harper, 1993.
International Encyclopedia of Communications. 4 vols. New York: Oxford, 1989.

Journalism: A Guide to the Reference Literature. Englewood, CO: Libraries Unlimited, 1990.
Journalism Biographies: Master Index. Detroit: Gale, 1979. Supplements.
Media Law: A Legal Handbook for the Working Journalist. Berkeley: Nolo, 1984.
News Media and Public Policy: An Annotated Bibliography. 2 vols. New York: Garland, 1985.
Radio and Television: A Selected, Annotated Bibliography. Metuchen: Scarecrow, 1978. Supplements.
The Reporter's Handbook. New York: St. Martin's, 1990.
Violence and Terror in the Mass Media: An Annotated Bibliography. Westport: Greenwood, 1988.

INDEXES AND ELECTRONIC DATABASES

AP NEWS (E)
ARTS AND HUMANITIES SEARCH (E)
Business Periodicals Index. New York: Wilson, 1958–present. (P)(E)
Communications Abstracts. Beverly Hills: Sage, 1978–present.
Humanities Index. New York: Wilson, 1974–present. (P)(E—HUMANITIES ABSTRACTS FULL TEXT)

NATIONAL NEWSPAPER INDEX (E)
NEWSEARCH (E)
REUTERS (E)
SOCSCI SEARCH (E)
UPI NEWS (E)

LANGUAGE AND LITERATURE

GENERAL WORKS AND BIBLIOGRAPHIES

Contemporary Authors. Detroit: Gale, 1962–present.

Contemporary Literary Criticism. Detroit: Gale, 1973–present.

Dictionary of Literary Biography. Detroit: Gale, 1978–present (in progress).

A Glossary of Contemporary Literary Theory. New York: Routledge, 1992.

Handbook to Literature. New York: Macmillan, 1992.

Literary Criticism Index. 4 vols. Metuchen: Scarecrow, 1993.

Literary Research Guide. New York: MLA, 1993.

Reference Guide for English Studies. Berkeley: U of California P, 1990.

Research Guide for Undergraduate Students: English and American Literature. New York: MLA, 1985.

AFRICAN AMERICAN LITERATURE (SEE ALSO ETHNIC STUDIES)

Bibliographic Guide to Black Studies. Boston: Hall, 1980. Supplements.

A Bibliographic Guide to African-American Women Writers. Westport, CT: Greenwood, 1993.

Black American Literature: A Critical History. Totowa, NJ: Littlefield, 1974.

Black American Women in Literature. Jefferson, NC: McFarland, 1989.

Black American Women Novelists. Englewood Cliffs, NJ: Salem, 1989.

Black Americans in Autobiography: An Annotated Bibliography of Autobiographies and Autobiographical

Books Written since the Civil War. Durham: Duke UP, 1984.

Conjuring: Black Women, Fiction, and Literary Tradition. Bloomington: Indiana UP, 1985.

The Negro in American Literature and Bibliography of Literature by and about Negro Americans. Oshkosh: Wisconsin Council of Teachers of English, 1996.

Poetry of the Negro: 1746–1970. New York: Doubleday, 1970.

AMERICAN LITERATURE

American Literary Scholarship. Durham: Duke UP, 1963–present. Annually.

American Women Writers: A Critical Reference Guide from Colonial Times to the Present. 4 vols. New York: Ungar, 1979–82. Vol. 5, 1994.

American Writers. 4 vols. New York: Scribner's, 1961–81. Supplements.

Bibliographic Guide to the Study of Literature of the USA. Durham: Duke UP, 1984.

A Bibliographic Guide to the Study of Western American Literature. Lincoln: U of Nebraska P, 1982.

Bibliography of American Literature. 7 vols. New Haven: Yale UP, 1955–present.

Cambridge Handbook of American Literature. New York: Cambridge UP, 1986.

Literary History of the United States. 2 vols. New York: Macmillan, 1974.

Modern American Literature. New York: Unger, 1969–76. Supplements.

Oxford Companion to American Literature. New York: Oxford UP, 1995.

The Transcendentalists: A Review of Research and Criticism. New York: MLA, 1984.

Twentieth Century American Science Fiction Writers. New York: St. Martin's, 1981.

BRITISH LITERATURE

Anglo-Irish Literature: A Review of Research. New York: MLA, 1976. Supplement 1983.

British Writers. New York: Scribner's, 1979–92.

Cambridge Guide to English Literature. New York: Cambridge UP, 1983.

Cambridge History of English Literature. 15 vols. Cambridge: Cambridge: UP, 1907–33.

Encyclopedia of Victorian Britain. New York: Garland, 1987.

The English Romantic Poets: A Review of Research and Criticism. New York: MLA, 1985.

McGraw-Hill Guide to English Literature. 2 vols. New York: McGraw, 1985.

Modern British Literature. New York: Ungar, 1966–75. Supplements 1985–present.

New Cambridge Bibliography of English Literature. 5 vols. New York: Cambridge UP, 1969–77.

Oxford Companion to English Literature. Oxford: Clarendon, 1995.

Oxford History of English Literature. Oxford; Clarendon, 1945-present.

Romantic Movement: A Selective and Critical Bibliography. New York: Garland, 1980–present.

The Shakespeare Companion. New York; Scribner's, 1978.

Victorian Fiction: A Second Guide to Research. New York: MLA, 1978.

DRAMA AND THEATER

American Drama Criticism: Interpretations, 1890–1977. Hamden: Shoe String, 1979. Supplements 1984, 1989, 1992.

British Theatre, A Bibliography from the Beginning to 1985. Romsey, UK: Motley, 1989.

Cambridge Guide to American Theatre. New York: Cambridge UP, 1993.

Cambridge Guide to Theatre. New York: Cambridge UP, 1992.

Contemporary Dramatists. New York: St. Martin's, 1987.

Critical Survey of Drama. 8 vols. Englewood Cliffs: Salem, 1994.

Drama Criticism. 3 vols. Detroit: Gale, 1991–93.

Drury's Guide to Best Plays. Metuchen, NJ: Scarecrow, 1987.

A Guide to Reference and Bibliography for Theatre Research. Columbus: Ohio State UP, 1983.

Index to Full Length Plays: 1895–1964. 3 vols. Westwood: Faxon, 1956–65.

Index to Plays in Periodicals. Metuchen: Scarecrow, 1977–87. Supplement, 1990.

McGraw-Hill Encyclopedia of World Drama. New York: McGraw, 1984.

Oxford Companion to the Theatre. Fairlawn, NJ: Oxford UP, 1984.

Play Index. New York: Wilson, 1953–present.

A Survey and Bibliography of Renaissance Drama. 4 vols. Lincoln: U of Nebraska P, 1975–78.

LANGUAGE STUDIES

American Literature and Language: A Guide to Information Sources. Detroit: Gale, 1982.

Cambridge Encyclopedia of Language. New York: Cambridge UP, 1988.

Compendium of the World's Languages. 2 vols. New York: Routledge, 1991.

Dictionary of American Regional English. Cambridge: Harvard UP, 1985–present.

An Encyclopedic Dictionary of Language and Languages. Oxford: Blackwell, 1993.

Linguistics: A Guide to Reference Literature. Englewood CO: Libraries Unlimited, 1991.

Oxford English Dictionary. 20 vols. New York: Oxford UP, 1989. (P) (E)

The World's Major Languages. New York: Oxford UP, 1987.

MYTHOLOGY AND FOLKLORE

American Folklore: A Bibliography. Metuchen: Scarecrow, 1977.
The Arthurian Encyclopedia. New York: Bedrick, 1987.
Arthurian Legend and Literature: An Annotated Bibliography. New York: Garland, 1984–In progress.
Bullfinch's Mythology. New York: Avenel, 1978.
Dictionary of Celtic Myth and Legend. London: Thames & Hudson, 1992.
Dictionary of Classical Mythology. New York: Blackwell, 1986.
Dictionary of Native American Mythology. Santa Barbara, CA: ABC-Clio, 1982.
Fable Scholarship: An Annotated Bibliography. New York: Garland, 1985.
The Facts on File Encyclopedia of World Mythology and Legend. New York: Facts on File, 1988.

Folklore and Folklife: A Guide to English-Language Reference Sources. New York: Garland, 1992.
Folklore and Literature in the United States: An Annotated Bibliography. New York: Garland, 1984.
The Golden Bough. Sir James Frazer. 12 vols. New York: St. Martin's, 1955.
Handbook of American Folklore. Bloomington: Indiana UP, 1986.
Mythological and Fabulous Creatures: A Source Book and Research Guide. Westport: Greenwood, 1987.
Storyteller's Sourcebook. Detroit: Gale, 1982.
The Study of American Folklore. New York: Norton, 1987.

THE NOVEL

American Fiction: A Contribution Toward a Bibliography. 3 vols. San Marino: Huntington Library, 1969, 1979.
American Fiction 1900–1950: A Guide to Information Sources. Detroit: Gale, 1974.
The American Novel 1789–1959: A Checklist of Twentieth Century Criticism. Miami: Ohio UP, 1961.
Critical Survey of Long Fiction. Englewood Cliffs: Salem, 1983. Supplement 1987.

English Novel Explication: Criticism to 1972. Hamden, CT: Shoe String, 1973. Supplements, 1976-present.
Facts on File Bibliography of American Fiction, 1866–1918. 2 vols. New York: Facts on File, 1993.
Facts on File Bibliography of American Fiction, 1919–1988. 2 vols. New York: Facts on File, 1991.

POETRY

American and British Poetry: A Guide to the Criticism. Athens, OH: Swallow, 1984.
Columbia Granger's Index to Poetry. New York: Columbia UP, 1994.
Critical Survey of Poetry. 8 vols. Englewood Cliffs: Salem, 1982.

New Princeton Encyclopedia of Poetry and Poetics. Princeton: Princeton UP, 1993.
Poetry Explication: A Checklist of Interpretations since 1925 of British and American Poems Past and Present. Boston: Hall, 1980.

THE SHORT STORY

*American Short-Fiction Criticism and
  Scholarship, 1959–1977: A Checklist.*
Athens: Ohio UP, 1982.
Critical Survey of Short Fiction. 7 vols.
Englewood Cliffs: Salem, 1993.

Short Story Index. New York: Wilson, 1953.
Supplements.
Twentieth-Century Short Story Explication.
Hamden, CT: Shoe String, 1977.
Supplements. New series started in 1993.

WORLD LITERATURE

Benet's Reader's Encyclopedia. New York:
  Harper, 1987.
*Columbia Dictionary of Modern European
  Literature.* New York: Columbia UP, 1980.

*Encyclopedia of World Literature in the
  20th* Century. New York: Ungar, 1981–84.
Reader's Companion to World Literature.
  New York: NAL, 1973.

INDEXES AND ELECTRONIC DATABASES

Abstracts of English Studies. Urbana: NCTE,
  1958–present.
ACADEMIC INDEX ASAP (E)
ARTS AND HUMANITIES SEARCH (E)
Book Review Digest. New York: Wilson,
  1905–present. (P) (E-BOOK REVIEW
  INDEX)

Humanities Index. New York: Wilson,
  1974–present. (P) (E—HUMANITIES
  ABSTRACTS FULL TEXT)
*MLA International Bibliography of Books
  and Articles on Modern Language and
  Literature.* New York: MLA,
  1921–present. Annually. (P) (E)

MATHEMATICS

GENERAL WORKS AND BIBLIOGRAPHIES

*Biographical Dictionary of
  Mathematicians.* 4 vols. New York:
  Scribner's 1991.
Encyclopedia of Mathematics. 10 vols.
  Norwell, MA: Reidel/Kluwer,
  1988–present.
Encyclopedic Dictionary of Mathematics.
  4 vols. Cambridge: MIT Press, 1987.
*International Catalogue of Scientific
  Literature: 1901–1914.* Section A:
  Mathematics. Metuchen: Scarecrow, 1974.
*Mathematical Journals: An Annotated
  Guide.* Metuchen: Scarecrow, 1992.

The Mathematics Dictionary. New York:
  Reinhold, 1992.
Omega Bibliography of Mathematical Logic.
  New York: Springer-Verlag, 1987.
The Story of Mathematics. New York:
  Plenum, 1993.
*Using the Mathematical Literature: A
  Practical Guide.* New York: Dekker, 1979.
*The VNR Concise Encyclopedia of
  Mathematics.* New York: Reinhold, 1989.

INDEXES AND ELECTRONIC DATABASES

General Science Index. New York: Wilson,
  1978–present. (P) (E—GENERAL
  SCIENCE ABSTRACTS)

Mathematical Reviews. Providence, RI: AMS,
  1940–present.
MATHSCI (E)

MUSIC

GENERAL WORKS AND BIBLIOGRAPHIES

*Baker's Biographical Dictionary of
    Musicians.* New York: Schirmer, 1992.
Dictionary of Music. New York: Facts on
    File, 1983.
Dictionary of Music Technology. Westport,
    CT: Greenwood, 1992.
The Encyclopedia of Opera. New York:
    Scribner's, 1976.
Encyclopedia of Pop, Rock, and Soul. New
    York: St. Martin's, 1990.
General Bibliography for Music Research.
    Detroit: Information Coordinator's 1996.
*Information on Music: A Handbook of
    Reference Sources in European
    Languages.* 3 vols. Littleton, CO: Libraries
    Unlimited, 1975–84.
*International Encyclopedia of Women
    Composers.* New York: Books and Music
    USA, 1988.

Library Research Guide to Music. Ann
    Arbor: Pierian, 1982.
*Music Reference and Research Materials:
    An Annotated Bibliography.* New York:
    Schirmer, 1994.
Music Since 1900. New York: Schirmer,
    1992.
New Grove Dictionary of American Music.
    4 vols. New York: Grove, 1986.
*New Grove Dictionary of Music and
    Musicians.* 20 vols. New York: Macmillan,
    1980.
New Harvard Dictionary of Music.
    Cambridge: Harvard UP, 1986.
New Oxford History of Music. 10 vols. New
    York: Oxford UP, 1986–.
*Popular Music: An Annotated Index of
    American Popular Songs.* 6 vols. Detroit:
    Gale, 1963–present. In progress.

INDEXES AND ELECTRONIC DATABASES

ACADEMIC INDEX ASAP (E)
Humanities Index. New York: Wilson,
    1974–present. (P) (E—HUMANITIES
    ABSTRACTS FULL TEXT)
Music Article Guide. Philadelphia:
    Information Services, 1966–present.

Music Index. Warren, MI: Information
    Coordinators, 1949–present. (P) (E)
RILM ABSTRACTS (*Repertoire
    Internationale de Litterata Musicale*) (E)

PHILOSOPHY

GENERAL WORKS AND BIBLIOGRAPHIES

*The Classical World Bibliography of
    Philosophy, Religion, and Rhetoric.* New
    York: Garland, 1978.
A Companion to Aesthetics. Cambridge:
    Blackwell, 1993.
Dictionary of Philosophy. New York:
    Paul/Methuen, 1987.
Encyclopedia of Philosophy. New York:
    Macmillan, 1996.
Ethics: An Annotated Bibliography.
    Englewood Cliffs, NJ: Salem, 1991.
Great Thinkers of the Western World. New
    York: HarperCollins, 1992.

*Philosophy: A Guide to the Reference
    Literature.* Littleton, CO: Libraries
    Unlimited, 1986.
Research Guide to Philosophy. Chicago:
    ALA, 1983.
*World Philosophy: A Contemporary
    Bibliography.* Westport, CT: Greenwood,
    1993.
*World Philosophy: Essay Reviews of 225
    Major Works.* 5 vols. Englewood Cliffs,
    NJ: Salem, 1982.

INDEXES AND ELECTRONIC DATABASES

ACADEMIC INDEX ASAP (E) *Humanities Index*. New York: Wilson, 1974-present. (P) (E—HUMANITIES ABSTRACTS FULL TEXT)

Philosopher's Index. Bowling Green: Bowling Green UP, 1967–present. (P) (E)

PHYSICS

GENERAL WORKS AND BIBLIOGRAPHIES

American Institute of Physics Handbook. New York: McGraw, 1972.

Annual Review of Nuclear and Particle Science. Palo Alto: 1952–present.

The Astronomy and Astrophysics Encyclopedia. New York: Reinhold, 1992.

Concise Dictionary of Physics and Related Subjects. New York: Oxford UP, 1986.

Encyclopedia of Physics. New York: VCH, 1991.

Encyclopedia of Physics. New York: Reinhold, 1990.

Information Sources in Physics. London: Bowker-Saur, 1994.

Magill's Survey of Science: Physical Science Series. 6 vols. Englewood Cliffs, NJ: Salem, 1992.

Physics Abstracts. London: IEE, 1898–present.

Soild State Physics Literature Guide. New York: Plenum, 1972–present.

Sources of History of Quantum Physics. Philadelphia: APS, 1967.

Space Almanac. New York: Arcsoft, 1992.

INDEXES AND ELECTRONIC DATABASES

Applied Science and Technology Index. New York: Wilson, 1958–present.

Current Papers in Physics. London: IEE, 1966–present.

Current Physics Index. New York: AIP, 1975–present. Quarterly.

INSPEC (E)

SCISEARCH (E)

SPIN (Searchable Physics Information Notices) (E)

POLITICAL SCIENCE

GENERAL WORKS AND BIBLIOGRAPHIES

Basic Documents on Human Rights. Oxford: Clarendon, 1981.

Blackwell Encyclopedia of Political Institutions. Oxford: Blackwell, 1987.

Communism in the World since 1945. Santa Barbara: ABC-Clio, 1987.

Congress A to Z. Washington, DC: Congressional Quarterly, 1993.

Definitive Guide to the New Language of Politics. By William Safire. New York: Random, 1993.

Dorsey Dictionary of American Government and Politics. Belmont, CA: Dorsey, 1988.

Dictionary of Modern Political Ideologies. New York: St. Martin's, 1987.

Encyclopedia of the American President. 4 vols. New York: Simon, 1994.

Encyclopedia of Government and Politics. 2 vols. New York: Routledge, 1992.

Europa World Yearbook. 2 vols. London: Europa, 1899—Annual.

Guide to Official Publications of Foreign
Countries. Chicago: ALA, 1990.
Europa World Yearbook. 2 vols. London:
Europa, 1899–(Annual).
Information Sources of Political Science.
Santa Barbara: ABC-Clio, 1986.
Introduction to United States Information
Sources. Littleton, CO: Libraries
Unlimited, 1992.
Political Handbook of the World. New York:
McGraw, 1975–present. Annually.
Political Science: A Guide to Reference and
Information Sources. Littleton, CO:
Libraries Unlimited, 1990.
The Presidents: A Reference History. New
York: Scribner's, 1984.

Russia and Eastern Europe, 1789–1985: A
Bibliographical Guide. Manchester, UK:
Manchester UP, 1989.
Sources of information in the Social
Sciences. Chicago: ALA, 1986.
The Statesman's Yearbook. New York: St.
Martin's, 1964–present. Annually.
Thomas Legislative Information on the
Internet. Internet. Available:
http://thomas.loc.gov.
Yearbook of the United Nations. Lake
Success, NY: United Nations,
1947–present. Annually.

INDEXES AND ELECTRONIC SOURCES

ABC: Pol Sci. Santa Barbara: ABC-Clio,
1969–present.
CONGRESSIONAL RECORD ABSTRACTS
(E)
FEDERAL REGISTER ABSTRACTS (E)
GPO MONTHLY CATALOG (E)
International Political Science Abstracts.
Oslo: International Political Science Assn.,
1951–present.

PAIS Bulletin. New York: Public Affairs
Information Service, 1954–present. (P)
(E—PAIS INTERNATIONAL)
Social Sciences Index. New York: Wilson,
1974–present. (P) (E)

PSYCHOLOGY

GENERAL WORKS AND BIBLIOGRAPHIES

American Handbook of Psychiatry. 8 vols.
New York: Basic, 1974–81.
Annual Reviews of Psychology. Palo Alto:
Annual Reviews, 1950–present.
Bibliographic Guide to Psychology. Boston:
Hall, 1975–present.
Diagnostic and Statistical Manual of
Mental Disorders. Washington, DC: APA,
1994.
Dictionary of Behavioral Science. New York:
Academic P, 1989.
Encyclopedia of Psychology. 4 vols. New
York: Wiley, 1994.

How to Find Out in Psychology. Elsevier
Science, 1986.
International Handbook of Psychology.
Westport: Greenwood, 1987.
Library Use: A Handbook for Psychology.
Washington, DC: APA, 1992.
Oxford Companion to the Mind. New York:
Oxford UP, 1987.
Research Guide for Psychology. Westport:
Greenwood, 1982.
Survey of Social Science Psychology Series.
6 vols. Englewood Cliffs, NJ: Salem, 1993.

INDEXES AND ELECTRONIC DATABASES

ACADEMIC INDEX ASAP (E)
*Child Development Abstracts and
Bibliography.* Chicago: U of Chicago P,
1927–present.
Psychological Abstracts. Washington, DC:
APA, 1927–present.

MENTAL HEALTH ABSTRACTS (E)
PSYCINFO (E)
SOCIAL SCISEARCH (E)
SOCIAL SCIENCES INDEX (E)

RELIGION

GENERAL WORKS AND BIBLIOGRAPHIES

The Anchor Bible Dictionary. 6 vols. New
York: Doubleday, 1992.
A Basic Library for Bible Students. Grand
Rapids, MI: Baker, 1981.
Concise Encyclopedia of Islam. San
Francisco: Harper, 1989.
Eliade Guide to World Religions. San
Francisco: Harper, 1991.
*Encyclopedia of African American
Religions.* New York: Garland, 1993.
Encyclopedia of American Religions.
Detroit: Gale, 1994.
Encyclopedia Judaica. 16 vols. New York:
Macmillan, 1972. Annual supplements.
Encyclopedia of Religion. New York:
Macmillan, 1993.
Guide to Hindu Religion. Boston: Hall, 1981.
Harper Atlas of the Bible. New York: Harper,
1987.

Introduction to Theological Research.
Chicago: Moody, 1982.
*Library Research Guide to Religion and
Theology.* Ann Arbor: Pierian, 1984.
New Catholic Encyclopedia. 17 vols. New
York: McGraw, 1977–79. Supplement,
1989.
Oxford Dictionary of the Christian Church.
New York: Oxford UP, 1974.
*Reference Works for Theological Research:
Annotated Selective Bibliographical
Guide.* Lanham, MD: UP of America,
1981.
Religious Books and Serials in Print. New
York: Bowker, 1978. Biennial.
Research Guide to Religious Studies.
Chicago: ALA, 1982.

INDEXES AND ELECTRONIC DATABASES

ACADEMIC INDEX ASAP (E)
*The Catholic Periodical and Literature
Index.* New York: Catholic Library Assn.,
1934–present.
Humanities Index. New York: Wilson,
1974–present. (P) (E—HUMANITIES
ABSTRACTS FULL TEXT)

RELIGION INDEX (E)
*Religion: Index One: Periodicals, Religion
and Theological Abstracts.* Chicago:
ATLA, 1949–present.

SOCIOLOGY AND SOCIAL WORK

GENERAL WORKS AND BIBLIOGRAPHIES

*American Families: A Research Guide and
Historical Handbook.* Westport:
Greenwood, 1991.

Crime Dictionary. New York: Facts on File,
1988.
A Critical Dictionary of Sociology. Chicago:
U of Chicago P, 1989.

Encyclopedia of Adolescence. 2 vols. New
York: Garland, 1991.
Encyclopedia of Homosexuality. 2 vols. New
York: Garland, 1990.
Encyclopedia of Social Work. New York:
NASW, 1988. Supplement, 1990.
Handbook of Sociology. Newbury Park, CA:
Sage, 1988.
*Library Research Guide to Sociology:
Illustrated Search Strategy and Sources.*
Ann Arbor: Pierian, 1981.

*Reference Sources in Social Work: An
Annotated Bibliography.* Metuchen:
Scarecrow, 1982.
Social Work Almanac. Silver Spring, MD:
NASW, 1992.
*Sociology: A Guide to Reference and
Information Sources.* Littleton, CO:
Libraries Unlimited, 1987.
*Statistical Handbook on the American
Family.* Phoenix: Oryx, 1992.
Student Sociologist's Handbook. New York:
McGraw, 1986.

Indexes and Electronic Databases

ACADEMIC INDEX ASAP (E)
CHILD ABUSE AND NEGLECT (E)
FAMILY RESOURCES (E)
POPULATION BIBLIOGRAPHY (E)
SOCIAL SCISEARCH (E)
Social Work Research and Abstracts. New
York: NASW, 1977–. Quarterly.

Social Sciences Index. New York: Wilson,
1974–present. (P) (E)
Sociological Abstracts. New York:
Sociological Abstracts, 1952–present. (P)
(E).

WOMEN'S STUDIES
GENERAL WORKS AND BIBLIOGRAPHIES

*American Women in Politics: A Selected
Bibliography and Research Guide.* New
York: Garland, 1983.
*American Women Writers: A Critical
Reference Guide.* 4 vols. New York:
Continuum, 1982. Supplement 1993.
*Annotated Bibliography of Feminist
Criticism.* Boston: Hall, 1987.
*Bibliographic Guide to Studies on the
Status of Women: Development and
Population Trends.* Paris: UNESCO, 1983.
Biographies of American Women. Santa
Barbara: ABC-Clio, 1990.
*Feminist Resources for Schools and
Colleges: A Guide.* Westbury, NY: Feminist
Press, 1980.
*Guide to Social Science Resources in
Women's Studies.* Santa Barbara: ABC-
Clio, 1978.
Handbook of American Women's History.
New York: Garland, 1990.

Index-Directory of Women's Media.
Washington, DC: Women's Institute for
Freedom of the Press, 1975–present.
*Introduction to Library Research in
Women's Studies.* Boulder, CO: Westview,
1985.
*Statistical Handbook on Women in
America.* Phoenix: Oryx, 1991.
Statistical Handbook of Women Worldwide.
Detroit: Gale, 1991.
*Women in America: A Guide to
Information Sources.* Detroit: Gale, 1980.
*Women and Work: Paid and Unpaid: A
Selected Annotated Bibliography.* New
York: Garland, 1987.
*Women's Studies: A Guide to Information
Sources.* Jefferson, NC: McFarland, 1990.
*Women's Studies: A Recommended Core
Bibliography.* Littleton, CO: Libraries
Unlimited, 1987.
Women's Studies Encyclopedia. 3 vols.
Westport: Greenwood, 1989–present.

INDEXES AND ELECTRONIC DATABASES

ACADEMIC INDEX ASAP (E)
Social Sciences Index. New York: Wilson,
   1974–present. (P) (E)
SOCIAL SCISEARCH (E)
SOCIOLOGICAL ABSTRACTS (E)

Women Studies Abstracts. Rush, NY: Rush,
   1972–present.
Women's Studies Index (1989–present).
   Boston: Hall, 1992–present. Annually.

Acknowledgments

Figure 4, from Lawrence Lundgren, *Environmental Geology*, © 1986, p. v. Prentice Hall, Upper Saddle River, New Jersey. Reprinted by permission.

Figure 5, from Lawrence Lundgren, *Environmental Geology*, © 1986, p. 569. Prentice Hall, Upper Saddle River, New Jersey. Reprinted by permission.

Figure 6, reprinted with permission from *Encyclopaedia Britannica*, 15th edition, © 1988 by Encyclopaedia Britannica, Inc.

Figure 7, reprinted with permission from *Encyclopaedia Britannica*, 15th edition, © 1988 by Encyclopaedia Britannica, Inc.

Figure 8, reprinted with permission from *Encyclopaedia Britannica*, 15th edition, © 1988 by Encyclopaedia Britannica, Inc.

Figure 9, from Magazine Index Plus™ Copyright © 1997 Information Access Company. Reprinted by permission.

Figure 17, from *Subject Guide to Books in Print* online. Copyright © R.R. Bowker. Reprinted with permission.

Figure 18, from the *Bibliographic Index*, 1984. Reprinted by permission of H. W. Wilson Company.

Figure 19, from the *Essay and General Literature Index*. Reprinted by permission of H. W. Wilson Company.

Figure 20, from *The Reader's Guide to Periodical Literature*. Reprinted by permission of H.W. Wilson Company.

Figure 21, from Expanded Academic ASAP™. Copyright © 1997 Information Access Company. Reprinted by permission.

Figure 22, from *The New York Times Index*, 1925. Copyright © 1925 by The New York Times Co. Reprinted by permission.

Figure 23, from the *Humanities Index*. Reprinted by permission of H. W. Wilson Company.

Figure 24, from *Biology Digest*, Volume 15, #2, October 1988; used by permission of Plexus Publishing, Inc., 143 Old Marlton Pike, Medford, NJ 08055, 609/654–6500.

Figure 25, reprinted by permission of the Modern Language Association from the online *MLA International Bibliography*.

Figure 26, from "The Impact of Racial Diversity and Involvement on College Students' Social Concern Values," *Dissertation Abstracts International*. The dissertation titles and abstracts contained here are published with per-

Index